AMERICA IN LITERATURE

The South

AMERICA IN LITERATURE

General Editor, Max Bogart

The Northeast, James Lape, editor
The South, Sara Marshall, editor
The West, Peter Monahan, editor
The Midwest, Ronald Szymanski, editor
The Small Town, Flory Jones Schultheiss, editor
The City, Adele Stern, editor

AMERICA IN LITERATURE

The South

EDITED BY

Sara Marshall

Palmetto High School
Palmetto, Florida

CHARLES SCRIBNER'S SONS • NEW YORK

Library of Congress Cataloging in Publication Data
Main entry under title:
America in literature: the South.
  Includes index.
  1. American literature—Southern States.
I. Marshall, Sara.
PS551.A4   810'.9'975   78-25615
ISBN 0-684-16136-2 pbk.

Cover Illustration: *Rafting Downstream* (artist unknown). Courtesy of the Indiana University
  Art Museum. Ken Strothman, Photographer.

Picture Research: Yvonne Freund

ACKNOWLEDGMENTS

STEPHEN VINCENT BENÉT, "Cudjo," "Aunt Bess," and "Mary Lou Wingate" from: *John
  Brown's Body* by Stephen Vincent Benét. Holt, Rinehart & Winston. Copyright, 1927,
  1928 by Stephen Vincent Benét. Copyright renewed ©, 1955, 1956 by Rosemary Carr
  Benét. Reprinted by permission of Brandt & Brandt Literary Agency, Inc.
JOSEPHINE PINCKNEY, "The Misses Poar Drive to Church." Reprinted from *Sea-Drinking
  Cities:* Poems by Josephine Pinckney. Copyright, 1927 by Harper & Row, Publishers,
  Inc.; renewed, 1955 by Josephine Pinckney. By permission of Harper & Row, Publishers,
  Inc.
JOHN CROWE RANSOM, "Dead Boy." Copyright 1927 by Alfred A. Knopf, Inc. and renewed
  1955 by John Crowe Ransom. Reprinted from *Selected Poems*, Third Edition, Revised and
  Enlarged, by John Crowe Ransom, by permission of Alfred A. Knopf, Inc.
Acknowledgments continue on page 243, an extension of the copyright page.

CONTENTS

AMERICA IN LITERATURE

The South

Introduction

Anyone who has read or seen the movie of Margaret Mitchell's *Gone with the Wind* can point to that distinctive American culture which is the South—or at least to its best-known stereotype. But this region is far too complex to be caught up in any single statement. In this anthology we shall try to expand the stereotyped view of the region by looking at the writing that has been inspired by, and reflects, the culture and environment of the South.

The Mason-Dixon Line has generally been regarded as the division between North and South because it separated slave-holding states from "free" states. However, Missouri, Kentucky, West Virginia, and Maryland—all south of that line—never joined the Confederacy. And of those eleven states who did, Arkansas and Texas have, since the War between the States, become more western than southern in their cultural development. This volume will focus on those nine states—Louisiana, Mississippi, Alabama, Georgia, Florida, the Carolinas, Virginia, and Tennessee—known as the "Deep South," the area which particularly carries the southern image. The writers included in this volume were either born in the South or spent a portion of their lives there; some few others who do not hail from the area have been included because their writing nonetheless reflects the southern milieu.

The South is a diverse region. Nearly any Southerner will tell you that there is no such thing as "a southern culture," no common denominator; and each will tell you how different his or her home state is from the others. Even when you mention a certain way of speaking as a mark of identification, a Southerner will remind you that Alabamans don't talk like Virginians, that Tennesseeans and Georgians sound quite different from each other, that in the metropolitan areas south of Tallahassee, Floridians have no accent at all.

Still, when viewed from the perspective of the entire United States, the

South is a unique and distinct region. When Southerners use the word *Yankee*, their reactions may range from hostile to friendly to comic; but however subtly, to them that word communicates "other." Conversely, a Yankee recognizes a Southerner at once by the way he talks. What Northerner would fail to notice the softening of the *r*'s, the andante rhythms, the use of "y'all" for second-person plural?

The "southern accent" is harder to detect on the printed page than in the spoken language, but there does seem to be some essence of *South* which knits together—however loosely—such diverse subcultures as Faulkner's Yoknapatawpha County, the Creole mystique of New Orleans, the foxfires of North Carolina, the subtropics of Florida. In this anthology we hope to show through the literature something of the essence as well as the diversity of the South, and, in addition, the place of southern writing in the American literary experience.

Until the mid-twentieth century, most southern writers dealt with a few major themes: the romance of the old plantation, its passing with the Civil War, the subsequent wearing away of its ideals. The literature also has reflected other main currents and concerns of the region: its rural, agrarian make-up; the importance of religion; and, especially in the last fifty years, race relations.

The antebellum or "Romantic South" was a strictly rural society dominated by plantations. The plantation was a small, stratified community with the white landowner at the center, surrounded by sharecroppers and slaves. It was a closed world in which each person knew his or her place, as illustrated in the selections from Stephen Vincent Benét's *John Brown's Body*. In antebellum society everyone recognized *quality*, the southern word for those elite who were set apart from (and above) the rest of the population.

Although historians tell us that there were very few plantations as magnificent as those in romantic fiction—perhaps less than a dozen—it was these few that gave rise to the genteel tradition of southern living that still prevails. All admired and envied the elegant and graceful manner of plantation life among the rich and powerful landowners, and their devotion to a life of pleasure; and all sought to emulate them as much as their more modest places would allow. Perhaps because of the relatively mild climate—especially as one moves farther south—leisurely tempos have always prevailed, and leisurely pursuits. Scholarship and diligence are admired, but

Out for a Days Shooting (Off for the Woods), Currier and Ives

for most they do not hold a candle to the joys of hospitality, social graces, family connections, personal charm (note how often Miss America is a southern belle), and just plain "goin' fishin'."

The Romantic South was abolished by the War between the States (as Southerners almost always refer to that conflict), but not the stratified social system which had sustained it. The Misses Poar (an obvious play on words) in the poem by Josephine Pinckney, still occupied the front pew in church, seeming "no finer, really, before the War/ When money was free in the house. . . ." Deference to quality still exists in the South. John Crowe Ransom's "Dead Boy" may have been "a pig with a pasty face" but he was, after all, "a green bough from Virginia's aged tree," and his death is genuinely mourned. Richard Wright's "Bigger" grows from the frustrations of those—both black and white—who find themselves categorically excluded from quality.

The South today is still largely a land of small communities and rural areas. Even its big cities seem to take their flavor and tempo more from small-town ways than from urban pressures of time and space and anonymity. There are few "city slickers" in southern fiction. It is George Webber in Thomas Wolfe's "The Child by Tiger" awakened in the middle of the night by the firebell ringing from City Hall, and young Melitte in Kate Chopin's "Aunt Lympy's Interference" choosing to be a village school teacher rather than a fashionable belle in New Orleans, who set the tone.

A line from Carson McCullers's *Ballad of the Sad Café* reads, "If you walk along the main street on an August afternoon there is nothing whatsoever to do." There follows an unforgettable, bizarre tale in which a great deal takes place; and this is the paradox of rural society which has inspired the creative imagination of many of our best writers. Little comedies and tragedies that might be lost in the affairs of crowded cities and corporations and nations become, in a small town, matters of real interest and concern in which everybody's opinions and sentiments become a part of the event.

Within southern rural society the clan spirit has always been very strong. Mark Twain's Grangerfords and Shepherdsons in the selection from *Huckleberry Finn* demonstrate a bitter example of clan loyalty; but in milder forms this same loyalty leads also to a policy of "taking care of one's own" which generates great personal kindness, a warmth and generosity for which Southerners are well known. Lily Daw's plight in the story by Eudora Welty is not left to chance or to government agencies, but is naturally assumed by three ladies in her home town who look out for her happiness as cheerfully and unselfishly as if she were "family."

The importance of religion in the culture of the South has provided another rich vein for dramatic expression. Flannery O'Connor, for example, wrote of little else. In this area writers have a full spectrum of experience from which to choose. Church affiliation—whether one actually attends services regularly or not—has always been something of a status symbol in the South, ever since the plantation lords sanctioned it in antebellum days. The South teems with churches of every denomination, and belonging to any organized church is accepted as a mark of respectability—as avowed atheism is definitely *not* in most southern circles.

Outside the metropolitan areas, the church becomes the social as well as the moral center of activity. Sunday school picnics, meetings of the Ladies' Aid Society, and church suppers are important social events. But none are as special as the revival meetings sponsored by the less formal churches. These are highly publicized and generally well attended. Usually they last for several days, and more often than not they are held out-of-doors. Excitement often mounts to frenzy as the revivalist preacher urges the crowds to higher and higher levels of emotionalism. The music becomes louder and more abandoned as the sinners (which includes everybody) scream and weep and clap their hands and sing; some may even fall to the floor and speak in Unknown Tongues. In between these moments of joyous, unrestrained religious convictions, there is plenty of time for an abundance of good food and drink, visiting with friends, and romancing among the young.

Race relations for many years has been an important and volatile national issue that has focused on the South. Before the War between the States, blacks were part of "their white families," upon which they were totally dependent. Not so frequently remembered is that whites were in many ways dependent upon the blacks also. They provided the whites with comfort and leisure and the means of prosperity. They tended the houses and the cotton and tobacco fields and the young whites; and their own wealth of folklore and myth and music passed naturally into the mainstream of southern culture. Whether the black's lot in this symbiotic relationship was ever a happy one depends upon which piece you are reading. Nonetheless, the black experience is a rich and important vein of southern literature.

Peachtree Center, Atlanta, Georgia

The War between the States was, until the middle of the present century, the single most important event in southern history and culture. It ended the period known as the Romantic South and opened up an era of great transition and social upheaval, and bitterness on the part of many. After a time blacks began to write about the ignominy of the role in which they had been cast. Some southern whites hated the blacks who tried to change that role; and some even hated themselves for being unwilling, or perhaps incapable, of changing theirs; and *they* wrote a good deal about *that*. It was Faulkner's deep and compassionate expression of their ambivalence which has made him one of our great contemporary authors.

The Civil Rights movement beginning in the late 1950s seems to mark the beginning of the New South, and a new generation of writers both black and white appeared about this time. They, too, grew up in southern small towns among genteel traditions and religious revivals and leisurely tempos, and they still write about these things occasionally. But for the most part they have turned their attention to new themes: nostalgia, personal identity, an age "on wheels" and on to outer space. Perhaps they are tired of the limitations of the genteel tradition, the regional burdens of bitterness and guilt among whites, the indignation of blacks against their inferior status. Perhaps they sense, as artists, that these themes have already been exhausted by the literary giants of the South. Or perhaps they simply reflect in their craft the general purging of traditional values in every area of American life, which seems to characterize the present period in the cultural history of our nation. The southern literary heritage has been preserved and cherished by them, but primarily as a sort of nostalgic security from which they venture into the presence of the New South.

The most significant changes in the South have come about because of the Civil Rights movement and recent legislation. Many racial barriers have been broken down, such as school segregation; others still remain and tensions still exist. But, for the most part the social fabric of the South has been permanently altered.

The South has also recently experienced great industrial and economic growth. Business and industry have rediscovered the potential of the South; it is now home to many corporations and industries—aerospace, shipbuilding, and the arts, among others. Along with industrialization has come urbanization; cities and towns have grown apace. Atlanta is now one of

America's major cities; others are growing rapidly. Still, the small town, agrarian flavor remains predominant in much of the region.

The South has produced some of America's greatest writers—Mark Twain and Langston Hughes and Tennessee Williams, Sidney Lanier and Thomas Wolfe and William Faulkner, to name just a few. Reading the works of southern writers can tell us much about the heritage of the South—its culture and environment, its great diversity and its uniqueness. More importantly, however, it provides us with a rich vein of the American literary experience.

The Pride

Southern pride, almost a regional stereotype, began, like most southern traditions, in the "Big House" which was the center of plantation life. The supremacy of the master and his family was never questioned in their own minds, or in the minds of those who served them. In fact, the gentility of the master lent a certain prestige to his slaves, among whom there developed, also, a highly stratified society. Those who worked in the master's house held more status than those employed in the stables; and they, in turn, felt themselves "above" the field hands. Each knew his *place*, the southern term for social position.

For many years the system worked by common consent, probably because of its built-in concept of *noblesse oblige*—a paradoxical notion that while nobility carries privileges not allowed to others, it also implies certain obligations—honor between "equals" and largesse to all.

The War between the States legally destroyed the feudal society of the South, but its aristocratic lifestyle continued to prevail in southern consciousness. The notion of quality was, of course, inextricable from the genteel—but not confined to them. Each class contained its own quality, an important part of which was the understanding of one's place. The Wingates in Benét's *John Brown's Body* and the Grangerfords and Shepherdsons in *Huckleberry Finn* are prototypes of southern quality. But so are Jeff and Jennie Patton in Arna Bontemps's "A Summer Tragedy," and Jeff York in Robert Penn Warren's "The Patented Gate and the Mean Hamburger," who will sacrifice himself for his wife's happiness but not his hard-won place, symbolized in the story by his marvellous gate.

The Pride

The Civil Rights movement which began much earlier but did not become a national issue until the late 1950s presented in the still aristocratically oriented South a sort of legal checkmate; but laws cannot immediately effect changes in the heart. In the South contemptuous epithets still exist for those who forget their place.

Southern pride is mainly the outgrowth of these two time-honored regional concepts—quality and place. Its expression has sometimes taken the form of arrogance, and even violence. At the same time it has also reinforced, within the limitations of an aristocratic lifestyle, a classic emphasis on personal worth which is also an integral part of southern pride.

FROM *John Brown's Body*

STEPHEN VINCENT BENÉT

CUDJO

Cudjo, the negro, watched from the pantry
The smooth glissades of the dancing gentry,
His splay-feet tapping in time to the tune
While his broad face beamed like a drunken moon
At candles weeping in crystal sconces,
Waxed floors glowing like polished bronzes,
Sparkles glinting on Royal Worcester
And all the stir and color and luster
Where Miss Louisa and Miss Amanda,
Proud dolls scissored from silver paper,
With hoopskirts wide as the front veranda
And the gypsy eyes of a caged frivolity,
Pointed their toes in a satin caper
To the nonchalant glory of the Quality.
And there were the gentlemen, one and all,
Friends and neighbors of Wingate Hall—
Old Judge Brooke from Little Vermillion
With the rusty voice of a cracked horse-pistol
And manners as stiff as a French cotillion.
Huger Shepley and Wainscott Bristol,
Hawky arrogant sons of anger
Who rode like devils and fought like cocks
And watched, with an ineffable languor
Their spoilt youth tarnish a dicing-box .
The Casanova boys and the Cotter brothers,
Pepperalls from Pepperall Ride.

Wormsloe Plantation, Savannah, Georgia

Cummings and Crowls and a dozen others,
Every one with a name and a pride.
Sallow young dandies in shirts with ruffles,
Each could dance like a blowing feather,
And each had the voice that Georgia muffles
In the lazy honey of her May weather.

Cudjo watched and measured and knew them,
Seeing behind and around and through them
With the shrewd, dispassionate, smiling eye
Of the old-time servant in days gone by.
He couldn't read and he couldn't write,
But he knew Quality, black or white,
And even his master could not find
The secret place in the back of his mind
Where witch-bones talked to a scarlet rag
And a child's voice spoke from a conjur-bag.
For he belonged to the hidden nation,
The mute, enormous confederation
Of the planted earth and the burden borne
And the horse that is ridden and given corn.
The wind from the brier-patch brought him news
The never went walking in white men's shoes
And the grapevine whispered its message faster
Than a horse could gallop across a grave,
Till, long ere the letter could tell the master,
The doomsday rabbits had told the slave.

He was faithful as bread or salt,
A flawless servant without a fault,
Major-domo of Wingate Hall,
Proud of his white folks, proud of it all.
They might scold him, they might let him scold them,
And he might know things that he never told them,

The Pride

But there was a bond, and the bond would hold,
On either side until both were cold.

.   .   .

AUNT BESS

Fat Aunt Bess is older than Time
But her eyes still shine like a bright, new dime,
Though two generations have gone to rest
On the sleepy mountain of her breast.
Wingate children in Wingate Hall,
From the first weak cry in the bearing-bed
She has petted and punished them, one and all,
She has closed their eyes when they lay dead.
She raised Marse Billy when he was puny,
She cared for the Squire when he got loony,
Fed him and washed him and combed his head,
Nobody else would do instead.
The matriarch of the weak and the young,
The lazy crooning, comforting tongue.
She has had children of her own,
But the white-skinned ones are bone of her bone.

They may not be hers, but she is theirs,
And if the shares were unequal shares,
She does not know it, now she is old.
They will keep her out of the rain and cold.
And some were naughty, and some were good,
But she will be warm while they have wood,
Rule them and spoil them and play physician
With the vast, insensate force of tradition,
Half a nuisance and half a mother
And legally neither one nor the other,
Till at last they follow her to her grave,
The family-despot, and the slave.
—Curious blossom from bitter-ground,

14

Master of masters who left you bound,
Who shall unravel the mingled strands
Or read the anomaly of your hands?
They have made you a shrine and a humorous fable,
But they kept you a slave while they were able,
And yet, there was something between the two
That you shared with them and they shared with you,
Brittle and dim, but a steak of gold,
A genuine kindness, unbought, unsold,
Graciousness founded on hopeless wrong
But queerly loving and queerly strong. . . .

There were three stout pillars that held up all
The weight and tradition of Wingate Hall.
One was Cudjo and one was you
And the third was the mistress, Mary Lou.

.   .   .

MARY LOU WINGATE

Mary Lou Wingate, as slightly made
And as hard to break as a rapier-blade.
Bristol's daughter and Wingate's bride,
Never well since the last child died
But staring at pain with courteous eyes.
When the pain outwits it, the body dies.
Meanwhile the body bears the pain.
She loved her hands and they made her vain,
The tiny hands of her generation
That gathered the reins of the whole plantation;
The velvet sheathing the steel demurely
In the trained, light grip that holds so surely.

She was at work by candlelight,
She was at work in the dead of night,
Smoothing out troubles and healing schisms

15

The Pride

And doctoring phthisics and rheumatisms,
Guiding the cooking and watching the baking,
The sewing, the soap-and-candle-making,
The brewing, the darning, the lady-daughters,
The births and deaths in the negro-quarters,
Seeing that Suke had some new, strong shoes
And Joe got a week in the calaboose,
While Dicey's Jacob escaped a whipping
And the jellybag dripped with its proper dripping,
And the shirts and estrangements were neatly mended,
And all of the tasks that never ended.
Her manner was gracious but hardly fervent
And she seldom raised her voice to a servant.
She was often mistaken, not often blind,
And she knew the whole duty of womankind,
To take the burden and have the power
And seem like the well-protected flower,
To manage a dozen industries
With a casual gesture in scraps of ease.
To hate the sin and to love the sinner
And to see that the gentlemen got their dinner
Ready and plenty and piping hot
Whether you wanted to eat or not.
And always, always, to have the charm
That makes the gentlemen take your arm
But never the bright, unseemly spell
That makes strange gentlemen love too well,
Once you were married and settled down
With a suitable gentleman of your own.

And when that happened, and you had bred
The requisite children, living and dead,
To pity the fool and comfort the weak
And always let the gentlemen speak.
To succor your love from deep-struck roots

16

When gentlemen went to bed in their boots,
And manage a gentleman's whole plantation
In the manner befitting your female station.

This was the creed that her mother taught her
And the creed that she taught to every daughter.
She knew her Bible—and how to flirt
With a swansdown fan and a brocade skirt.
For she trusted in God but she liked formalities
And the world and Heaven were both realities.
—In Heaven, of course, we should all be equal,
But, until we came to that golden sequel,
Gentility must keep to gentility
Where God and breeding had made things stable,
While the rest of the cosmos deserved civility
But dined in its boots at the second-table.
This view may be reckoned a trifle narrow,
But it had the driving force of an arrow,
And it helped Mary Lou to stand up straight,
For she was gentle, but she could hate
And she hated the North with the hate of Jael
When the dry hot hands went seeking the nail,
The terrible hate of women's ire,
The smoky, the long-consuming fire.
The Yankees were devils, and she could pray,
For devils, no doubt, upon Judgment Day,
But now in the world, she would hate them still
And send the gentlemen out to kill.

The gentlemen killed and the gentlemen died,
But she was the South's incarnate pride
That mended the broken gentlemen
And sent them out to the war again,
That kept the house with the men away
And baked the bricks where there was no clay,

The Pride

Made courage from terror and bread from bran
And propped the South on a swansdown fan
Through four long years of ruin and stress,
The pride—and the deadly bitterness.

Why Harney Rode
Away for His Hat*

MARK TWAIN

Col. Grangerford was a gentleman, you see. He was a gentleman all over; and so was his family. He was well born, as the saying is, and that's worth as much in a man as it is in a horse, so the Widow Douglas said, and nobody ever denied that she was of the first aristocracy in our town; and pap he always said it, too, though he warn't no more quality than a mudcat himself. Col. Grangerford was very tall and very slim, and had a darkish-paly complexion, not a sign of red in it anywheres; he was clean-shaved every morning all over his thin face, and he had the thinnest kind of lips, and the thinnest kind of nostrils, and a high nose, and heavy eyebrows, and the blackest kind of eyes, sunk so deep back that they seemed like they was looking out of caverns at you, as you may say. His forehead was high, and his hair was gray and straight and hung to his shoulders. His hands was long and thin, and every day of his life he put on a clean shirt and a full suit from head to foot made out of linen so white it hurt your eyes to look at it; and on Sundays he wore a blue tail-coat with brass buttons on it. He carried a mahogany cane with a silver head to it. There warn't no frivolishness about him, not a bit, and he warn't ever loud. He was as kind as he could be—you could feel that, you know, and so you had confidence. Sometimes he smiled, and it was good to see; but when he straightened himself up like a liberty-pole, and the lightning begun to flicker out from under his eyebrows, you wanted to climb a tree first, and find out what the matter was afterwards. He didn't ever have to tell anybody to mind their manners—everybody was always good-mannered where he was. Everybody loved to have him around, too; he was sunshine most always—I mean he made it seem like good weather. When he turned into a cloud-bank it was awful dark for half a minute, and that was enough; there wouldn't nothing go wrong again for a week.

*Chapter XVII of *The Adventures of Huckleberry Finn.*

19

Caricature of Mark Twain by Max Beerbohm

When him and the old lady come down in the morning all the family got up out of their chairs and give them good day, and didn't set down again till they had set down. Then Tom and Bob went to the sideboard where the decanter was, and mixed a glass of bitters and handed it to him, and he held it in his hand and waited till Tom's and Bob's was mixed, and then they bowed and said, "Our duty to you, sir, and madam"; and *they* bowed the least bit in the world and said thank you, and so they drank, all three, and Bob and Tom poured a spoonful of water on the sugar and the mite of whisky or apple-brandy in the bottom of their tumblers, and give it to me and Buck, and we drank to the old people too.

Bob was the oldest and Tom next—tall, beautiful men with very broad shoulders and brown faces, and long black hair and black eyes. They dressed in white linen from head to foot, like the old gentleman, and wore broad Panama hats.

Then there was Miss Charlotte; she was twenty-five, and tall and proud and grand, but as good as she could be when she warn't stirred up; but when she was she had a look that would make you wilt in your tracks, like her father. She was beautiful.

So was her sister, Miss Sophia, but it was a different kind. She was gentle and sweet like a dove, and she was only twenty.

Each person had their own nigger to wait on them—Buck too. My nigger had a monstrous easy time, because I warn't used to having anybody to do anything for me, but Buck's was on the jump most of the time.

This was all there was of the family now, but there used to be more—three sons; they got killed; and Emmeline that died.

The old gentleman owned a lot of farms and over a hundred niggers. Sometimes a stack of people would come there, horseback, from ten or fifteen mile around, and stay five or six days, and have such junketings round about and on the river, and dances and picnics in the woods daytimes, and balls at the house nights. These people was mostly kinfolks of the family. The men brought their guns with them. It was a handsome lot of quality, I tell you.

There was another clan of aristocracy around there—five or six families—mostly of the name of Shepherdson. They was as high-toned and well born and rich and grand as the tribe of Grangerfords. The Shepherdsons and Grangerfords used the same steamboat-landing, which was about two mile above our house; so sometimes when I went up there with a lot of our folks I used to see a lot of the Shepherdsons there on their fine horses.

One day Buck and me was away out in the woods hunting, and heard a horse coming. We was crossing the road. Buck says:

"Quick! jump for the woods!"

We done it, and then peeped down the woods through the leaves. Pretty soon a splendid young man came galloping down the road, setting his horse easy and looking like a soldier. He had his gun across his pommel. I had seen him before. It was young Harney Shepherdson. I heard Buck's gun go off at my ear, and Harney's hat tumbled off from his head. He grabbed his gun and rode straight to the place where we was hid. But we didn't wait. We started through the woods on a run. The woods warn't thick, so I looked over my shoulder to dodge the bullet, and twice I seen Harney cover Buck with his gun; and then he rode away the way he come— to get his hat, I reckon, but I couldn't see. We never stopped running till we got home. The old gentleman's eyes blazed a minute—'twas pleasure, mainly, I judged—then his face sort of smoothed down, and he says, kind of gentle:

"I don't like that shooting from behind a bush. Why didn't you step into the road, my boy?"

"The Shepherdsons don't, father. They always take advantage."

Miss Charlotte she held her head up like a queen while Buck was telling his tale, and her nostrils spread and her eyes snapped. The two young men looked dark, but never said nothing. Miss Sophia she turned pale, but the color came back when she found the man warn't hurt.

Soon as I could get Buck down by the corn-cribs under the trees by ourselves, I says:

"Did you want to kill him, Buck?"

"Well, I bet I did."

"What did he do to you."

"Him? He never done nothing to me."

"Well, then, what did you want to kill him for?"

"Why, nothing—only it's on account of the feud."

"What's a feud?"

"Why, where was you raised? Don't you know what a feud is?"

"Never heard of it before—tell me about it."

"Well," says Buck, "a feud is this way: A man has a quarrel with another man, and kills him; then that other man's brother kills *him;* then the other brothers, on both sides, goes for one another; then the *cousins* chip in—and by and by everybody's killed off, and there ain't no more feud. But it's kind of slow, and takes a long time."

"Has this one been going on long, Buck?"

"Well, I should *reckon!* It started thirty year ago, or som'ers along there. There was trouble 'bout something, and then a lawsuit to settle it; and the suit went agin one of the men, and so he up and shot the man that won the suit—which he would naturally do, of course. Anybody would."

"What was the trouble about, Buck?—land?"

"I reckon maybe—I don't know."

"Well, who done the shooting? Was it a Grangerford or a Sheperdson?"

"Laws, how do *I* know? It was so long ago."

"Don't anybody know?"

"Oh, yes, pa knows, I reckon, and some of the other old people; but they don't know now what the row was about in the first place."

"Has there been many killed, Buck?"

"Yes; right smart chance of funerals. But they don't always kill. Pa's got a few buckshot in him; but he don't mind it 'cuz he don't weigh much, anyway. Bob's been carved up some with a bowie, and Tom's been hurt once or twice."

"Has anybody been killed this year, Buck?"

"Yes; we got one and they got one. 'Bout three months ago my cousin Bud, fourteen year old, was riding through the woods on t'other side of the river, and didn't have no weapon with him, which was blame' foolishness, and in a lonesome place he hears a horse a-coming behind him, and sees old Baldy Shepherdson a-linkin' after him with his gun in his hand and his white hair a-flying in the wind; and 'stead of jumping off and taking to the brush, Bud 'lowed he could outrun him; so they had it, nip and tuck, for five mile or more, the old man a-gaining all the time; so at last Bud seen it warn't any use, so he stopped and faced around so as to have the bullet-holes in front, you know, and the old man he rode up and shot him down. But he didn't git much chance to enjoy his luck, for inside of a week our folks laid *him* out."

"I reckon that old man was a coward, Buck."

"I reckon he *warn't* a coward. Not by a blame' sight. There ain't a coward amongst them Shepherdsons—not a one. And there ain't no cowards amongst the Grangerfords either. Why, that old man kep' up his end in a fight one day for half an hour against three Grangerfords, and come out winner. They was all a-horseback; he lit off of his horse and got behind a little woodpile, and kep' his horse before him to stop the bullets; but the Grangerfords stayed on their horses and capered around the old man, and peppered away at him, and he peppered away at them. Him and his horse both went home pretty leaky and crippled, but the Grangerfords had to be *fetched* home—and one of 'em was dead, and another died the next day. No, sir; if a body's out hunting for cowards he don't want to fool away any time amongst them Shepherdsons, becuz they don't breed any of that *kind*."

Next Sunday we all went to church, about three mile, everybody a-horseback. The men took their guns along, so did Buck, and kept them between their knees or stood them handy against the wall. The Shepherdsons done the same. It was pretty ornery preaching—all about brotherly love, and such-like tiresomeness; but everybody said it was a good sermon, and they all talked it over going home and had such a powerful lot to say about faith and good works and free grace and preforeordestination, and I don't know what all, that it did seem to me to be one of the roughest Sundays I had run across yet.

About an hour after dinner everybody was dozing around, some in their chairs and some in their rooms, and it got to be pretty dull. Buck and a dog was stretched out on the grass in the sun sound asleep. I went up to our room, and judged I would take a nap myself. I found that sweet Miss Sophia standing in her door, which was next to ours, and she took me in her room and shut the door very soft, and asked me if I liked her, and I said I did; and she asked me if I would do something for her and not tell anybody, and I said I would. Then she said she'd forgot her Testament, and left it in the seat at church between two other books, and would I slip out quiet and go there and fetch it to her, and not say nothing to nobody. I said I would. So I slid out and slipped off up the road, and there warn't anybody at the church, except maybe a hog or two, for there warn't any lock on the door, and hogs likes a puncheon floor in summer-time because it's cool. If you notice, most folks don't go to church only when they've got to; but a hog is different.

Says I to myself, something's up; it ain't natural for a girl to be in such a sweat about a Testament. So I give it a shake, and out drops a little piece of

24

paper with *"Half past two"* wrote on it with a pencil. I ransacked it, but couldn't find anything else. I couldn't make anything out of that, so I put the paper in the book again, and when I got home and upstairs there was Miss Sophia in her door waiting for me. She pulled me in and shut the door; then she looked in the Testament till she found the paper, and as soon as she read it she looked glad; and before a body could think she grabbed me and give me a squeeze, and said I was the best boy in the world, and not to tell anybody. She was mighty red in the face for a minute, and her eyes lighted up, and it made her powerful pretty. I was a good deal astonished, but when I got my breath I asked her what the paper was about, and she asked me if I had read it, and I said no, and she asked me if I could read writing, and I told her "no, only coarse-hand," and then she said the paper warn't anything but a book-mark to keep her place, and I might go and play now.

I went off down to the river, studying over this thing. . . .

I don't want to talk much about the next day. I reckon I'll cut it pretty short. I waked up about dawn, and was a-going to turn over and go to sleep again when I noticed how still it was—didn't seem to be anybody stirring. That warn't usual. Next I noticed that Buck was up and gone. Well, I gets up, a-wondering, and goes down-stairs—everything as still as a mouse. Just the same outside. Thinks I, what does it mean? Down by the woodpile I comes across my Jack and says:

"What's it all about?"

Says he:

"Don't you know, Mars Jawge?"

"No," says I, "I don't."

"Well, den, Miss Sophia's run off! 'deed she has. She run off in de night some time—nobody don't know jis' when; run off to get married to dat young Harney Shepherdson, you know—leastways, so dey 'spec. De fambly foun' it out 'bout half an hour ago—maybe a little mo'—en' I *tell* you dey warn't no time los'. Sich another hurryin' up guns en hosses *you* never see! De women folks has gone for to stir up de relations, en ole Mars Saul en de boys tuck dey guns en rode up de river road for to try to ketch dat young man en kill him 'fo' he kin git acrost de river wid Miss Sophia. I reck'n dey's gwyne to be mighty rough times."

"Buck went off 'thout waking me up."

"Well, I reck'n he *did!* Dey warn't gwyne to mix you up in it. Mars

Buck he loaded up his gun en 'lowed he's gwyne to fetch home a Shepherd-son or bust. Well, dey'll be plenty un 'm dah, I reck'n, en you bet you he'll fetch one ef he gits a chanst."

I took up the river road as hard as I could put. By and by I begin to hear guns a good ways off. When I came in sight of the log store and the wood-pile where the steamboats lands I worked along under the trees and brush till I got to a good place, and then I clumb up into the forks of a cottonwood that was out of reach, and watched. There was a wood-rank four foot high a little ways in front of the tree, and first I was going to hide behind that; but maybe it was luckier I didn't.

There was four or five men cavorting around on their horses in the open place before the log store, cussing and yelling, and trying to get at a couple of young chaps that was behind the wood-rank alongside of the steamboat-landing; but they couldn't come it. Every time one of them showed himself on the river side of the wood-pile he got shot at. The two boys was squatting back to back behind the pile, so they could watch both ways.

By and by the men stopped cavorting around and yelling. They started riding towards the store; then up gets one of the boys, draws a steady bead over the wood-rank, and drops one of them out of his saddle. All the men jumped off of their horses and grabbed the hurt one and started to carry him to the store; and that minute the two boys started on the run. They got half-way to the tree I was in before the men noticed. Then the men see them, and jumped on their horses and took out after them. They gained on the boys, but it didn't do no good, the boys had too good a start; they got to the woodpile that was in front of my tree, and slipped in behind it, and so they had the bulge on the men again. One of the boys was Buck, and the other was a slim young chap about nineteen years old.

The men ripped around awhile, and then rode away. As soon as they was out of sight I sung out to Buck and told him. He didn't know what to make of my voice coming out of the tree at first. He was awful surprised. He told me to watch out sharp and let him know when the men come in sight again; said they was up to some devilment or other—wouldn't be gone long. I wished I was out of that tree, but I dasn't come down. Buck begun to cry and rip, and 'lowed that him and his cousin Joe (that was the other young chap) would make up for this day yet. He said his father and his two brothers was killed, and two or three of the enemy. Said the Shepherdsons laid for them in ambush. Buck said his father and brothers ought to waited for their relations—the Shepherdsons was too strong for them. I asked him what was become of young Harney and Miss Sophia. He said they'd got across the river and was safe. I was glad of that; but the way Buck did take on because he didn't manage to kill Harney that day he shot at him—I hain't ever heard anything like it.

All of a sudden, bang! bang! bang! goes three or four guns—the men had slipped around through the woods and come in from behind without their horses! The boys jumped for the river—both of them hurt—and as they swum down the current the men run along the bank shooting at them and singing out, "Kill them, kill them!" It made me so sick I most fell out of the tree. I ain't a-going to tell *all* that happened—it would make me sick again if I was to do that. I wished I hadn't ever come ashore that night to see such things. I ain't ever going to get shut of them—lots of times I dream about them.

I stayed in the tree till it begun to get dark, afraid to come down. Sometimes I heard guns away off in the woods; and twice I seen little gangs of men gallop past the log store with guns; so I reckoned the trouble was still a-going on. I was mighty downhearted; so I made up my mind I wouldn't ever go anear that house again, because I reckoned I was to blame, somehow. I judged that that piece of paper meant that Miss Sophia was to meet Harney somewheres at half past two and run off; and I judged I ought to told her father about that paper and the curious way she acted, and then maybe he would 'a' locked her up, and this mess wouldn't ever happened.

When I got down out of the tree I crept along down the river-bank a piece and found the two bodies laying in the edge of the water, and tugged at them till I got them ashore; then I covered up their faces, and got away as quick as I could. I cried a little when I was covering up Buck's face, for he was mighty good to me.

It was just dark now. I never went near the house, but struck through the woods and made for the swamp.

The Misses Poar Drive to Church

JOSEPHINE PINCKNEY

Out from the tall plantation gate
Issue the Misses Poar in state.
Neatly darned are their black silk mitts,
And straight each stately sister sits.
Their carriage-dresses, brushed and steamed,
Cover their decent limbs; they seemed
No finer, really, before the War
When money was free in the house of Poar.
The negro coachman in beaver hat,
Slightly nibbled by moth and rat,
Smooths his frock-coat of greenish hue,—
But fitting as trim as when it was new—
With which he stiffens his spine of pride
By tightly buttoning himself inside
To drive in this elegant equipage
A yoke of oxen of doubtful age.
(They've had no horses since sixty-four
When the Yankees stopped at the house of Poar.)

The ladies move to the square front pew,
Their Christian meekness in ample view,
And follow the youthful parson's word
With reverence meet for a legate of God
Up to the moment when he prates
Of the President of the United States;
Then, knowing full well that Heaven can't
Expect them to pray for General Grant,

They bury their noses' partrician hook
In dear Great-grandpapa's prayer-book,
Wherein are found urban petitions
To guard the Crown against seditions
And rest King Charles the Martyr's soul.
Not that they hold King Charles so dear,
Although their blood is Cavalier,
But it suits their piety, on the whole,
Better to pray for the Restoration
Than the overseer of a patch-work nation.

Dead Boy

JOHN CROWE RANSOM

The little cousin is dead, by foul subtraction,
A green bough from Virginia's aged tree,
And none of the county kin like the transaction,
Nor some of the world of outer dark, like me.

A boy not beautiful, nor good, nor clever,
A black cloud full of storms too hot for keeping,
A sword beneath his mother's heart—yet never
Woman bewept her babe as this is weeping.

A pig with a pasty face, so I had said,
Squealing for cookies, kinned by poor pretense
With a noble house. But the little man quite dead,
I see the forbears' antique lineaments.

The elder men have strode by the box of death
To the wide flag porch, and muttering low send round
The bruit of the day. O friendly waste of breath!
Their hearts are hurt with a deep dynastic death.

He was pale and little, the foolish neighbors say;
The first fruits, saith the Preacher, the Lord hath taken;
But this was the old tree's late branch wrenched away,
Grieving the sapless limbs, the shorn and shaken.

A Summer Tragedy

ARNA BONTEMPS

Old Jeff Patton, the black share farmer, fumbled with his bow tie. His fingers trembled and the high stiff collar pinched his throat. A fellow loses his hand for such vanities after thirty or forty years of simple life. Once a year, or maybe twice if there's a wedding among his kinfolks, he may spruce up; but generally fancy clothes do nothing but adorn the wall of the big room and feed the moths. That had been Jeff Patton's experience. He had not worn his stiff-bosomed shirt more than a dozen times in all his married life. His swallow-tailed coat lay on the bed beside him, freshly brushed and pressed, but it was as full of holes as the overalls in which he worked on weekdays. The moths had used it badly. Jeff twisted his mouth into a hideous toothless grimace as he contended with the obstinate bow. He stamped his good foot and decided to give up the struggle.

"Jennie," he called.

"What's that, Jeff?" His wife's shrunken voice came out of the adjoining room like an echo. It was hardly bigger than a whisper.

"I reckon you'll have to he'p me wid this heah bow tie, baby," he said meekly. "Dog if I can hitch it up."

Her answer was not strong enough to reach him, but presently the old woman came to the door, feeling her way with a stick. She had a wasted, dead-leaf appearance. Her body, as scrawny and gnarled as a string bean, seemed less than nothing in the ocean of frayed and faded petticoats that surrounded her. These hung an inch or two above the tops of her heavy unlaced shoes and showed little grotesque piles where the stockings had fallen down from her negligible legs.

"You oughta could do a heap mo' wid a thing like that'n me—beingst as you got yo' good sight."

"Looks like I oughta could," he admitted. "But ma fingers is gone democrat on me. I get all mixed up in the looking glass an' can't tell wicha way to twist the devilish thing."

Jennie sat on the side of the bed and old Jeff Patton got down on one knee while she tied the bow knot. It was a slow and painful ordeal for each of them in this position. Jeff's bones cracked, his knee ached, and it was only after a half dozen attempts that Jennie worked a semblance of a bow into the tie.

"I got to dress maself now," the old woman whispered. "These is ma old shoes an' stockings, and I ain't so much as unwrapped ma dress."

"Well, don't worry 'bout me no mo', baby," Jeff said. "That 'bout finishes me. All I gotta do now is slip on that old coat 'n ves' an' I'll be fixed to leave."

Jennie disappeared again through the dim passage into the shed room. Being blind was no handicap to her in that black hole. Jeff heard the cane placed against the wall beside the door and knew that his wife was on easy ground. He put on his coat, took a battered top hat from the bedpost and hobbled to the front door. He was ready to travel. As soon as Jennie could get on her Sunday shoes and her old black silk dress, they would start.

Outside the tiny log house, the day was warm and mellow with sunshine. A host of wasps were humming with busy excitement in the trunk of a dead sycamore. Gray squirrels were searching through the grass for hickory nuts and blue jays were in the trees, hopping from branch to branch. Pine woods stretched away to the left like a black sea. Among them were scattered scores of log houses like Jeff's, houses of black share farmers. Cows and pigs wandered freely among the trees. There was no danger of loss. Each farmer knew his own stock and knew his neighbor's as well as he knew his neighbor's children.

Down the slope to the right were the cultivated acres on which the colored folks worked. They extended to the river, more than two miles away, and they were today green with the unmade cotton crop. A tiny thread of a road, which passed directly in front of Jeff's place, ran through these green fields like a pencil mark.

Jeff, standing outside the door, with his absurd hat in his left hand, surveyed the wide scene tenderly. He had been forty-five years on these acres. He loved them with the unexplained affection that others have for the countries to which they belong.

The sun was hot on his head, his collar still pinched his throat, and the Sunday clothes were intolerably hot. Jeff transferred the hat to his right hand and began fanning with it. Suddenly the whisper that was Jennie's voice came out of the shed room.

"You can bring the car round front whilst you's waitin'," it said feebly. There was a tired pause; then it added, "I'll soon be fixed to go."

"A'right, baby," Jeff answered. "I'll get it in a minute."

But he didn't move. A thought struck him that made his mouth fall open. The mention of the car brought to his mind, with new intensity, the trip he and Jennie were about to take. Fear came into his eyes; excitement took his breath. Lord, Jesus!

"Jeff . . . O Jeff," the old woman's whisper called.

He awakened with a jolt. "Hunh, baby?"

"What you doin'?"

"Nuthin. Jes studyin'. I jes been turnin' things round'n round in ma mind."

"You could be gettin' the car," she said.

"Oh yes, right away, baby."

He started round to the shed, limping heavily on his bad leg. There were three frizzly chickens in the yard. All his other chickens had been killed or stolen recently. But the frizzly chickens had been saved somehow. That was fortunate indeed, for these curious creatures had a way of devouring "Poison" from the yard and in that way protecting against conjure and black luck and spells. But even the frizzly chickens seemed now to be in a stupor. Jeff thought they had some ailment; he expected all three of them to die shortly.

The shed in which the old T-model Ford stood was only a grass roof held up by four corner poles. It had been built by tremulous hands at a time when the little rattletrap car had been regarded as a peculiar treasure. And, miraculously, despite wind and downpour it still stood.

Jeff adjusted the crank and put his weight upon it. The engine came to life with a sputter and bang that rattled the old car from radiator to taillight. Jeff hopped into the seat and put his foot on the accelerator. The sputtering and banging increased. The rattling became more violent. That was good. It was good banging, good sputtering and rattling, and it meant that the aged car was still in running condition. She could be depended on for this trip.

Again Jeff's thought halted as if paralyzed. The suggestion of the trip fell into the machinery of his mind like a wrench. He felt dazed and weak. He swung the car out into the yard, made a half turn and drove around to the front door. When he took his hands off the wheel, he noticed that he was trembling violently. He cut off the motor and climbed to the ground to wait for Jennie.

A few minutes later she was at the window, her voice rattling against the pane like a broken shutter.

"I'm ready, Jeff."

He did not answer, but limped into the house and took her by the arm. He led her slowly through the big room, down the step and across the yard.

"You reckon I'd oughta lock the do'?" he asked softly.

They stopped and Jennie weighted the question. Finally she shook her head.

"Ne' mind the do'," she said. "I don't see no cause to lock up things."

"You right," Jeff agreed. "No cause to lock up."

Jeff opened the door and helped his wife into the car. A quick shudder passed over him. Jesus! Again he trembled.

"How come you shaking so?" Jennie whispered.

"I don't know," he said.

"You mus' be scairt, Jeff."

"No, baby, I ain't scairt."

He slammed the door after her and went around to crank up again. The motor started easily. Jeff wished that it had not been so responsive. He would have liked a few more minutes in which to turn things around in his head. As it was, with Jennie chiding him about being afraid, he had to keep going. He swung the car into the little pencil-mark road and started off toward the river, driving very slowly, very cautiously.

Chugging across the green countryside, the small battered Ford seemed tiny indeed. Jeff felt a familiar excitement, a thrill, as they came down the first slope to the immense levels on which the cotton was growing. He could not help reflecting that the crops were good. He knew what that meant, too; he had made forty-five of them with his own hands. It was true that he had worn out nearly a dozen mules, but that was the fault of old man Stevenson, the owner of the land. Major Stevenson had the odd notion that one mule was all a share farmer needed to work a thirty-acre plot. It was an expensive notion, the way it killed mules from overwork, but the old man held to it. Jeff thought it killed a good many share farmers as well as mules, but he had no sympathy for them. He had always been strong, and he had been taught to have no patience with weakness in men. Women or children might be tolerated if they were puny, but a weak man was a curse. Of course, his own children—

Jeff's thought halted there. He and Jennie never mentioned their dead children any more. And naturally he did not wish to dwell upon them in his mind. Before he knew it, some remark would slip out of his mouth and that would make Jennie feel blue. Perhaps she would cry. A woman like Jennie could not easily throw off the grief that comes from losing five grown children within two years. Even Jeff was still staggered by the blow. His memory had not been much good recently. He frequently talked to himself. And, although he had kept it a secret, he knew that his courage had left him. He was terrified by the least unfamiliar sound at night. He was reluctant to venture far from home in the daytime. And that habit of trembling when he felt fearful was now far beyond his control. Sometimes he became afraid and trembled without knowing what had frightened him. The feeling would just come over him like a chill.

The car rattled slowly over the dusty road. Jennie sat erect and silent, with a little absurd hat pinned to her hair. Her useless eyes seemed very large, very white in their deep sockets. Suddenly Jeff heard her voice, and he inclined his head to catch the words.

"Is we passed Delia Moore's house yet?" she asked.

"Not yet," he said.

"You must be drivin' mighty slow, Jeff."

"We might just as well take our time, baby."

There was a pause. A little puff of steam was coming out of the radiator of the car. Heat wavered above the hood. Delia Moore's house was nearly half a mile away. After a moment Jennie spoke again.

"You ain't really scairt, is you, Jeff?"

"Nah, baby, I ain't scairt."

"You know how we agreed—we gotta keep on goin'."

Jewels of perspiration appeared on Jeff's forehead. His eyes rounded, blinked, became fixed on the road.

"I don't know," he said with a shiver. "I reckon it's the only thing to do."

"Hm."

A flock of guinea fowls, pecking in the road, were scattered by the passing car. Some of them took to their wings; others hid under bushes. A blue jay, swaying on a leafy twig, was annoying a roadside squirrel. Jeff held an even speed till he came near Delia's place. Then he slowed down noticeably.

Delia's house was really no house at all, but an abandoned store building converted into a dwelling. It sat near a crossroads, beneath a single black cedar tree. There Delia, a cattish old creature of Jennie's age, lived alone. She had been there more years than anybody could remember, and long ago had won the disfavor of such women as Jennie. For in her young days Delia had been gayer, yellower and saucier than seemed proper in those parts. Her ways with menfolks had been dark and suspicious. And the fact that she had had as many husbands as children did not help her reputation.

"Yonder's old Delia," Jeff said as they passed.

"What she doin'?"

"Jes sittin' in the do'," he said

"She see us?"

"Hm," Jeff said. "Musta did."

That relieved Jennie. It strengthened her to know that her old enemy had seen her pass in her best clothes. That would give the old she-devil something to chew her gums and fret about, Jennie thought. Wouldn't she have a fit if she didn't find out? Old evil Delia! This would be just the thing for her. It would pay her back for being so evil. It would also pay her, Jennie thought, for the way she used to grin at Jeff—long ago when her teeth were good.

The road became smooth and red, and Jeff could tell by the smell of the air that they were nearing the river. He could see the rise where the road turned and ran along parallel to the stream. The car chugged on monotonously. After a long silent spell, Jennie leaned against Jeff and spoke.

"How many bale o' cotton you think we got standin'?" she said.

Jeff wrinkled his forehead as he calculated.

" 'Bout twenty-five, I reckon."

"How many you make las' year?"

"Twenty-eight," he said. "How come you ask that?"

"I's jes thinkin'," Jennie said quietly.

"It don't make a speck o' difference though," Jeff reflected. "If we get much or if we get little, we still gonna be in debt to old man Stevenson when

36

he gets through counting up agin us. It's took us a long time to learn that."

Jennie was not listening to these words. She had fallen into a trance-like meditation. Her lips twitched. She chewed her gums and rubbed her gnarled hands nervously. Suddenly she leaned forward, buried her face in the nervous hands and burst into tears. She cried aloud in a dry cracked voice that suggested the rattle of fodder on dead stalks. She cried aloud like a child, for she had never learned to suppress a genuine sob. Her slight old frame shook heavily and seemed hardly able to sustain such violent grief.

"What's the matter, baby?" Jeff asked awkwardly. "Why you cryin' like all that?"

"I's jes thinkin'," she said.

"So you the one what's scairt now, hunh?"

"I ain't scairt, Jeff. I's jes thinkin' 'bout leavin' eve'thing like this— eve'thing we been used to. It's right sad-like."

Jeff did not answer, and presently Jennie buried her face again and cried.

The sun was almost overhead. It beat down furiously on the dusty wagon-path road, on the parched roadside grass and the tiny battered car. Jeff's hands, gripping the wheel, became wet with perspiration; his forehead sparkled. Jeff's lips parted. His mouth shaped a hideous grimace. His face suggested the face of a man being burned. But the torture passed and his expression softened again.

"You mustn't cry, baby," he said to his wife. "We gotta be strong. We can't break down."

Jennie waited a few seconds, then said, "You reckon we oughta do it, Jeff? You reckon we oughta go 'head an' do it, really?"

Jeff's voice choked; his eyes blurred. He was terrified to hear Jennie say the thing that had been in his mind all morning. She had egged him on when he had wanted more than anything in the world to wait, to reconsider, to think things over a little longer. Now she was getting cold feet. Actually there was no need of thinking the question through again. It would only end in making the same painful decision once more. Jeff knew that. There was no need of fooling around longer.

"We jes as well to do like we planned," he said. "They ain't nothin' else for us now—it's the bes' thing."

Jeff thought of the handicaps, the near impossibility, of making another crop with his leg bothering him more and more each week. Then there was always the chance that he would have another stroke, like the one that had made him lame. Another one might kill him. The least it could do would be to leave him helpless. Jeff gasped—Lord, Jesus! He could not bear to think of being helpless, like a baby, on Jennie's hands. Frail, blind Jennie.

The little pounding motor of the car worked harder and harder. The puff of steam from the cracked radiator became larger. Jeff realized that they were climbing a little rise. A moment later the road turned abruptly and he looked down upon the face of the river.

"Jeff."

"Hunh?"

"Is that the water I hear?"

"Hm. Tha's it."

"Well, which way you goin' now?"

"Down this-a way," he said. "The road runs 'long 'side o' the water a lil piece."

She waited a while calmly. Then she said, "Drive faster."

"A'right, baby," Jeff said.

The water roared in the bed of the river. It was fifty or sixty feet below the level of the road. Between the road and the water there was a long smooth slope, sharply inclined. The slope was dry, the clay hardened by prolonged summer heat. The water below, roaring in a narrow channel, was noisy and wild.

"Jeff."

"Hunh?"

"How far you goin'?"

"Jes a lil piece down the road."

"You ain't scairt, is you, Jeff?"

"Nah, baby," he said trembling. "I ain't scairt."

"Remember how we planned it, Jeff. We gotta do it like we said. Brave-like."

"Hm."

Jeff's brain darkened. Things suddenly seemed unreal, like figures in a dream. Thoughts swam in his mind foolishly, hysterically, like little blind fish in a pool within a dense cave. They rushed, crossed one another, jostled, collided, retreated and rushed again. Jeff soon became dizzy. He shuddered violently and turned to his wife.

"Jennie, I can't do it. I can't." His voice broke pitifully.

She did not appear to be listening. All the grief had gone from her face. She sat erect, her unseeing eyes wide open, strained and frightful. Her glossy black skin had become dull. She seemed as thin, as sharp and bony, as a starved bird. Now, having suffered and endured the sadness of tearing herself away from beloved things, she showed no anguish. She was absorbed with her own thoughts, and she didn't even hear Jeff's voice shouting in her ear.

Jeff said nothing more. For an instant there was light in his cavernous brain. The great chamber was, for less than a second, peopled by characters he knew and loved. They were simple, healthy creatures, and they behaved in a manner that he could understand. They had quality. But since he had already taken leave of them long ago, the remembrance did not break his heart again. Young Jeff Patton was among them, the Jeff Patton of fifty years ago who went down to New Orleans with a crowd, boys with candy-striped shirts and rouged-brown girls in noisy silks, was like a picture in his head. Yet it did not make him sad. On that very trip Slim Burns had killed Joe Beasley—the crowd had been broken up. Since then Jeff Patton's world had been the Greenbriar Plantation. If there had been other Mardi Gras carnivals, he had not heard of them. Since then there had been no time; the years had fallen on him like waves. Now he was old, worn out. Another paralytic stroke (like the one he had already suffered) would put him on his back for keeps. In that condition, with a frail blind woman to look after him, he would be worse off than if he were dead.

Suddenly Jeff's hands became steady. He actually felt brave. He slowed down the motor of the car and carefully pulled off the road. Below, the water of the stream boomed, a soft thunder in the deep channel. Jeff ran the car onto the clay slope, pointed it directly toward the stream and put his foot heavily on the accelerator. The little car leaped furiously down the steep incline toward the water. The movement was nearly as swift and direct as a fall. The two old black folks, sitting quietly side by side, showed no excitement. In another instant the car hit the water and dropped immediately out of sight.

A little later it lodged in the mud of a shallow place. One wheel of the crushed and upturned little Ford became visible above the rushing water.

Aripeko, Fernando County, Florida

The Patented Gate and the Mean Hamburger

ROBERT PENN WARREN

You have seen him a thousand times. You have seen him standing on the street corner on Saturday afternoon, in the little county-seat towns. He wears blue jean pants, or overalls washed to a pale pastel blue like the color of sky after a shower in spring, but because it is Saturday he has on a wool coat, an old one, perhaps the coat left from the suit he got married in a long time back. His long wrist bones hang out from the sleeves of the coat, the tendons showing along the bone like the dry twist of grapevine still corded on the stove-length of a hickory sapling you would find in his wood box beside his cookstove among the split chunks of gum and red oak. The big hands, with the knotted, cracked joints and the square, horn-thick nails, hang loose off the wrist bone like clumsy, home-made tools hung on the wall of a shed after work. If it is summer, he wears a straw hat with a wide brim, the straw fraying loose around the edge. If it is winter, he wears a felt hat, black once, but now weathered with streaks of dark gray and dull purple in the sunlight. His face is long and bony, the jawbone long under the drawn-in cheeks. The flesh along the jawbone is nicked in a couple of places where the unaccustomed razor has been drawn over the leather-coarse skin. A tiny bit of blood crusts brown where the nick is. The color of the face is red, a dull red like the red clay mud or clay dust which clings to the bottom of his pants and to the cast-iron-looking brogans on his feet, or a red like the color of a piece of hewed cedar which has been left in the weather. The face does not look alive. It seems to be molded from the clay or hewed from the cedar. When the jaw moves, once, with its deliberate, massive motion on the quid of tobacco, you are still not convinced. That motion is but the cunning triumph of a mechanism concealed within.

But you see the eyes. You see that the eyes are alive. They are pale blue or gray, set back under the deep brows and thorny eyebrows. They are not wide, but are squinched up like eyes accustomed to wind or sun or to measuring the stroke of the ax or to fixing the object over the rifle sights.

41

When you pass, you see that the eyes are alive and are warily and dispassionately estimating you from the ambush of the thorny brows. Then you pass on, and he stands there in that stillness which is his gift.

With him may be standing two or three others like himself, but they are still, too. They do not talk. The young men, who will be like these men when they get to be fifty or sixty, are down at the beer parlor, carousing and laughing with a high, whickering laugh. But the men on the corner are long past all that. They are past many things. They have endured and will endure in their silence and wisdom. They will stand on the street corner and reject the world which passes under their level gaze as a rabble passes under the guns of a rocky citadel around whose base a slatternly town has assembled.

I had seen Jeff York a thousand times, or near, standing like that on the street corner in town, while the people flowed past him, under the distant and wary and dispassionate eyes in ambush. He would be waiting for his wife and the three tow-headed children who were walking around the town looking into store windows and at the people. After a while they would come back to him, and then, wordlessly, he would lead them to the store where they always did their trading. He would go first, marching with a steady bent-kneed stride, setting the cast-iron brogans down deliberately on the cement; then his wife, a small woman with covert, sidewise, curious glances for the world, would follow, and behind her the towheads bunched together in a dazed, glory-struck way. In the store, when their turn came, Jeff York would move to the counter, accept the clerk's greeting, and then bend down from his height to catch the whispered directions of his wife. He would straighten up and say, "Gimme a sack of flahr, if'n you please." Then when the sack of flour had been brought, he would lean again to his wife for the next item. When the stuff had all been bought and paid for with the grease-thick, wadded dollar bills which he took from an old leather coin purse with a metal catch to it, he would heave it all together into his arms and march out, his wife and towheads behind him and his eyes fixed level over the heads of the crowd. He would march down the street and around to the hitching lot where the wagons were, and put his stuff into his wagon and cover it with an old quilt to wait till he got ready to drive out to his place.

For Jeff York had a place. That was what made him different from the other men who looked like him and with whom he stood on the street corner on Saturday afternoon. They were croppers, but he, Jeff York, had a place. But he stood with them because his father had stood with their fathers and his grandfathers with their grandfathers, or with men like their fathers and grandfathers, in other towns, in settlements in the mountains, in towns beyond the mountains. They were the great-great-grandsons of men who, half woodsmen and half farmers, had been shoved into the sand hills, into the limestone hills, into the barrens, two hundred, two hundred and fifty years before and had learned there the way to grabble a life out of the sand and the stone. And when the soil had leached away into the sand or burnt off the stone, they went on west, walking with the bent-kneed stride over the mountains, their eyes squinching warily in the gaunt faces, the rifle over the crooked arm, hunting a new place.

But there was a curse on them. They only knew the life they knew, and that life did not belong to the fat bottom lands, where the cane was head-tall, and to the grassy meadows and the rich swale. So they passed those places by and hunted for the place which was like home and where they could pick up the old life, with the same feel in the bones and the squirrel's bark sounding the same after first light. They had walked a long way, to the sand hills of Alabama, to the red country of North Mississippi and Louisiana, to the Barrens of Tennessee, to the Knobs of Kentucky and the scrub country of West Kentucky, to the Ozarks. Some of them had stopped in Cobb County, Tennessee, in the hilly eastern part of the county, and had built their cabins and dug up the ground for the corn patch. But the land had washed away there, too, and in the end they had come down out of the high land into the bottoms—for half of Cobb County is a rich, swelling country—where the corn was good and the tobacco unfurled a leaf like a yard of green velvet and the white houses stood among cedars and tulip trees and maples. But they were not to live in the white houses with the limestone chimneys set strong at the end of each gable. No, they were to live in the shacks on the back of the farms, or in cabins not much different from the cabins they had once lived in two hundred years before over the mountains or, later, in the hills of Cobb County. But the shacks and the cabins now stood on somebody else's ground, and the curse which they had brought with them over the mountain trail, more precious than the bullet mold or grandma's quilt, the curse which was the very feeling in the bones and the habit in the hand, had come full circle.

Jeff York was one of those men, but he had broken the curse. It had taken him more than thirty years to do it, from the time when he was nothing but a big boy until he was fifty. It had taken him from sun to sun, year in and year out, and all the sweat in his body, and all the power of rejection he could muster, until the very act of rejection had become a kind of pleasure, a dark, secret, savage dissipation, like an obsessing vice. But those years had given him his place, sixty acres with a house and barn.

When he bought the place, it was not very good. The land was run-down from years of neglect and abuse. But Jeff York put brush in the gullies to stop the wash and planted clover on the run-down fields. He mended the fences, rod by rod. He patched the roof on the little house and propped up the porch, buying lumber and shingles almost piece by piece and one by one as he could spare the sweat-bright and grease-slick quarters and half-dollars out of his leather purse. Then he painted the house. He painted it white, for he knew that that was the color you painted a house sitting back from the road with its couple of maples, beyond the clover field.

Last, he put up the gate. It was a patented gate, the kind you can ride up to and open by pulling on a pull rope without getting off your horse or out of your buggy or wagon. It had a high pair of posts, well braced and with a high crossbar between, and the bars for the opening mechanism extending on each side. It was painted white, too. Jeff was even prouder of the gate than he was of the place. Lewis Simmons, who lived next to Jeff's place, swore he had seen Jeff come out after dark on a mule and ride in and out of that gate, back and forth, just for the pleasure of pulling on the rope and making the mechanism work. The gate was the seal Jeff York had put on all the years of sweat and rejection. He could sit on his porch on a Sunday afternoon in summer, before milking time, and look down the rise, down the winding dirt track, to the white gate beyond the clover, and know what he needed to know about all the years passed.

Meanwhile Jeff York had married and had had the three towheads. His wife was twenty years or so younger than he, a small, dark woman, who walked with her head bowed a little and from that humble and unprovoking posture stole sidewise, secret glances at the world from eyes which were brown or black—you never could tell which because you never remembered having looked her straight in the eye—and which were surprisingly bright in that sidewise, secret flicker, like the eyes of a small, cunning bird which surprises you from the brush. When they came to town she moved along the street, with a child in her arms or later with the three trailing behind her, and stole her looks at the world. She wore a calico dress, dun-colored, which hung loose to conceal whatever shape her thin body had, and in winter over the dress a brown wool coat with a scrap of fur at the collar which looked like some tattered growth of fungus feeding on old wood. She wore black high-heeled shoes, slippers of some kind, which she kept polished and which surprised you under that dress and coat. In the slippers she moved with a slightly limping, stealthy gait, almost sliding them along the pavement, as though she had not fully mastered the complicated trick required to use them properly. You knew that she wore them only when she came to town, that she carried them wrapped up in a piece of newspaper until their wagon had reached the first house on the outskirts of town, and that, on the way back, at the same point, she would take them off and wrap them up again and hold the bundle in her lap until she got home. If the weather happened to be bad, or if it was winter, she would have a pair of old brogans under the wagon seat.

It was not that Jeff York was a hard man and kept his wife in clothes that were as bad as those worn by the poorest of the women of the croppers. In fact, some of the cropper women, poor or not, black or white, managed to buy dresses with some color in them and proper hats, and went to the moving picture show on Saturday afternoon. But Jeff still owed a little money on his place, less than two hundred dollars, which he had had to borrow to rebuild his barn after it was struck by lightning. He had, in fact, never been entirely out of debt. He had lost a mule which had got out on the highway and been hit by a truck. That had set him back. One of his towheads had been sickly for a couple of winters. He had not been in deep, but he was not a man, with all those years of rejection behind him, to forget the meaning of those years. He was good enough to his family. Nobody ever said the contrary. But he was good to them in terms of all the years he had lived through. He did what he could afford. He bought the towheads a ten-cent bag of colored candy every Saturday afternoon for them to suck on during the ride home in the wagon, and the last thing before they left town, he always took the lot of them over to the dogwagon to get hamburgers and orange pop.

The towheads were crazy about hamburgers. And so was his wife, for that matter. You could tell it, even if she didn't say anything, for she would lift her bowed-forward head a little, and her face would brighten, and she would run her tongue out to wet her lips just as the plate with the hamburger would be set on the counter before her. But all those folks, like Jeff York and his family, like hamburgers, with pickle and onions and mustard and tomato catsup, the whole works. It is something different. They stay out in the country and eat hog-meat, when they can get it, and greens and corn bread and potatoes, and nothing but a pinch of salt to brighten it on the tongue, and when they get to town and get hold of beef and wheat bread and all the stuff to jack up the flavor, they have to swallow to keep the mouth from flooding before they even take the first bite.

So the last thing every Saturday, Jeff York would take his family over to Slick Hardin's Dew Drop Inn Diner and give them the treat. The diner was built like a railway coach, but it was set on a concrete foundation on a lot just off the main street of town. At each end the concrete was painted to show wheels. Slick Hardin kept the grass just in front of the place pretty well mowed and one or two summers he even had a couple of flower beds in the middle of that shirttail-size lawn. Slick had a good business. For a few years he had been a prelim fighter over in Nashville and had got his name in the papers a few times. So he was a kind of hero, with the air of romance about him. He had been born, however, right in town and, as soon as he had found out he wasn't ever going to be good enough to be a real fighter, he had come back home and started the dogwagon, the first one ever in town. He was a slick-skinned fellow, about thirty-five, prematurely bald, with his head slick all over. He had big eyes, pale blue and slick looking like agates. When he said something that he thought smart, he would roll his eyes around, slick in his head like marbles, to see who was laughing. Then he'd wink. He had done very well with his business, for despite the fact that he had picked up city ways and a lot of city talk, he still remembered enough to deal with the country people, and they were the ones who brought the dimes in. People who lived right there in town, except for school kids in the afternoon and the young toughs from the pool room or men on the night shift down at the railroad, didn't often get around to the dogwagon.

Slick Hardin was perhaps trying to be smart when he said what he did to Mrs. York. Perhaps he had forgotten, just for that moment, that people like Jeff York and his wife didn't like to be kidded, at least not in that way. He said what he did, and then grinned and rolled his eyes around to see if some of the other people present were thinking it was funny.

Mrs. York was sitting on a stool in front of the counter, flanked on one side by Jeff York and on the other by the three towheads. She had just sat down to wait for the hamburger—there were several orders in ahead of the York order—and had been watching in her sidewise fashion every move of Slick Hardin's hands as he patted the pink meat onto the hot slab and wiped the split buns over the greasy iron to make them ready to receive it. She always watched him like that, and when the hamburger was set before her she would wet her lips with her tongue.

That day Slick set the hamburger down in front of Mrs. York, and said, "Anybody likes hamburger much as you, Mrs. York, ought to git him a hamburger stand."

Mrs. York flushed up, and didn't say anything, staring at her plate. Slick rolled his eyes to see how it was going over, and somebody down the counter snickered. Slick looked back at the Yorks, and if he had not been so encouraged by the snicker he might, when he saw Jeff York's face, have hesitated before going on with his kidding. People like Jeff York are touchous, and they are especially touchous about their women-folks, and you do not make jokes with or about their women-folks unless it is perfectly plain that the joke is a very special kind of friendly joke. The snicker down the counter had defined the joke as not entirely friendly. Jeff was looking at Slick, and something was growing slowly in that hewed-cedar face, and back in the gray eyes in the ambush of thorny brows.

But Slick did not notice. The snicker had encouraged him, and so he said, "Yeah, if I liked them hamburgers much as you, I'd buy me a hamburger stand. Fact, I'm selling this one. You want to buy it?"

There was another snicker, louder, and Jeff York, whose hamburger had been about half way to his mouth for another bite, laid it down deliberately on his plate. But whatever might have happened at that moment did not happen. It did not happen because Mrs. York lifted her flushed face, looked straight at Slick Hardin, swallowed hard to get down a piece of the hamburger or to master her nerve, and said in a sharp strained voice, "You sellen this place?"

There was complete silence. Nobody had expected her to say anything. The chances were she had never said a word in that diner in the couple of hundred times she had been in it. She had come in with Jeff York and, when a stool had come vacant, had sat down, and Jeff had said, "Gimme five hamburgers, if'n you please, and make 'em well done, and five bottles of orange pop." Then, after the eating was over he had always laid down seventy-five cents on the counter—that is, after there were five hamburger-eaters in the family—and walked out, putting his brogans down slow, and his wife and kids following without a word. But now she spoke up and asked the question, in that strained, artificial voice, and everybody, including her husband, looked at her with surprise.

As soon as he could take it in, Slick Hardin replied, "Yeah, I'm selling it."

She swallowed hard again, but this time it could not have been hamburger, and demanded, "What you asken fer hit?"

Slick looked at her in the new silence, half shrugged, a little contemptuously, and said, "Fourteen hundred and fifty dollars."

She looked back at him, while the blood ebbed from her face. "Hit's a lot of money," she said in a flat tone, and returned her gaze to the hamburger on her plate.

"Lady," Slick said defensively, "I got that much money tied up here. Look at that there stove. It is a Heat Master and they cost. Them coffee urns, now. Money can't buy no better. And this here lot, lady, the diner sets on. Anybody knows I got that much money tied up here, I got more. This lot cost me more'n . . ." He suddenly realized that she was not listening to him. And he must have realized, too, that she didn't have a dime in the world and couldn't buy his diner, and that he was making a fool of himself, defending his price. He stopped abruptly, shrugged his shoulders, and then swung his wide gaze down the counter to pick out somebody to wink to.

But before he got the wink off, Jeff York had said, "Mr. Hardin."

Slick looked at him and asked, "Yeah?"

"She didn't mean no harm," Jeff York said. "She didn't mean to be messen in your business."

Slick shrugged. "Ain't no skin off my nose," he said. "Ain't no secret I'm selling out. My price ain't no secret neither."

Mrs. York bowed her head over her plate. She was chewing a mouthful of her hamburger with a slow, abstracted motion of her jaw, and you knew that it was flavorless on her tongue.

That was, of course, on a Saturday. On Thursday afternoon of the next week, Slick was in the diner alone. It was the slack time, right in the middle of the afternoon. Slick, as he told it later, was wiping off the stove and wasn't noticing. He was sort of whistling to himself, he said. He had a way of whistling soft through his teeth. But he wasn't whistling loud, he said, not so loud he wouldn't have heard the door open or the steps if she hadn't come gum-shoeing in on him to stand there waiting in the middle of the floor until he turned round and was so surprised he nearly had heart failure. He had thought he was there alone, and there she was, watching every move he was making, like a cat watching a goldfish swim in a bowl.

"Howdy-do," he said, when he got his breath back.

"This place still fer sale?" she asked him.

"Yeah, lady," he said.

"What you asken fer hit?"

"Lady, I done told you," Slick replied, "fourteen hundred and fifty dollars."

"Hit's a heap of money," she said.

Slick started to tell her how much money he had tied up there, but before he had got going, she had turned and slipped out of the door.

"Yeah," Slick said later to the men who came into the diner, "me like a fool starting to tell her how much money I got tied up here when I knowed she didn't have a dime. That woman's crazy. She must walked that five or six miles in here just to ask me something she already knowed the answer to. And then turned right round and walked out. But I am selling me this place. I'm tired of slinging hash to them hicks. I got me some connections over in Nashville and I'm gonna open me a place over there. A cigar stand and about three pool tables and maybe some beer. I'll have me a sort of club in the back. You know, membership cards to get in, where the boys will play a little game. Just sociable, I got good connections over in Nashville. I'm selling this place. But that woman, she ain't got a dime. She ain't gonna buy it."

But she did.

On Saturday Jeff York led his family over to the diner. They ate hamburgers without a word and marched out. After they had gone, Slick said, "Looks like she ain't going to make the invest-mint. Gonna buy a block of bank stock instead." Then he rolled his eyes, located a brother down the counter, and winked.

It was almost the end of the next week before it happened. What had been going on inside the white house out on Jeff York's place nobody knew or was to know. Perhaps she just starved him out, just not doing the cooking or burning everything. Perhaps she just quit attending to the children prop-

erly and he had to come back tired from work and take care of them.
Perhaps she just lay in bed at night and talked and talked to him, asking
him to buy it, nagging him all night long, while he would fall asleep and
then wake up with a start to hear her voice still going on. Or perhaps she
just turned her face away from him and wouldn't let him touch her. He was
a lot older than she, and she was probably the only woman he had ever had.
He had been too ridden by his dream and his passion for rejection during all
the years before to lay even a finger on a woman. So she had him there.
Because he was a lot older and because he had never had another woman.
But perhaps she used none of these methods. She was a small, dark, cunning woman, with a sidewise look from her lowered face, and she could
have thought up ways of her own, no doubt.

Whatever she thought up, it worked. On Friday morning Jeff York went
to the bank. He wanted to mortgage his place, he told Todd Sullivan, the
president. He wanted fourteen hundred and fifty dollars, he said. Todd
Sullivan would not let him have it. He already owed the bank one hundred
and sixty dollars and the best he could get on a mortgage was eleven
hundred dollars. That was in 1935 and then farmland wasn't worth much
and half the land in the country was mortgaged anyway. Jeff York sat in the
chair by Todd Sullivan's desk and didn't say anything. Eleven hundred
dollars would not do him any good. Take off the hundred and sixty dollars
he owed and it wouldn't be but a little over nine hundred dollars clear to
him. He sat there quietly for a minute, apparently turning that fact over in
his head. Then Todd Sullivan asked him, "How much you say you need?"

Jeff York told him.

"What you want it for?" Todd Sullivan asked.

He told him that.

"I tell you," Todd Sullivan said, "I don't want to stand in the way of a
man bettering himself. Never did. That diner ought to be a good proposi-
tion, all right, and I don't want to stand in your way if you want to come to
town and better yourself. It will be a step up from that farm for you, and I
like a man has got ambition. The bank can't lend you the money, not on that
piece of property. But I tell you what I'll do. I'll buy your place. I got me
some walking horses I'm keeping out on my father's place. But I could use
me a little place of my own. For my horses. I'll give you seventeen hundred
for it. Cash."

50

Jeff York did not say anything to that. He looked slow at Todd Sullivan as though he did not understand.

"Seventeen hundred," the banker repeated. "That's a good figure. For these times."

Jeff was not looking at him now. He was looking out the window, across the alleyway—Todd Sullivan's office was in the back of the bank. The banker, telling about it later when the doings of Jeff York had become for a moment a matter of interest, said, "I thought he hadn't even heard me. He looked like he was half asleep or something. I coughed to sort of wake him up. You know the way you do. I didn't want to rush him. You can't rush those people, you know. But I couldn't sit there all day. I had offered him a fair price."

It was, as a matter of fact, a fair price for the times, when the bottom was out of everything in the section.

Jeff York took it. He took the seventeen hundred dollars and bought the dogwagon with it, and rented a little house on the edge of town and moved in with his wife and the towheads. The first day after they got settled, Jeff York and his wife went over to the diner to get instructions from Slick about running the place. He showed Mrs. York all about how to work the coffee machine and the stove, and how to make up the sandwiches, and how to clean the place up after herself. She fried up hamburgers for all of them, herself, her husband, and Slick Hardin, for practice, and they ate the hamburgers while a couple of hangers-on watched them. "Lady," Slick said, for he had money in his pocket and was heading out for Nashville on the seven o'clock train that night, and was feeling expansive, "lady, you sure fling a mean hamburger."

He wiped the last crumbs and mustard off his lips, got his valise from behind the door, and said, "Lady, git in there and pitch. I hope you make a million hamburgers." Then he stepped out into the bright fall sunshine and walked away whistling up the street, whistling through his teeth and rolling his eyes as though there were somebody to wink to. That was the last anybody in town ever saw of Slick Hardin.

The next day, Jeff York worked all day down at the diner. He was scrubbing up the place inside and cleaning up the trash which had accumulated behind it. He burned all the trash. Then he gave the place a good coat of paint outside, white paint. That took him two days. Then he

51

touched up the counter inside with varnish. He straightened up the sign out front, which had begun to sag a little. He had that place looking spic and span.

Then on the fifth day after they got settled—it was Sunday—he took a walk in the country. It was along toward sundown when he started out, not late, as a matter of fact, for by October the days are shortening up. He walked out the Curtisville pike and out the cut-off leading to his farm. When he entered the cut-off, about a mile from his own place, it was still light enough for the Bowdoins, who had a filling station at the corner, to see him plain when he passed.

The next time anybody saw him was on Monday morning about six o'clock. A man taking milk into town saw him. He was hanging from the main cross bar of the white patented gate. He had jumped off the gate. But he had propped the thing open so there wouldn't be any chance of clambering back up on it if his neck didn't break when he jumped and he should happen to change his mind.

But that was an unnecessary precaution, as it developed. Dr. Stauffer said that his neck was broken very clean. "A man who can break a neck as clean as that could make a living at it," Dr. Stauffer said. And added, "if he's damned sure it ain't ever his own neck."

Mrs. York was much cut up by her husband's death. People were sympathetic and helpful, and out of a mixture of sympathy and curiosity she got a good starting trade at the diner. And the trade kept right on. She got so she didn't hang her head and look sidewise at you and the world. She would look straight at you. She got so she could walk in high heels without giving the impression that it was a trick she was learning. She wasn't a bad-looking woman, as a matter of fact, once she had caught on how to fix herself up a little. The railroad men and the pool hall gang liked to hang out there and kid with her. Also, they said, she flung a mean hamburger.

The Bitterness

Bitterness is a universal human response to real or imagined injustice, hardly confined to any particular region. However, in the South there has been a regional bitterness which resulted from the War between the States. Its presence is witnessed even in the syntax of southern speech. Only the young and "liberated" or Yankee immigrants refer to that conflict as the Civil War, or to themselves as Rebels. Both terms imply a resistance to the authority of established tradition which is anathema to most adult Southerners even today.

Southerners who fought in that war were not conscripted; they *chose* to fight for a way of life which they cherished. Their valiant armies were defeated, but their indomitable pride was not. The result was a regional bitterness which touched almost everybody.

Its most obvious manifestation came from the families of plantation masters. Bereft of their wealth, which was the original source of their power, they held more tenaciously than ever to their genteel image. Former slaves found themselves the winners of a joyous independence for which they were unprepared. Many were exploited by carpetbaggers and corporate northern interests who, unlike their former owners, felt no responsibility for their welfare. Sharecroppers moved in eagerly—only to find they still had no financial security and no more place than they had held before.

The South was impoverished, its resources depleted. All that was left was the land; there was no money, little manpower, and no economic structure for rebuilding it. A terrible sense of bitterness pervaded the land. Southerners had not lost sight of their proper place, but they had lost the power to maintain it; and it was the only social and economic order which they knew.

To all this we add the bitterness of southern Indians. The lament for their place, lost long before the War, was now heard as another small voice echoing the chaos of a proud people in the face of defeat.

Charleston in the 1860's
(Derived from the Diaries of Mary Boykin Chestnut)

ADRIENNE RICH

He seized me round the waist and kissed my throat . . .
Your eyes, dear, are they grey or blue,
eyes of an angel?
The carts have passed already with their heaped
night-soil, we breathe again,
Is this what war is? Nitrate . . .
But smell the pear,
the jasmine, the violets.
Why does this landscape always sadden you?
Now the freshet is up on every side,
the river comes to our doors,
limbs of primeval trees dip in the swamp.

So we fool on into the black
cloud ahead of us.
Everything human glitters fever-bright,
the thrill of waking up
out of a stagnant life?
There seems a spell upon
your lovers—all dead of wounds
or blown to pieces . . . Nitrate!
I'm writing blind with tears of rage.
In vain. Years, death, depopulation, fears,
bondage: these shall all be borne.
No imagination to forestall woe.

Nocturne At Bethesda

ARNA BONTEMPS

I thought I saw an angel flying low.
I thought I saw the flicker of a wing
above the mulberry trees—but not again.
Bethesda sleeps. This ancient pool that healed
a host of bearded Jews does not awake.
This pool that once the angels troubled does not move.
No angel stirs it now, no Savior comes
with healing in His hands to raise the sick
and bid the lame man leap upon the ground.

The golden days are gone. Why do we wait
so long upon the marble steps, blood
falling from our open wounds? And why
do our black faces search the empty sky?
Is there something we have forgotten? some precious thing
we have lost, wandering in strange lands?

There was a day, I remember now,
I beat my breast and cried 'Wash me God,
wash me with a wave of wind upon
the barley; O quiet One, draw near, draw near!
walk upon the hills with lovely feet
and in the waterfall stand and speak.

Dip white hands in the lily pool and mourn
upon the harps still hanging in the trees
near Babylon along the river's edge,
but oh, remember me, I pray, before
the summer goes and rose leaves lose their red.'

Prisoners from the Front, Winslow Homer

The Bitterness

The old terror takes my heart, the fear
of quiet waters and of faint twilights.
There will be better days when I am gone
and healing pools where I cannot be healed.
Fragrant stars will gleam forever and ever
above the place where I lie desolate.

Yet I hope, still I long to live.
And if there can be returning after death
I shall come back. But it will not be here:
if you want me you must search for me
beneath the palms of Africa. Or if
I am not there you may call to me
across the shining dunes, perhaps I shall
be following a desert caravan.

I may pass through centuries of death
with quiet eyes, but I'll remember still
a jungle tree with burning scarlet birds.
There is something I have forgotten, some precious thing.
I shall be seeking ornaments of ivory,
I shall be dying for a jungle fruit.

You do not hear, Bethesda,
O still green water in a stagnant pool!
Love abandoned you and me alike.
There was a day you held a rich full moon
upon your heart and listened to the words
of men now dead and saw the angels fly.
There is a simple story on your face:
years have wrinkled you. I know, Bethesda!
You are sad. It is the same with me.

The Child By Tiger*

THOMAS WOLFE

One day after school, Monk and several of the boys were playing with a football in the yard at Randy Shepperton's. Randy was calling signals and handling the ball. Nebraska Crane was kicking it. Augustus Potterham was too clumsy to run or kick or pass, so they put him at center where all he'd have to do would be to pass the ball back to Randy when he got the signal. To the other boys, Gus Potterham was their freak child, their lame duck, the butt of their jokes and ridicule, but they also had a sincere affection for him; he was something to be taken in hand, to be protected and cared for.

There were several other boys who were ordinarily members of their group. They had Harry Higginson and Sam Pennock, and two boys named Howard Jarvis and Jim Redmond. It wasn't enough to make a team, of course. They didn't have room enough to play a game even if they had had team enough. What they played was really a kind of skeletonized practice game, with Randy and Nebraska back, Gus at center, two other fellows at the ends, and Monk and two or three more on the other side, whose duty was to get in and "break it up" if they could.

It was about four o'clock in the afternoon, late in October, and there was a smell of smoke, of leaves, of burning in the air. Bras had just kicked to Monk. It was a good kick too—a high, soaring punt that spiraled out above Monk's head, behind him. He ran back and tried to get it, but it was far and away "over the goal line"—that is to say, out in the street. It hit the street and bounded back and forth with that peculiarly erratic bounce a football has.

The ball rolled away from Monk down towards the corner. He was running out to get it when Dick Prosser, Sheppertons' new Negro man, came along, gathered it up neatly in his great black paw, and tossed it to him. Dick turned in then, and came on around the house, greeting the boys as he came. He called all of them "Mister" except Randy, and Randy was

*Chapter Eight of *The Web and the Rock*.

always "Cap'n"—"Cap'n Shepperton." This formal address—"Mr." Crane, "Mr." Potterham, "Mr." Webber, "Cap'n" Shepperton—pleased them immensely, gave them a feeling of mature importance and authority.

"Cap'n Shepperton" was splendid! It was something more to all of them than a mere title of respect. It had a delightful military association, particularly when Dick Prosser said it. Dick had served a long enlistment in the U.S. army. He had been a member of a regiment of crack Negro troops upon the Texas border, and the stamp of the military man was evident in everything he did. It was a joy just to watch him split up kindling. He did it with a power, a clean precision, a kind of military order, that was astounding. Every stick he cut seemed to be exactly the same length and shape as every other. He had all of them neatly stacked against the walls of the Shepperton basement with such regimented faultness that it almost seemed a pity to disturb their symmetry for the use for which they were intended.

It was the same with everything else he did. His little whitewashed basement room was as spotless as a barracks room. The bare board floor was always cleanly swept, a plain, bare table and a plain, straight chair were stationed exactly in the center of the room. On the table there was always just one object—an old Bible with a limp cover, almost worn out by constant use, for Dick was a deeply religious man. There was a little cast-iron stove and a little wooden box with a few lumps of coal and a neat stack of kindling in it. And against the wall, to the left, there was an iron cot, always precisely made and covered cleanly with a coarse grey blanket.

The Sheppertons were delighted with him. He had come there looking for work just a month or two before, "gone around to the back door" and modestly presented his qualifications. He had, he said, only recently received his discharge from the army, and was eager to get employment, at no matter what wage. He could cook, he could tend the furnace, he could do odd jobs, he was handy at carpentry, he knew how to drive a car—in fact, it seemed to the boys that there was very little that Dick Prosser could not do.

He could certainly shoot. He gave a modest demonstration of his prowess one afternoon, with Randy's "twenty-two," that left them gasping. He just lifted that little rifle in his powerful black hands as if it were a toy, without seeming to take aim, pointed it towards a strip of tin on which they had crudely marked out some bull's eye circles, and he simply peppered the center of the bull's eye, putting twelve holes through a space one inch square, so fast they could not even count the shots.

60

He knew how to box, too. Randy said he had been a regimental champion. At any rate, he was as cunning and crafty as a cat. He never boxed with the boys, of course, but Randy had two sets of gloves, and Dick used to coach them while they sparred. There was something amazingly tender and watchful about him. He taught them many things, how to lead, to hook, to counter, and to block, but he was careful to see that they did not hurt each other. Nebraska, who was the most powerful of the lot, could hit like a mule. He would have killed Gus Potterham in his simple, honest way if he had ever been given a free hand. But Dick, with his quick watchfulness, his gentle and persuasive tact, was careful to see this did not happen.

He knew about football, too, and that day, as Dick passed the boys, he paused, a powerful, respectable-looking Negro of thirty years or more, and watched them for a moment as they played.

Randy took the ball and went up to him.

"How do you hold it, Dick?" he said. "Is this right?"

Dick watched him attentively as he gripped the ball and held it back above his shoulder. The Negro nodded approvingly and said:

"That's right, Cap'n Shepperton. You've got it. Only," he said gently, and now took the ball in his own powerful hand, "when you gits a little oldah, yo' handses gits biggah and you gits a bettah grip."

His own great hand, in fact, seemed to hold the ball as easily as if it were an apple. And, holding it so a moment, he brought it back, aimed over his outstretched left hand as if he were pointing a gun, and rifled it in a beautiful, whizzing spiral thirty yards or more to Gus. He then showed them how to kick, how to get the ball off of the toe in such a way that it would rise and spiral cleanly.

He showed them how to make a fire, how to pile the kindling, where to place the coal, so that the flames shot up cone-wise, cleanly, without smoke or waste. He showed them how to strike a match with the thumbnail of one hand and keep and hold the flame in the strongest wind. He showed them how to lift a weight, how to "tote" a burden on their shoulders in the easiest way. There was nothing that he did not know. They were all so proud of him. Mr. Shepperton himself declared that Dick was the best man he'd ever had, the smartest darky that he'd ever known.

And yet? He went too softly, at too swift a pace. He was there upon them sometimes like a cat. Looking before them sometimes, seeing nothing but the world before them, suddenly they felt a shadow at their back, and, looking up, would find that Dick was there. And there was something moving in the night. They never saw him come or go. Sometimes they would waken, startled, and feel that they had heard a board creak, the soft clicking of a latch, a shadow passing swiftly. All was still.

"Young white fokes—O young white gentlemen"—his soft voice ending in a moan, a kind of rhythm in his lips—"O young white fokes, I'se tellin' *you*—" that soft, low moan again—"you gotta love each othah like a brothah." He was deeply religious and went to church three times a week. He read his Bible every night.

Sometimes Dick would come out of his little basement room and his eyes would be red, as if he had been weeping. They would know, then, that he had been reading his Bible. There would be times when he would almost moan when he talked to them, a kind of hymnal chant, a religious ecstasy, that came from some deep intoxication of the spirit, and that transported him. For the boys, it was a troubling and bewildering experience. They tried to laugh it off and make jokes about it. But there was something in it so dark and strange and full of a feeling they could not fathom that their jokes were hollow, and the trouble in their minds and in their hearts remained.

Sometimes on these occasions his speech would be made up of some weird jargon of Biblical phrases and quotations and allusions, of which he seemed to have hundreds, and which he wove together in the strange pattern of his emotion in a sequence that was meaningless to them but to which he himself had the coherent clue.

"O young white fokes," he would begin, moaning gently, "de dry bones in de valley. I tell you, white fokes, de day is comin' when He's comin' on dis earth again to sit in judgment. He'll put de sheep upon de right hand and de goats upon de left—O white fokes, white fokes—de Armageddon day's a-comin', white fokes—an' de dry bones in de valley."

Or again, they could hear him singing as he went about his work, in his deep rich voice, so full of warmth and strength, so full of Africa, singing hymns that were not only of his own race, but that were familiar to them all. They didn't know where he learned them. Perhaps they were remembered from his army days. Perhaps he had learned them in the service of former masters. He drove the Sheppertons to church on Sunday morning, and would wait for them throughout the service. He would come up to the side door of the church while the service was going on, neatly dressed in his good, dark suit, holding his chauffeur's hat respectfully in his hand, and stand humbly and listen during the course of the entire sermon.

And then when the hymns were sung, and the great rich sound would swell and roll out into the quiet air of Sunday, Dick would stand and listen, and sometimes he would join quietly in the song. A number of these favorite hymns the boys heard him singing many times in a low, rich voice, as he went about his work around the house. He would sing "Who Follows in His Train?"—or "Alexander's Glory Song," or "Rock of Ages," or "Onward, Christian Soldiers."

And yet? Well, nothing happened—there was just "a flying hint from here and there"—and the sense of something passing in the night.

Turning into the Square one day, as Dick was driving Mr. Shepperton to town, Lon Pilcher skidded murderously around the corner, side-swiped Dick, and took the fender off. The Negro was out of the car like a cat and got his master out. Mr. Shepperton was unhurt. Lon Pilcher climbed out and reeled across the street, drunk as a sot in mid-afternoon. He swung viciously, clumsily, at the Negro, smashed him in the face. Blood trickled from the fat black nostrils and from the thick, liver-colored lips. Dick did not move. But suddenly the whites of his eyes were shot with red, his bleeding lips bared for a moment over the white ivory of his teeth. Lon smashed at him again. The Negro took it full in the face again; his hands twitched slightly but he did not move. They collared the drunken sot and hauled him off and locked him up. Dick stood there for a moment, then he wiped his face and turned to see what damage had been done to the car. No more now, but there were those who saw it, who remembered later how the eyes went red.

Another thing. The Sheppertons had a cook named Pansy Harris. She was a comely Negro wench, young, plump, black as the ace of spades, a good-hearted girl with a deep dimple in her cheeks and faultless teeth, bared in a most engaging smile. No one ever saw Dick speak to her. No one ever saw her glance at him, or him at her—and yet that dimpled, plump, and smilingly good-natured wench became as mournful-silent and as silent-sullen as midnight pitch. She sang no more. No more was seen the gleaming ivory of her smile. No more was heard the hearty and infectious exuberance of her warm, full-throated laugh. She went about her work as mournfully as if she were going to a funeral. The gloom deepened all about her. She answered sullenly now when spoken to.

One night towards Christmas she announced that she was leaving. In response to all entreaties, all efforts to find the reason for her sudden and unreasonable decision, she had no answer except a sullen repetition of the assertion that she had to leave. Repeated questionings did finally wring from her a statement that her husband wanted her to quit, that he needed her at home. More than this she would not say, and even this excuse was highly suspected, because her husband was a Pullman porter, home only two days a week, and well accustomed to do himself such housekeeping tasks as she might do for him.

The Sheppertons were fond of her. The girl had been with them for several years. They tried again to find the reason for her leaving. Was she dissatisfied? "No'm"—an implacable monosyllable, mournful, unrevealing as the night. Had she been offered a better job elsewhere? "No'm"—as untelling as before. If they offered her more wages, would she stay with them? "No'm"—again and again, sullen and unyielding; until finally the exasperated mistress threw her hands up in a gesture of defeat and said: "All right then, Pansy. Have it your own way, if that's the way you feel. Only for heaven's sake, don't leave us in the lurch. Don't leave us until we get another cook."

This, at length, with obvious reluctance, the girl agreed to. Then, putting on her hat and coat, and taking the paper bag of "leavings" she was allowed to take home with her at night, she went out the kitchen door and made her sullen and morose departure.

This was on Saturday night, a little after eight o'clock.

That same afternoon Randy and Monk had been fooling around the Shepperton basement, and, seeing that Dick's door was slightly ajar, they stopped at the opening and looked in to see if he was there. The little room was empty, and swept and spotless as it had always been.

But they did not notice that! That saw *it!* At the same moment their breaths caught sharply in a gasp of startled wonderment. Randy was the first to speak.

"Look!" he whispered. "Do you see it?"

See it? Monk's eyes were glued upon it. Had he found himself staring suddenly at the flat head of a rattlesnake his hypnotized surprise could have been no greater. Squarely across the bare boards of the table, blue-dull, deadly in its murderous efficiency, lay an automatic army rifle. They both knew the type. They had seen them all when Randy went to buy his little "twenty-two" at Uncle Morris Teitlebaum's. Beside it was a box containing one hundred rounds of ammunition, and behind it, squarely in the center, face downward, open on the table, was the familiar cover of Dick's old, worn Bible.

Then he was on them like a cat. He was there like a great, dark shadow before they knew it. They turned, terrified. He was there above them, his thick lips bared above his gums, his eyes gone small and red as rodents'.

"Dick!" Randy gasped, and moistened his dry lips. "Dick!" he fairly cried now.

It was all over like a flash. Dick's mouth closed. They could see the whites of his eyes again. He smiled and said softly, affably, "Yes, suh, Cap'n Shepperton. Yes suh! You gent-mun lookin' at my rifle?"—and he stepped across the sill into the room.

Monk gulped and nodded his head and couldn't say a word, and Randy whispered, "Yes." And both of them still stared at him with an expression of appalled and fascinated interest.

Dick shook his head and chuckled. "Can't do without my rifle, white fokes. No suh!" He shook his head good-naturedly again, "Ole Dick, he's—he's—he's an ole *ahmy* man, you know. He's gotta have his rifle. If they take his rifle away from him, why that's jest lak takin' candy away from a little baby. Yes suh!" he chuckled again, and picked the weapon up affectionately. "Ole Dick felt Christmas comin' on—he—he—I reckon he must have felt it in his bones," he chuckled, "so I been savin' up my money—I jest thought I'd hide this heah and keep it as a big surprise fo' the young white fokes," he said. "I was jest gonna put it away heah and keep it untwill Christmas morning. Then I was gonna take the young white fokes out and show 'em how to shoot."

They had begun to breathe more easily now, and, almost as if they were under the spell of the Pied Piper of Hamelin, they had followed him step by step into the room.

"Yes suh," Dick chuckled, "I was jest fixin' to hide this gun away and keep it hid twill Christmas day, but Cap'n Shepperton—hee!" he chuckled heartily and slapped his thigh—"you can't fool ole Cap'n Shepperton! He was too quick fo' me. He jest must've smelled this ole gun right out. He comes right in and sees it befo' I has a chance to tu'n around. . . . Now, white fokes," Dick's voice fell to a tone of low and winning confidence,

65

"Ah's hopin' that I'd git to keep this gun as a little supprise fo' you. Now that you's found out, I'll tell you what I'll do. If you'll jest keep it a supprise from the other white fokes twill Christmas day, I'll take all you gent'mun out and let you shoot it. Now cose," he went on quietly, with a shade of resignation, "if you want to tell on me you can—but"—here his voice fell again, with just the faintest yet most eloquent shade of sorrowful regret— "Ole Dick was lookin' fahwad to this. He was hopin' to give all the white fokes a supprise Christmas day."

They promised earnestly that they would keep his secret as if it were their own. They fairly whispered their solemn vow. They tiptoed away out of the little basement room, as if they were afraid their very footsteps might betray the partner of their confidence.

This was four o'clock on Saturday afternoon. Already, there was a somber moaning of the wind, grey storm clouds sweeping over. The threat of snow was in the air.

Snow fell that night. It began at six o'clock. It came howling down across the hills. It swept in on them from the Smokies. By seven o'clock the air was blind with sweeping snow, the earth was carpeted, the streets were numb. The storm howled on, around houses warm with crackling fires and shaded light. All life seemed to have withdrawn into thrilling isolation. A horse went by upon the street with muffled hoofs.

George Webber went to sleep upon this mystery, lying in the darkness, listening to that exultancy of storm, to that dumb wonder, that enormous and attentive quietness of snow, with something dark and jubilant in his soul he could not utter.

Snow in the South is wonderful. It has a kind of magic and a mystery that it has nowhere else. And the reason for this is that it comes to people in the South not as the grim, unyielding tenant of the Winter's keep, but as a strange and wild visitor from the secret North. It comes to them from darkness, to their own special and most secret soul there in the South. It brings to them the thrilling isolation of its own white mystery. It brings them something that they lack, and that they have to have; something that they have lost, but now have found; something that they have known utterly, but had forgotten until now.

In every man there are two hemispheres of light and dark, two worlds discrete, two countries of his soul's adventure. And one of these is the dark land, the other half of his heart's home, the unvisited domain of his father's earth.

And this is the land he knows the best. It is the earth unvisited—and it is his, as nothing he has seen can ever be. It is the world intangible that he has never touched—yet more his own than something he has owned forever. It is the great world of his mind, his heart, his spirit, built there in his imagination, shaped by wonder and unclouded by the obscuring flaws of accident and actuality, the proud, unknown earth of the lost, the found, the never-here, the ever-real America, unsullied, true, essential, built there in the brain, and shaped to glory by the proud and flaming vision of a child.

Thus, at the head of those two poles of life will lie the real, the truthful image of its immortal opposite. Thus, buried in the dark heart of the cold and secret North, abides forever the essential image of the South; thus, at the dark heart of the moveless South, there burns forever the immortal splendor of the North.

So had it always been with George. The other half of his heart's home, the world unknown that he knew the best, was the dark North. And snow swept in that night across the hills, demonic visitant, to restore that land to him, to sheet it in essential wonder. Upon this mystery he fell asleep.

A little after two o'clock next morning he was awakened by the ringing of a bell. It was the fire bell of the City Hall, and it was beating an alarm—a hard, fast stroke that he had never heard before. Bronze with peril, clangorous through the snow-numbed silence of the air, it had a quality of instancy and menace he had never known before. He leaped up and ran to the window to look for the telltale glow against the sky. But it was no fire. Almost before he looked, those deadly strokes beat in upon his brain the message that this was no alarm for fire. It was a savage, brazen tongue calling the town to action, warning mankind against the menace of some peril—secret, dark, unknown, greater than fire or flood could ever be.

He got instantly, in the most overwhelming and electric way, the sense that the whole town had come to life. All up and down the street the houses were beginning to light up. Next door, the Shepperton house was ablaze with light, from top to bottom. Even as he looked Mr. Shepperton, wearing an overcoat over his pajamas, ran down the steps and padded out across the snow-covered walk towards the street.

People were beginning to run out of doors. He heard excited cries and shouts and questions everywhere. He saw Nebraska Crane come pounding up the middle of the street. He knew that he was coming for him and Randy. As Bras ran by Shepperton's, he put his fingers to his mouth and whistled piercingly. It was a signal they all knew.

Monk was already almost dressed by the time he came running in across the front yard. He hammered at the door; Monk was already there. They both spoke at once. He had answered Monk's startled question before he got it out.

"Come on!" he said, panting with excitement, his Cherokee black eyes burning with an intensity Monk had never seen before. "Come on!" he cried. They were halfway out across the yard by now. "It's that nigger! He's gone crazy and is running wild!"

"Wh-wh-what nigger?" Monk gasped, pounding at his heels.

Even before he spoke Monk had the answer. Mr. Crane had already come out of his house and crossed the street, buttoning his heavy policeman's overcoat and buckling his girdle as he came. He had paused to speak for a moment to Mr. Shepperton, and Monk heard Mr. Shepperton say quickly, in a low voice:

"Which way did he go?"

Then he heard somebody cry, "It's that nigger of Shepperton's!"

Mr. Shepperton turned and went quickly back across his yard towards the house. His wife and two girls stood huddled in the open doorway. The snow had drifted in across the porch. The three women stood there, white, trembling, holding themselves together, their arms thrust in the wide sleeves of their kimonos.

The telephone in Shepperton's house was ringing like mad but no one was paying any attention to it. Monk heard Mrs. Shepperton say quickly as her husband ran up the steps, "Is it Dick?" He nodded and passed her brusquely, going towards the phone.

At this moment, Nebraska whistled piercingly again upon his fingers, and Randy Shepperton ran past his mother and sped down the steps. She called sharply to him. He paid no attention to her. When he came up, Monk saw that his fine, thin face was white as a sheet. He looked at Monk and whispered:

"It's—it's Dick!" And in a moment, "They say he's killed four people!"

"With—?" Monk couldn't finish.

Randy nodded dumbly, and they both stared there for a minute, two white-faced boys, aware now of the full and murderous significance of the secret they had kept, the confidence they had not violated, with a sudden sense of guilt and fear as if somehow the crime lay on their shoulders.

Across the street a window banged up in the parlor of Suggs' house and Old Man Suggs appeared in the window clad only in his nightgown, his brutal old face inflamed with excitement, his shock of silvery white hair awry, his powerful shoulders and his thick hands gripping his crutches.

"He's coming this way!" he bawled to the world in general. "They say he lit out across the Square! He's heading out in this direction!"

Mr. Crane paused to yell back impatiently over his shoulder, "No, he went down South Main Street. He's heading for Wilton and the river. I've already heard from headquarters."

Automobiles were beginning to roar and sputter all along the street. Even at that time, over half the people on the street had them. Across the street Monk could hear Mr. Potterham sweating with his Ford. He would whirl the crank a dozen times or more, the engine would catch for a moment, cough and splutter, and then die again. Gus ran out of doors with a kettle of boiling water and began to pour it feverishly down the radiator spout.

Mr. Shepperton was already dressed. They saw him run down the back steps towards the carriage house. Randy, Bras, and Monk streaked down the driveway to help him. They got the old wooden doors open. He went in and cranked the car. It was a new Buick. It responded to their prayers and started up at once. Mr. Shepperton backed out into the snowy drive. They all clambered up onto the running board. He spoke absently, saying:

"You boys stay here. Randy, your mother's calling you."

But they all tumbled in and he didn't say a word.

He came backing down the driveway at top speed. They turned into the street and picked up Mr. Crane. As they took the corner into Charles Street, Fred Sanford and his father roared past them in their Oldsmobile. They lit out for town, going at top speed. Every house along Charles Street was lighted up. Even the hospital was ablaze with light. Cars were coming out of alleys everywhere. They could hear people shouting questions and replies at one another. Monk heard one man shout, "He's killed six men!"

Monk didn't know how fast they went, but it was breakneck speed with streets in such condition. It didn't take them over five minutes to reach the Square, but when they got there it seemed as if the whole town was there ahead of them. Mr. Shepperton pulled the car up and parked in front of the City Hall. Mr. Crane leaped out and went pounding away across the Square without another word to them.

Everyone was running in the same direction. From every corner, every street that led into the Square, people were streaking in. One could see the dark figures of running men across the white carpet of the Square. They were all rushing in to one focal point.

The southwest corner of the Square where South Main Street came into it was like a dog fight. Those running figures streaking towards that dense crowd gathered there made Monk think of nothing else so much as a fight between two boys upon the playgrounds of the school at recess time. The way the crowd was swarming in was just the same.

But then he *heard* a difference. From that crowd came a low and growing mutter, an ugly and insistent growl, of a tone and quality he had never heard before, but, hearing it now, he knew instantly what it meant. There was no mistaking the blood note in that foggy growl. And the three of them, the three boys, looked at one another with the same question in the eyes of all.

Nebraska's coal black eyes were shining now with a savage sparkle even they had never had before. The awakened blood of the Cherokee was smoking in him. "Come on," he said in a low tone, exultantly. "They mean business this time, sure. Let's go!" And he darted away towards the dense and sinister darkness of the crowd.

Even as they followed him they heard behind them, at the edge of Niggertown, coming towards them now, growing, swelling at every instant, one of the most savagely mournful and terrifying sounds that night can know. It was the baying of the hounds as they came up upon the leash from Niggertown. Full-throated, howling deep, the savagery of blood was in it, and the savagery of man's guilty doom, was in it, too.

They came up swiftly, fairly baying at the boys' heels as they sped across the snow-white darkness of the Square. As they got up to the crowd they saw that it had gathered at the corner where Mark Joyner's hardware store stood. Monk's uncle had not yet arrived but they had phoned for him; he was already on the way. But Monk heard Mr. Shepperton swear beneath his breath in vexation:

"Damn, if I'd only thought—we could have taken him!"

Facing the crowd which pressed in on them so close and menacing that

70

they were almost flattened out against the glass, three or four men were standing with arms stretched out in a kind of chain, as if trying to protect with the last resistance of their strength and eloquence the sanctity of private property.

George Gallatin was Mayor at that time, and he was standing there shoulder to shoulder and arm to arm with Hugh McPherson. Monk could see Hugh, taller by half a foot than anyone around him, his long, gaunt figure, the gaunt passion of his face, even the attitude of his outstretched bony arms, strangely, movingly Lincolnesque, his one good eye (for he was blind in the other) blazing in the cold glare of the corner lamp with a kind of cold, inspired, Scotch passion.

"Wait a minute! Stop! You men wait a minute!" he cried. His words cut out above the shouts and clamor of the mob like an electric spark. "You'll gain nothing, you'll help nothing if you do this thing."

They tried to drown him out with an angry and derisive roar. He shot his big fist up into the air and shouted at them, blazed at them with that cold single eye, until they had to hear. "Listen to me!" he cried. "This is no time for mob law. This is no case for lynch law. This is a time for law and order. Wait till the sheriff swears you in. Wait until Mark Joyner comes. Wait—"

He got no further. "Wait, hell!" cried someone. "We've waited long enough! We're going to get that nigger!"

The mob took up the cry. The whole crowd was writhing angrily now, like a tormented snake. Suddenly there was a flurry in the crowd, a scattering. Somebody yelled a warning at Hugh McPherson. He ducked quickly, just in time. A brick whizzed past him, smashing the plate-glass window into fragments.

And instantly a bloody roar went up. The crowd surged forward, kicked the fragments of jagged glass away. In a moment the whole mob was storming into the dark store. Mark Joyner got there just too late. He said later that he heard the smash of broken glass just as he turned the corner to the Square from College Street. He arrived in time to take out his keys and open the front doors, but as he grimly remarked, with a convulsive movement of his lips, it was like closing the barn doors after the horse had been stolen.

The mob was in and they looted him. They helped themselves to every rifle they could find. They smashed open cartridge boxes and filled their pockets with the loose cartridges. Within ten minutes they had looted the store of every rifle, every cartridge in the stock. The whole place looked as if a hurricane had hit it. The mob was streaming out into the street, was already gathering around the dogs a hundred feet or so away, who were picking up the scent at that point, the place where Dick had halted last before he had turned and headed south, downhill along South Main Street, towards the river.

The hounds were scampering about, tugging at the leash, moaning softly with their noses pointed to the snow, their long ears flattened down. But in that light and in that snow it almost seemed no hounds were needed to follow Dick. Straight down the middle, in a snow-white streak, straight as a string right down the center of the sheeted car tracks, the Negro's footsteps led away. By the light of the corner lamps one could follow them until they vanished downhill in the darkness.

But now, although the snow had stopped, the wind was swirling through the street and making drifts and eddies in the snow. The footprints were fading rapidly. Soon they would be gone.

The dogs were given their head. They went straining on, softly, sniffing at the snow; behind them the dark masses of the mob closed in and followed. The three boys stood there watching while they went. They saw them go on down the street and vanish. But from below, over the snow-numbed stillness of the air, the vast, low mutter of the mob came back to them.

Men were clustered now in groups. Mark Joyner stood before his shattered window, ruefully surveying the ruin. Other men were gathered around the big telephone pole at the corner, measuring, estimating its width and thickness, pointing out two bullet holes that had been drilled cleanly through.

And swiftly, like a flash, running from group to group, like a powder train of fire, the full detail of that bloody chronicle of night was pieced together.

This was what had happened.

Somewhere between nine and ten o'clock that night, Dick Prosser had gone to Pansy Harris' shack in Niggertown. Some said he had been drinking when he went there. At any rate, the police had later found the remnants of a gallon jug of raw corn whiskey in the room.

72

What had happened in the shack from that time on was never clearly known. The woman evidently had protested, had tried to keep him out, but eventually, as she had done before, succumbed. He went in. They were alone. What happened then, what passed between them, was never known. And, besides, no one was greatly interested. It was a crazy nigger with a nigger wench. She was "another nigger's woman"; probably she had "gone with" Dick. This was the general assumption, but no one cared. Adultery among Negroes was assumed.

At any rate, some time after ten o'clock that night—it must have been closer to eleven, because the train of the Negro porter, Harris, was late and did not pull into the yards until 10:20—the woman's husband appeared upon the scene. The fight did not start then. According to the woman, the real trouble did not come until an hour or more after his return.

The men drank together. Each was in an ugly temper. Dick was steadily becoming more savagely inflamed. Shortly before midnight they got into a fight. Harris slashed at Dick with a razor. In a second they were locked together, rolling about and fighting like two madmen on the floor. Pansy Harris went screaming out of doors and across the street into a dingy little grocery store.

A riot call was telephoned at once to police headquarters at the City Hall. The news came in that a crazy nigger had broken loose on Valley Street in Niggertown, and to send help at once. Pansy Harris ran back across the street towards her little shack.

As she got there, her husband, with blood streaming from his face, staggered out across the little lean-to porch into the street, with his hands held up protectively behind his head in a gesture of instinctive terror. At the same moment, Dick Prosser appeared in the doorway of the shack, deliberately took aim with his rifle, and shot the fleeing Negro squarely through the back of the head. Harris dropped forward on his face into the snow. He was dead before he hit the ground. A huge dark stain of blood-soaked snow widened out around him. Dick Prosser took one step, seized the terrified Negress by the arm, hurled her into the shack, bolted the door, pulled down the shades, blew out the lamp, and waited.

A few minutes later, two policemen arrived from town. They were a young constable named Willis, who had but recently got on the force and John Grady, a lieutenant. The policemen took one look at the bloody figure in the snow, questioned the frightened keeper of the grocery store, and then, after consulting briefly, produced their weapons and walked out into the street.

Young Willis stepped softly down onto the snow-covered porch of the shack, flattened himself against the wall between the window and the door, and waited. Grady went around to the side, produced his flashlight, flashed it against the house and through the window, which on this side was shadeless. At the same moment Grady said in a loud voice:

"Come out of there!"

Dick's answer was to shoot him cleanly through the wrist. At the same moment Willis kicked the door in with a powerful thrust of his foot, and, without waiting, started in with pointed revolver. Dick shot him just above the eyes. The policeman fell forward on his face.

Grady came running out around the house, crossed the street, rushed into the grocery store, pulled the receiver of the old-fashioned telephone off the hook, rang frantically for headquarters, and yelled out across the wire that a crazy nigger had killed Sam Willis and a Negro man, and to send help.

At this moment Dick, coatless and without a hat, holding his rifle crosswise in his hands, stepped out across the porch into the street, aimed swiftly through the dirty window of the dingy little store and shot John Grady as he stood there at the phone. Grady fell dead with a bullet that entered just below his left temple and went out on the other side.

Dick, now moving in a long, unhurried stride that covered the ground with catlike speed, turned up the snow-covered slope of Valley Street and began his march towards town. He moved right up the center of the street, shooting cleanly from left to right as he went. Halfway up the hill, the second-story window of a Negro tenement flew open. An old Negro man, the janitor of an office building in the Square, stuck out his ancient head of cotton wool. Dick swiveled and shot casually from his hip. The shot tore the top of the old Negro's head off.

By the time Dick reached the head of Valley Street, they knew he was coming. He moved steadily along, leaving his big tread cleanly in the middle of the sheeted street, shifting a little as he walked, swinging his gun crosswise before him. This was the Negro Broadway of the town, the center of the night life of the Negro settlement. But where those pool rooms, barber shops, drug stores, and fried-fish places had been loud with dusky life ten minutes before, they were now silent as the ruins of Egypt. The word was flaming through the town that a crazy nigger was on the way. No one showed his head.

Dick moved on steadily, always in the middle of the street, reached the end of Valley Street and turned into South Main—turned right, uphill, in the middle of the car tracks, and started towards the Square. As he passed the lunchroom on the left he took a swift shot through the window at the counter man. The fellow ducked behind the counter. The bullet crashed into the wall above his head.

Meanwhile, the news that Dick was coming was crackling through the town. At the City Club on Sondley Street, three blocks away, a group of the town's leading gamblers and sporting men was intent in a haze of smoke above a green baize table and some stacks of poker chips. The phone rang. The call was for Wilson Redmond, the police court magistrate.

Wilson listened for a moment, then hung the phone up casually. "Come on, Jim," he said in casual tones to a crony, Jim McIntyre, "there's a crazy nigger loose. He's shooting up the town. Let's go get him." And with the same nonchalance he thrust his arms into the overcoat which the white-jacketed Negro held for him, put on his tall silk hat, took up his cane, pulled out his gloves, and started to depart. Wilson, like his comrade, had been drinking.

As if they were going to a wedding party, the two men went out into the deserted, snow-white streets, turned at the corner by the post office, and started up the street towards the Square. As they reached the Square and turned into it they heard Dick's shot into the lunchroom and the crash of glass.

"There he is, Jim!" said Wilson Redmond happily. "Now I'll have some fun. Let's go get him." The two gentlemen moved rapidly across the Square and into South Main Street.

Dick kept coming on, steadily, at his tireless, easy stride, straight up the middle of the street. Wilson Redmond started down the street to get him. He lifted his gold-headed cane and waved it at Dick Prosser.

"You're under arrest!" Wilson Redmond said.

Dick shot again, and also from the hip, but something faltered this time by the fraction of an inch. They always thought it was Wilson Redmond's tall silk hat that fooled him. The bullet drilled a hole right through the top of Judge Redmond's tall silk hat, and it went flying away. Wilson Redmond faded into the doorway of a building and fervently wished that his too, too solid flesh would melt.

Jim McIntyre was not so lucky. He started for the doorway but Wilson got there first. Dick shot cleanly from the hip again and blew Jim's side in with a fast shot. Poor Jim fell sprawling to the ground, to rise and walk again, it's true, but ever thereafter with a cane. Meanwhile, on the other side of the Square, at police headquarters, the sergeant had sent John Chapman out to head Dick off. Mr. Chapman was perhaps the best-liked man on the force. He was a pleasant, florid-faced man of forty-five, with curling brown mustaches, congenial and good-humored, devoted to his family, courageous, but perhaps too kindly and too gentle for a good policeman.

John Chapman heard the shots and ran forward. He came up to the corner by Joyner's hardware store just as Dick's shot sent poor Jim McIntyre sprawling to the ground. Mr. Chapman took up his position there at the corner behind the telephone pole. From this vantage point he took out his revolver and shot directly at Dick Prosser as he came up the street.

By this time Dick was not over thirty yards away. He dropped quietly upon one knee and aimed. Mr. Chapman shot again and missed. Dick fired. The high-velocity bullet bored through the post a little to one side. It grazed the shoulder of John Chapman's uniform and knocked a chip out of the monument sixty yards or more behind him in the center of the Square.

Mr. Chapman fired again and missed. And Dick, still coolly poised upon his knee, as calm and steady as if he were engaging in a rifle practice, fired again, drilled squarely through the center of the pole, and shot John Chapman through the heart. Mr. Chapman dropped dead. Then Dick rose, pivoted like a soldier in his tracks, and started back down the street, right down the center of the car tracks, straight as a string, right out of town.

This was the story as they got it, pieced together like a train of fire among the excited groups of men that clustered there in trampled snow before the shattered glass of Joyner's store.

And the rifle? Where did he get it? From whom had he purchased it? The answer to this, too, was not long in coming.

Mark Joyner denied instantly that the weapon had come from his store. At this moment there was a flurry in the crowd and Uncle Morris Teitlebaum, the pawnbroker, appeared, gesticulating volubly, clinging to a policeman. Baldheaded, squat, with the face of an old monkey, he protested shrilly, using his hands eloquently, and displaying craggy nuggins of gold teeth as he spoke.

"Vell," he said, "vhat could I do? His moaney vas good!" he said plaintively, lifting his hands and looking around with an expression of finality. "He comes with his moaney, he pays it down like everybodies—I should say no?" he cried, with such an accent of aggrieved innocence that, in spite of the occasion, a few people smiled.

Uncle Morris Teitlebaum's pawn shop, which was on the right-hand side of South Main Street, and which Dick had passed less than an hour before in his murderous march towards town, was, unlike Joyner's hardware store, securely protected at night by strong bars over the doors and show windows.

But now, save for these groups of talking men, the town again was silent. Far off, in the direction of the river and the Wilton Bottoms, they could hear the low and mournful baying of the hounds. There was nothing more to see or do. Mark Joyner stooped, picked up some fragments of the shattered glass, and threw them in the window. A policeman was left on guard, and presently all five of them—Mr. Shepperton, Mark Joyner, and the three boys—walked back across the Square and got into the car and drove home again.

But there was no more sleep for anyone that night. Black Dick had murdered sleep. Towards daybreak snow began to fall again. It continued through the morning. It was piled deep in gusting drifts by noon. All footprints were obliterated. The town waited, eager, tense, wondering if the man could get away.

They did not capture him that day, but they were on his trail. From time to time throughout the day news would drift back to them. Dick had turned east along the river to the Wilton Bottoms and, following the river banks as closely as he could, he had gone out for some miles along the Fairchilds road. There, a mile or two from Fairchilds, he crossed the river at the Rocky Shallows.

Shortly after daybreak a farmer from the Fairchilds section had seen him cross a field. They picked the trail up there again and followed it across the field and through a wood. He had come out on the other side and got down into the Cane Creek section, and there, for several hours, they lost him.

Dick had gone right down into the icy water of the creek and walked upstream a mile or so. They brought the dogs down to the creek, to where he broke the trail, took them over to the other side and scented up and down.

Towards five o'clock that afternoon they picked the trail up on the other side, a mile or more upstream. From that point on they began to close in on him. He had been seen just before nightfall by several people in the Lester township. The dogs followed him across the fields, across the Lester road, into a wood. One arm of the posse swept around the wood to head him off. They knew they had him. Dick, freezing, hungry, and unsheltered, was hiding in that wood. They knew he couldn't get away. The posse ringed the wood and waited until morning.

At seven-thirty the next morning he made a break for it. He almost got away. He got through the line without being seen, crossed the Lester road, and headed back across the fields in the direction of Cane Creek. And there they caught him. They saw him plunging through the snowdrift of a field. A cry went up. The posse started after him.

Part of the posse were on horseback. The men rode in across the field. Dick halted at the edge of the wood, dropped deliberately upon one knee, and for some minutes held them off with rapid fire. At two hundred yards he dropped Doc Lavender, a deputy, with a bullet through the throat.

The posse came in slowly, in an encircling, flank-wise movement. Dick got two more of them as they closed in, and then, as slowly and deliberately as a trained soldier retreating in good order, still firing as he went, he fell back through the wood. At the other side he turned and ran down through a sloping field that bordered on Cane Creek. At the creek edge he turned again, knelt once more in the snow, and aimed.

It was Dick's last shot. He didn't miss. The bullet struck Wayne Foraker, another deputy, dead center in the forehead and killed him in his saddle. Then the posse saw the Negro aim again, and nothing happened. Dick snapped the cartridge breech open savagely, then hurled the gun away. A cheer went up. The posse came charging forward. Dick turned, stumblingly, and ran the few remaining yards that separated him from the cold and rock-bright waters of the creek.

And here he did a curious thing—a thing that in later days was a subject of frequent and repeated speculation, a thing that no one ever wholly understood. It was thought that he would make one final break for freedom, that he would wade the creek and try to get away before they got to him.

78

Instead, arrived at the creek, he sat down calmly on the bank, and, as quietly and methodically as if he were seated on his cot in an army barracks, he unlaced his shoes, took them off, placed them together neatly at his side, and then stood up like a soldier, erect, in his bare feet, and faced the mob.

The men on horseback reached him first. They rode up around him and discharged their guns into him. He fell forward in the snow, riddled with bullets. The men dismounted, turned him over on his back, and all the other men came in and riddled him. They took his lifeless body, put a rope around his neck, and hung him to a tree. Then the mob exhausted all their ammunition on the riddled carcass.

By nine o'clock that morning the news had reached the town. Around eleven o'clock the mob came back, along the river road. A good crowd had gone out to meet it at the Wilton Bottoms. The sheriff rode ahead. Dick's body had been thrown like a sack and tied across the saddle of the horse of one of the deputies he had killed.

It was in this way, bullet-riddled, shot to pieces, open to the vengeful and the morbid gaze of all, that Dick came back to town. The mob came back right to its starting point in South Main Street. They halted there before an undertaking parlor, not twenty yards away from where Dick had halted last and knelt to kill John Chapman. They took that ghastly mutilated thing and hung it in the window of the undertaker's place, for every woman, man, and child in town to see.

And it was so they saw him last. Yes, they all had their look. In the end, they had their look. They said they wouldn't look, Randy and Monk. But in the end they went. And it has always been the same with people. It has never changed. It never will. They protest. They shudder. And they say they will not go. But in the end they always have their look.

Nebraska was the only one of the boys who didn't lie about it. With that forthright honesty that was part of him, so strangely wrought of innocence and of brutality, of heroism, cruelty, and tenderness, he announced at once that he was going, and then waited impatiently, spitting briefly and contemptuously from time to time, while the others argued out their own hypocrisy.

At length they went. They saw it—that horrible piece of torn bait—tried wretchedly to make themselves believe that once this thing had spoken to them gently, had been partner to their confidence, object of their affection and respect. And they were sick with nausea and fear, for something had come into their lives they could not understand.

The snow had stopped. The snow was going. The streets had been pounded into dirty mush, and before the shabby undertaking place the crowd milled and jostled, had their fill of horror, could not get enough.

Within, there was a battered roll-top desk, a swivel chair, a cast-iron stove, a wilted fern, a cheap diploma cheaply framed, and, in the window, that ghastly relic of man's savagery, that horrible hunk of torn bait. The boys looked and whitened to the lips, and craned their necks and looked away, and brought unwilling, fascinated eyes back to the horror once again, and craned and turned again, and shuffled in the slush uneasily, but could not go. And they looked up at the leaden reek of day, the dreary vapor of the sky, and, bleakly, at these forms and faces all around them—the people come to gape and stare, the pool-room loafers, the town toughs, the mongrel conquerors of earth—and yet, familiar to their lives and to the body of their whole experience, all known to their landscape, all living men.

And something had come into life—into their lives—that they had never known about before. It was a kind of shadow, a poisonous blackness filled with bewildered loathing. The snow would go, they knew; the reeking vapors of the sky would clear away. The leaf, the blade, the bud, the bird, then April, would come back again—and all of this would be as if it had never been. The homely light of day would shine again familiarly. And all of this would vanish as an evil dream. And yet not wholly so. For they would still remember the old dark doubt and loathing of their kind, of something hateful and unspeakable in the souls of men. They knew that they would not forget.

Beside them a man was telling the story of his own heroic accomplishments to a little group of fascinated listeners. Monk turned and looked at him. He was a little ferret-faced man with a furtive and uneasy eye, a mongrel mouth, and wiry jaw muscles.

"I was the first one to git in a shot," he said. "You see that hole there?" He pointed with a dirty finger. "That big hole right above the eye?"

They turned and goggled with a drugged and feeding stare.

"That's mine," the hero said, and turned briefly to the side and spat tobacco juice into the slush. "That's where I got him. Hell, after that he didn't know what hit him. The son-of-a-bitch was dead before he hit the ground. We all shot him full of holes then. The whole crowd came and let him have it. But that first shot of mine was the one that got him. But, boy!" he paused a moment, shook his head, and spat again. "We sure did fill him full of lead. Why, hell yes," he declared positively, with a decisive movement of his head, "we counted up to 287. We must have put 300 holes in him."

And Nebraska, fearless, blunt, outspoken, as he always was, turned abruptly, put two fingers to his lips and spat between them, widely and contemptuously.

"Yeah—*we!*" he grunted. "*We* killed a big one! *We*—we killed a b'ar, we did! . . . Come on, boys," he said gruffly, "let's be on our way!"

And, fearless and unshaken, untouched by any terror or any doubt, he moved away. And two white-faced, nauseated boys went with him.

A day or two went by before anyone could go into Dick's room again. Monk went in with Randy and his father. The little room was spotless, bare, and tidy as it had always been. Nothing had been changed or touched. But even the very bare austerity of that little room now seemed terribly alive with the presence of its recent black tenant. It was Dick's room. They all knew that. And somehow they all knew that no one else could ever live there again.

Mr. Shepperton went over to the table, picked up Dick's old Bible that still lay there, open and face downward, held it up to the light and looked at it, at the place that Dick had marked when he last read in it. And in a moment, without speaking to them, he began to read in a quiet voice:

"The Lord is my shepherd; I shall not want. He maketh me to lie down in green pastures: He leadeth me beside the still waters. He restoreth my soul; He leadeth me in the paths of righteousness for His name's sake. Yea, though I walk through the valley of the shadow of death, I will fear no evil: for Thou art with me. . . ."

Then Mr. Shepperton closed the book and put it down upon the table, the place where Dick had left it. And they went out the door, he locked it, and they went back into that room no more, forever.

The years passed, and all of them were given unto time. They went their ways. But often they would turn and come again, these faces and these voices of the past, and burn there in George Webber's memory again, upon the muted and immortal geography of time.

The Bitterness

And all would come again—the shout of the young voices, the hard thud of the kicked ball, and Dick moving, moving steadily, Dick moving, moving silently, a storm-white world and silence, and something moving, moving in the night. Then he would hear the furious bell, the crowd a-clamor and the baying of the dogs, and feel the shadow coming that would never disappear. Then he would see again the little room, the table and the book. And the pastoral holiness of that old psalm came back to him, and his heart would wonder with perplexity and doubt.

For he had heard another song since then, and one that Dick, he knew, had never heard and would not have understood, but one whose phrases and whose imagery, it seemed to him, would suit Dick better:

> Tiger! Tiger! burning bright
> In the forests of the night,
> What immortal hand or eye
> Could shape thy fearful symmetry?
>
> What the hammer? what the chain?
> In what furnace was thy brain?
> What the anvil? what dread grasp
> Dare its deadly terrors clasp?
>
> When the stars threw down their spears,
> And water'd heaven with their tears,
> Did he smile his work to see?
> Did he who made the Lamb make thee?

What the hammer? *What* the chain? No one ever knew. It was a mystery and a wonder. It was unexplained. There were a dozen stories, a hundred clues and rumors; all came to nothing in the end. Some said that Dick had come from Texas, others that his home had been in Georgia. Some said it was true that he had been enlisted in the army, but that he had killed a man while there and served a term at Leavenworth. Some said he had served in the army and had received an honorable discharge, but had later killed a man and had served a term in the state prison in Louisiana. Others said that he had been an army man but that he had "gone crazy," that he had served a period in an asylum when it was found that he was insane, that he had escaped from this asylum, that he had escaped from prison, that he was a fugitive from justice at the time he came to them.

But all these stories came to nothing. Nothing was ever proved. Nothing was ever found out. Men debated and discussed these things a thousand times—who and what he had been, what he had done, where he had come from—and all of it came to nothing. No one knew the answer.

He came from darkness. He came out of the heart of darkness, from the dark heart of the secret and undiscovered South. He came by night, just as he passed by night. He was night's child and partner, a token of the wonder and the mystery, the other side of man's dark soul, his nighttime partner, and his nighttime foal, a symbol of those things that pass by darkness and that still remain, of something still and waiting in the night that comes and passes and that will abide, a symbol of man's evil innocence, and the token of his mystery, a projection of his own unfathomed quality, a friend, a brother, and a mortal enemy, an unknown demon—our loving friend, our mortal enemy, two worlds together—a tiger and a child.

A Rose For Emily

WILLIAM FAULKNER

I

When Miss Emily Grierson died, our whole town went to her funeral: the men through a sort of respectful affection for a fallen monument, the women mostly out of curiosity to see the inside of her house, which no one save an old manservant—a combined gardener and cook—had seen in at least ten years.

It was a big, squarish frame house that had once been white, decorated with cupolas and spires and scrolled balconies in the heavily lightsome style of the seventies, set on what had once been our most select street. But garages and cotton gins had encroached and obliterated even the august names of that neighborhood; only Miss Emily's house was left, lifting its stubborn and coquettish decay above the cotton wagons and the gasoline pumps—an eyesore among eyesores. And now Miss Emily had gone to join the representatives of those august names where they lay in the cedar-bemused cemetery among the ranked and anonymous graves of Union and Confederate soldiers who fell at the battle of Jefferson.

Alive, Miss Emily had been a tradition, a duty, and a care; a sort of hereditary obligation upon the town, dating from that day in 1894 when Colonel Sartoris, the mayor—he who fathered the edict that no Negro woman should appear on the streets without an apron—remitted her taxes, the dispensation dating from the death of her father on into perpetuity. Not that Miss Emily would have accepted charity. Colonel Sartoris invented an involved tale to the effect that Miss Emily's father had loaned money to the town, which the town, as a matter of business, preferred this way of repaying. Only a man of Colonel Sartoris' generation and thought could have invented it, and only a woman could have believed it.

When the next generation, with its more modern ideas, became mayors and aldermen, this arrangement created some little dissatisfaction. On the first of the year they mailed her a tax notice. February came, and there was no reply. They wrote her a formal letter, asking her to call at the sheriff's office at her convenience. A week later the mayor wrote her himself, offering to call or to send his car for her, and received in reply a note on paper of an archaic shape, in a thin, flowing calligraphy in faded ink, to the effect that she no longer went out at all. The tax notice was also enclosed, without comment.

They called a special meeting of the Board of Aldermen. A deputation waited upon her, knocked at the door through which no visitor had passed since she ceased giving china-painting lessons eight or ten years earlier. They were admitted by the old Negro into a dim hall from which a stairway mounted into still more shadow. It smelled of dust and disuse—a close, dank smell. The Negro led them into the parlor. It was furnished in heavy, leather-covered furniture. When the Negro opened the blinds of one window, they could see that the leather was cracked; and when they sat down, a faint dust rose sluggishly about their thighs, spinning with slow motes in the single sun-ray. On a tarnished gilt easel before the fireplace stood a crayon portrait of Miss Emily's father.

They rose when she entered—a small, fat woman in black, with a thin gold chain descending to her waist and vanishing into her belt, leaning on an ebony cane with a tarnished gold head. Her skeleton was small and spare; perhaps, that was why what would have been merely plumpness in another was obesity in her. She looked bloated, like a body long submerged in motionless water, and of that pallid hue. Her eyes, lost in the fatty ridges of her face, looked like two small pieces of coal pressed into a lump of dough as they moved from one face to another while the visitors stated their errand.

She did not ask them to sit down. She just stood in the door and listened quietly until the spokesman came to a stumbling halt. Then they could hear the invisible watch ticking at the end of the gold chain.

Her voice was dry and cold. "I have no taxes in Jefferson. Colonel Sartoris explained it to me. Perhaps one of you can gain access to the city records and satisfy yourselves."

"But we have. We are the city authorities, Miss Emily. Didn't you get a notice from the sheriff, signed by him?"

"I received a paper, yes," Miss Emily said. "Perhaps he considers himself the sheriff. . . . I have no taxes in Jefferson."

"But there is nothing on the books to show that, you see. We must go by the—"

"See Colonel Sartoris. I have no taxes in Jefferson."

"But, Miss Emily—"

"See Colonel Sartoris." (Colonel Sartoris had been dead almost ten years.) "I have no taxes in Jefferson. Tobe!" The Negro appeared. "Show these gentlemen out."

II

So she vanquished them, horse and foot, just as she had vanquished their fathers thirty years before about the smell. That was two years after her father's death and a short time after her sweetheart—the one we believed would marry her—had deserted her. After her father's death she went out very little; after her sweetheart went away, people hardly saw her at all. A few of the ladies had the temerity to call, but were not received, and the only sign of life about the place was the Negro man—a young man then—going in and out with a market basket.

"Just as if a man—any man—could keep a kitchen properly," the ladies said; so they were not surprised when the smell developed. It was another link between the gross, teeming world and the high and mighty Griersons.

A neighbor, a woman, complained to the mayor, Judge Stevens, eighty years old.

"But what will you have me do about it, madam?" he said.

"Why, send her word to stop it," the woman said. "Isn't there a law?"

"I'm sure that won't be necessary," Judge Stevens said. "It's probably just a snake or a rat that nigger of hers killed in the yard. I'll speak to him about it."

The next day he received two more complaints, one from a man who came in diffident deprecation. "We really must do something about it, Judge. I'd be the last one in the world to bother Miss Emily, but we've got to do something." That night the Board of Aldermen met—three graybeards and a younger man, a member of the rising generation.

"It's simple enough," he said. "Send her word to have her place cleaned up. Give her a certain time to do it in, and if she don't. . . ."

"Dammit, sir," Judge Stevens said, "will you accuse a lady to her face of smelling bad?"

So the next night, after midnight, four men crossed Miss Emily's lawn and slunk about the house like burglars, sniffing along the base of the brickwork and at the cellar openings while one of them performed a regular sowing motion with his hand out of a sack slung from his shoulder. They broke open the cellar door and sprinkled lime there, and in all the outbuildings. As they recrossed the lawn, a window that had been dark was lighted and Miss Emily sat in it, the light behind her, and her upright torso motionless as that of an idol. They crept quietly across the lawn and into the shadow of the locusts that lined the street. After a week or two the smell went away.

That was when people had begun to feel really sorry for her. People in our town, remembering how old lady Wyatt, her great-aunt, had gone completely crazy at last, believed that the Griersons held themselves a little too high for what they really were. None of the young men were quite good enough for Miss Emily and such. We had long thought of them as a tableau; Miss Emily a slender figure in white in the background, her father a spraddled silhouette in the foreground, his back to her and clutching a horsewhip, the two of them framed by the backflung front door. So when she got to be thirty and was still single, we were not pleased exactly, but vindicated; even with insanity in the family she wouldn't have turned down all of her chances if they had really materialized.

When her father died, it got about that the house was all that was left to her; and in a way, people were glad. At last they could pity Miss Emily. Being left alone, and a pauper, she had become humanized. Now she too would know the old thrill and the old despair of a penny more or less.

The day after his death all the ladies prepared to call at the home and offer condolence and aid, as is our custom. Miss Emily met them at the door, dressed as usual and with no trace of grief on her face. She told them that her father was not dead. She did that for three days, with the ministers calling on her, and the doctors, trying to persuade her to let them dispose of the body. Just as they were about to resort to law and force, she broke down, and they buried her father quickly.

We did not say she was crazy then. We believed she had to do that. We remembered all the young men her father had driven away, and we knew that with nothing left, she would have to cling to that which had robbed her, as people will.

III

She was sick for a long time. When we saw her again, her hair was cut short, making her look like a girl, with a vague resemblance to those angels in colored church windows—sort of tragic and serene.

The town had just let the contracts for paving the sidewalks, and in the summer after her father's death they began the work. The construction company came with niggers and mules and machinery, and a foreman named Homer Barron, a Yankee—a big, dark, ready man, with a big voice and eyes lighter than his face. The little boys would follow in groups to hear him cuss the niggers, and the niggers singing in time to the rise and fall of picks. Pretty soon he knew everybody in town. Whenever you heard a lot of laughing anywhere about the square, Homer Barren would be in the center of the group. Presently we began to see him and Miss Emily on Sunday afternoons driving in the yellow-wheeled buggy and the matched team of bays from the livery stable.

At first we were glad that Miss Emily would have an interest, because the ladies all said, "Of course a Grierson would not think seriously of a Northerner, a day laborer." But there were still others, older people, who said that even grief could not cause a real lady to forget *noblesse oblige*—without calling it *noblesse oblige*. They just said, "Poor Emily. Her kinsfolk should come to her." She had some kin in Alabama; but years ago her father had fallen out with them over the estate of old lady Wyatt, the crazy woman, and there was no communication between the two families. They had not even been represented at the funeral.

And as soon as the old people said, "Poor Emily," the whispering began. "Do you suppose it's really so?" they said to one another. "Of course it is. What else could. . . ." This behind their hands; rustling of craned silk and satin behind jalousies closed upon the sun of Sunday afternoon as the thin, swift clop-clop of the matched team passed: "Poor Emily."

She carried her head high enough—even when we believed that she had fallen. It was as if she demanded more than ever the recognition of her dignity as the last Grierson; as if it had wanted that touch of earthiness to reaffirm her imperviousness. Like when she bought the rat poison, the arsenic. That was over a year after they had begun to say "Poor Emily," and while the two female cousins were visiting her.

"I want some poison," she said to the druggist. She was over thirty then, still a slight woman, though thinner than usual, with cold, haughty black eyes in a face the flesh of which was strained across the temples and about the eyesockets as you imagine a lighthouse-keeper's face ought to look. "I want some poison," she said.

"Yes, Miss Emily. What kind? For rats and such? I'd recom—"

"I want the best you have. I don't care what kind."

The druggist named several. "They'll kill anything up to an elephant. But what you want is—"

"Arsenic," Miss Emily said. "Is that a good one?"

"Is . . . arsenic? Yes, ma'am. But what you want—"

"I want arsenic."

The druggist looked down at her. She looked back at him, erect, her face like a strained flag. "Why, of course," the druggist said. "If that's what you want. But the law requires you to tell what you are going to use it for."

Miss Emily just stared at him her head tilted back in order to look him eye to eye, until he looked away and went and got the arsenic and wrapped it up. The Negro delivery boy brought her the package; the druggist didn't come back. When she opened the package at home there was written on the box, under the skull and bones: "For rats."

IV

So the next day we all said, "She will kill herself"; and we said it would be the best thing. When she had first begun to be seen with Homer Barron, we had said, "She will marry him." Then we said, "She will persuade him yet," because Homer himself had remarked—he liked men, and it was known that he drank with the younger men in the Elk's Club—that he was not a marrying man. Later we said, "Poor Emily," behind the jalousies as they passed on Sunday afternoon in the glittering buggy, Miss Emily with her head high and Homer Barron with his hat cocked and a cigar in his teeth, reins and whip in a yellow glove.

Then some of the ladies began to say that it was a disgrace to the town and a bad example to the young people. The men did not want to interfere, but at last the ladies forced the Baptist minister—Miss Emily's people were Episcopal—to call upon her. He would never divulge what happened during that interview, but he refused to go back again. The next Sunday they again drove about the streets, and the following day the minister's wife wrote to Miss Emily's relations in Alabama.

So she had blood-kin under her roof again and we sat back to watch developments. At first nothing happened. Then we were sure that they were to be married. We learned that Miss Emily had been to the jeweler's and ordered a man's toilet set in silver, with the letters H.B. on each piece. Two days later we learned that she had bought a complete outfit of men's clothing, including a nightshirt, and we said, "They are married." We were really glad. We were glad because the two female cousins were even more Grierson than Miss Emily had ever been.

So we were not surprised when Homer Barron—the streets had been finished some time since—was gone. We were a little disappointed that there was not a public blowing-off, but we believed that he had gone on to prepare for Miss Emily's coming, or to give her a chance to get rid of the cousins. (By that time it was a cabal, and we were all Miss Emily's allies to help circumvent the cousins.) Sure enough, after another week they departed. And, as we had expected all along, within three days Homer Barron was back in town. A neighbor saw the Negro man admit him at the kitchen door at dusk one evening.

And that was the last we saw of Homer Barron. And of Miss Emily for some time. The Negro man went in and out with the market basket, but the front door remained closed. Now and then we would see her at a window for a moment, as the men did that night when they sprinkled the lime, but for almost six months she did not appear on the streets. Then we knew that this was to be expected too; as if that quality of her father which had thwarted her woman's life so many times had been too virulent and too furious to die.

When we next saw Miss Emily, she had grown fat and her hair was turning gray. During the next few years it grew grayer and grayer until it attained an even pepper-and-salt iron-gray, when it ceased turning. Up to the day of her death at seventy-four it was still that vigorous iron-gray, like the hair of an active man.

From that time on her front door remained closed, save for a period of six or seven years, when she was about forty, during which she gave lessons in china-painting. She fitted up a studio in one of the downstairs rooms, where the daughters and granddaughters of Colonel Sartoris' contemporaries were sent to her with the same regularity and in the same spirit that they were sent on Sundays with a twenty-five cent piece for the collection plate. Meanwhile her taxes had been remitted.

Then the newer generation became the backbone and the spirit of the town, and the painting pupils grew up and fell away and did not send their children to her with boxes of color and tedious brushes and pictures cut from the ladies' magazines. The front door closed upon the last one and remained closed for good. When the town got free postal delivery Miss

Emily alone refused to let them fasten the metal numbers above her door and attach a mailbox to it. She would not listen to them.

Daily, monthly, yearly we watched the Negro grow grayer and more stooped, going in and out with the market basket. Each December we sent her a tax-notice, which would be returned by the post office a week later, unclaimed. Now and then we would see her in one of the downstairs windows—she had evidently shut up the top floor of the house—like the carven torso of an idol in a niche, looking or not looking at us, we could never tell which. Thus she passed from generation to generation—dear, inescapable, impervious, tranquil, and perverse.

And so she died. Fell ill in the house filled with dust and shadows, with only a doddering Negro man to wait on her. We did not even know she was sick; we had long since given up trying to get any information from the Negro. He talked to no one, probably not even to her, for his voice had grown harsh and rusty, as if from disuse.

She died in one of the downstairs rooms, in a heavy walnut bed with a curtain, her gray head propped on a pillow yellow and moldy with age and lack of sunlight.

V

The Negro met the first of the ladies at the front door and let them in, with their hushed, sibilant voices and their quick, curious glances, and then he disappeared. He walked right through the house and out the back and was not seen again.

The two female cousins came at once. They held the funeral on the second day, with the town coming to look at Miss Emily beneath a mass of bought flowers, with the crayon face of her father musing profoundly above the bier and the ladies sibilant and macabre; and the very old men—some in their brushed Confederate uniforms—on the porch and the lawn, talking of Miss Emily as if she had been a contemporary of theirs, believing that they had danced with her and courted her perhaps, confusing time with its mathematical progression, as the old do, to whom all the past is not a diminishing road, but, instead, a huge meadow which no winter ever quite touches, divided from them now by the narrow bottleneck of the most recent decade of years.

Already we knew that there was one room in that region above the stairs which no one had seen in forty years, and which would have to be forced. They waited until Miss Emily was decently in the ground before they opened it.

The violence of breaking down the door seemed to fill this room with pervading dust. A thin, acrid pall as of the tomb seemed to lie everywhere upon this room decked and furnished as for a bridal: upon the valance curtains of faded rose color, upon the rose-shaded lights, upon the dressing table, upon the delicate array of crystal and the man's toilet things backed with tarnished silver, silver so tarnished that the monogram was obscured. Among them lay a collar and tie, as if they had just been removed, which, lifted, left upon the surface a pale crescent in the dust. Upon a chair hung the suit, carefully folded; beneath it the two mute shoes and the discarded socks.

The man himself lay in the bed.

For a long while we just stood there, looking down at the profound and fleshless grin. The body had apparently once lain in the attitude of an embrace, but now the long sleep that outlasts love, that conquers even the grimace of love, had cuckolded him. What was left of him, rotted beneath what was left of the nightshirt, had become inextricable from the bed in which he lay; and upon him and upon the pillow beside him lay that even coating of the patient and biding dust.

Then we noticed that in the second pillow was the indentation of a head. One of us lifted something from it, and leaning forward, that faint and invisible dust dry and acrid in the nostrils, we saw a long strand of iron-gray hair.

The Long Stay Cut Short, or, The Unsatisfactory Supper

TENNESSEE WILLIAMS

THREE CHARACTERS

BABY DOLL

ARCHIE LEE

AUNT ROSE

The curtain rises on the porch and side yard of a shot-gun cottage in Blue Mountain, Mississippi. The frame house is faded and has a greenish-gray cast with dark streaks from the roof, and there are irregularities in the lines of the building. Behind it the dusky cyclorama is stained with the rose of sunset, which is stormy-looking, and the wind has a cat-like whine.

Upstage from the porch, in the center of the side yard, is a very large rose-bush, the beauty of which is somehow sinister-looking.

A Prokofief sort of music introduces the scene and sets a mood of grotesque lyricism.

The screen door opens with a snarl of rusty springs and latches: this stops the music.

MRS. "BABY DOLL" BOWMAN *appears. She is a large and indolent woman, but her amplitude is not benign, her stupidity is not comfortable. There is a suggestion of Egypt in the arrangement of her glossy black hair and the purple linen dress and heavy brass jewelry that she is wearing.*

ARCHIE LEE BOWMAN *comes out and sucks at his teeth. He is a large man with an unhealthy chalk-white face and slack figure.*

The Bitterness

[*The evenly cadenced lines of the dialogue between* BABY DOLL *and* ARCHIE
LEE *may be given a singsong reading, somewhat like a grotesque choral
incantation, and passages may be divided as strophe and antistrophe by*
BABY DOLL'S *movements back and forth on the porch.*]

ARCHIE LEE: The old lady used to could set a right fair table, but not any
more. The food has fallen off around here lately.

BABY DOLL: You're right about that, Archie Lee. I can't argue with you.

ARCHIE LEE: A good mess of greens is a satisfactory meal if it's cooked with
salt-pork an' left on th' stove till it's tender, but thrown in a platter ha'f
cooked an' unflavored, it ain't even fit for hog-slops.

BABY DOLL: It's hard t' spoil greens but the old lady sure did spoil 'em.

ARCHIE LEE: How did she manage t' do it?

BABY DOLL [*Slowly and contemptuously*]: Well, she had 'em on th' stove for
about an hour. Said she thought they wuh boilin'. I went in the kitchen.
The stove was stone-cold. The silly old thing had forgotten to build a
fire in it. So I called her back. I said, "Aunt Rose, I think I understand
why the greens aren't boilin'." "Why aren't they boilin'?" she says.
Well, I told her, "it might have something to do with the fack that the
stove issen lighted!"

ARCHIE LEE: What did she say about that?

BABY DOLL: Juss threw back her head an' cackled. "Why, I thought my
stove was lighted," she said. "I thought my greens wuh boilin'." Everything is *my*. My stove, my greens, my kitchen. She has taken possession
of everything on the place.

ARCHIE LEE: She's getting delusions of grandeur. [*A high, thin laugh is
heard inside.*] Why does she cackle that way?

BABY DOLL: How should I know why she cackles! I guess it's supposed to
show that she's in a good humor.

ARCHIE LEE: A thing like that can become awf'ly aggravating.

BABY DOLL: It gets on my nerves so bad I could haul off and scream. And
obstinate! She's just as obstinate as a mule.

ARCHIE LEE: A person can be obstinate and still cook greens.

BABY DOLL: Not if they're so obstinate they won't even look in a stove t' see
if it's lighted.

ARCHIE LEE: Why don't you keep the old lady out of the kitchen?

BABY DOLL: You get me a nigger and I'll keep her out of the kitchen. [*The*

94

screen door creaks open and AUNT ROSE *comes out on the porch. She is breathless with the exertion of moving from the kitchen, and clings to a porch column while she is catching her breath. She is the type of old lady, about eighty-five years old, that resembles a delicate white-headed monkey. She has on a dress of gray calico which has become too large for her shrunken figure. She has a continual fluttering in her chest which makes her laugh in a witless manner. Neither of the pair on the porch pays any apparent attention to her, though she nods and smiles brightly at each.*]

AUNT ROSE: I brought out m' scissors. Tomorrow is Sunday an' I can't stand for my house to be without flowers on Sunday. Besides if we don't cut the roses the wind'll just blow them away.

BABY DOLL [*Yawns ostentatiously.* ARCHIE LEE *sucks loudly at his teeth.* BABY DOLL, *venting her irritation*]: Will you quit suckin' your teeth?

ARCHIE LEE: I got something stuck in my teeth an' I can't remove it.

BABY DOLL: There's such a thing as a tooth-pick made for that purpose.

ARCHIE LEE: I told you at breakfast we didn't have any toothpicks. I told you the same thing at lunch and the same thing at supper. Does it have to appear in the paper for you to believe it?

BABY DOLL: There's other things with a point besides a toothpick.

AUNT ROSE [*Excitedly*]: Archie Lee, Son! [*She produces a spool of thread from her bulging skirt-pocket.*] You bite off a piece of this thread and run it between your teeth and if that don't dislodge a morsel nothing else will!

ARCHIE LEE [*Slamming his feet from porch-rail to floor*]: Now listen, you all, I want you both to get this. If I want to suck at my teeth, I'm going to suck at my teeth!

AUNT ROSE: That's right, Archie Lee, you go on and suck at your teeth as much as you want to. [BABY DOLL *grunts disgustedly.* ARCHIE LEE *throws his feet back on the rail and continues sucking loudly at his teeth.* AUNT ROSE, *hesitantly.*] Archie Lee, Son, you weren't satisfied with your supper. I noticed you left a lot of greens on your plate.

ARCHIE LEE: I'm not strong on greens.

AUNT ROSE: I'm surprised to hear you say that.

ARCHIE LEE: I don't see why you should be. As far as I know I never declared any terrible fondness for greens in your presence, Aunt Rose.

AUNT ROSE: Well, somebody did.

ARCHIE LEE: Somebody probably did sometime and somewhere but that don't mean it was me.

AUNT ROSE [*With a nervous laugh*]: Baby Doll, who is it dotes on greens so much?

BABY DOLL [*Wearily*]: I don't know who dotes on greens, Aunt Rose.

AUNT ROSE: All these likes and dislikes, it's hard to keep straight in your head. But Archie Lee's easy t' cook for, yes, he is, easy t' cook for! Jim's a complainer, oh, my, what a complainer. And Susie's household! What complainers! Every living one of them's a complainer! They're such complainers I die of nervous prostration when I'm cooking for them. But Archie Lee, here, he takes whatever you give him an' seems to love ev'ry bite of it! [*She touches his head.*] Bless you, honey, for being so easy t' cook for! [ARCHIE LEE *picks up his chair and moves it roughly away from* AUNT ROSE. *She laughs nervously and digs in her capacious pocket for the scissors.*] Now I'm goin' down there an' clip a few roses befo' th' wind blows 'em away 'cause I can't stand my house to be without flowers on Sunday. An' soon as I've finished with that, I'm goin' back in my kitchen an' light up my stove an' cook you some eggs Birmingham. I won't have my men-folks unsatisfied with their supper. Won't have it, I won't stand for it! [*She gets to the bottom of the steps and pauses for breath.*]

ARCHIE LEE: What is eggs Birmingham?

AUNT ROSE: Why, eggs Birmingham was Baby Doll's daddy's pet dish.

ARCHIE LEE: That don't answer my question.

AUNT ROSE [*As though confiding a secret*]: I'll tell you how to prepare them.

ARCHIE LEE: I don't care how you prepare them, I just want to know what they are.

AUNT ROSE [*Reasonably*]: Well, Son, I can't say what they are without telling how to prepare them. You cut some bread-slices and take the centers out of them. You put the bread-slices in a skillet with butter. Then into each cut-out center you drop one egg and on top of the eggs you put the cut-out centers.

ARCHIE LEE: [*Sarcastically*]: Do you build a fire in th' stove?

BABY DOLL: No, you forget to do that. That's why they call them eggs Birmingham, I suppose. [*She laughs at her wit.*]

AUNT ROSE [*Vivaciously*]: That's what they call them, they call them eggs Birmingham and Baby Doll's daddy was just insane about them. When

Baby Doll's daddy was not satisfied with his supper, he'd call for eggs Birmingham and would stomp his feet on the floor until I'd fixed 'em! [*This recollection seems to amuse her so that she nearly falls over.*] He'd stomp his feet on th' floor!—until I'd fixed 'em. . . . [*Her laughter dies out and she wanders away from the porch, examining the scissors.*]

BABY DOLL: That old woman is going out of her mind.

ARCHIE LEE: How long is she been with us?

BABY DOLL: She come in October.

ARCHIE LEE: No, it was August. She pulled in here last August.

BABY DOLL: Was it in August? Yes, it was, it was August.

ARCHIE LEE: Why don't she go an' cackle at Susie's awhile?

BABY DOLL: Susie don't have a bed for her.

ARCHIE LEE: Then how about Jim?

BABY DOLL: She was at Jim's direckly before she come here and Jim's wife said she stole from her and that's why she left.

ARCHIE LEE: I don't believe she stole from her. Do you believe she stole from her?

BABY DOLL: I don't believe she stole from her. I think it was just an excuse to get rid of her. [AUNT ROSE *has arrived at the rose-bush. The wind comes up and nearly blows her off her feet. She staggers around and laughs at her precarious balance.*]

AUNT ROSE: Oh, my gracious! Ha-ha! Oh! Ha-ha-ha!

BABY DOLL: Why, every time I lay my pocket-book down, the silly old thing picks it up and comes creeping in to me with it, and says, "Count the change."

ARCHIE LEE: What does she do that for?

BABY DOLL: She's afraid I'll accuse her of stealing like Jim's wife did.

AUNT ROSE [*Singing to herself as she creeps around the rose-bush*]:
> Rock of Ages, cleft for me,
> Let me hide myself in thee!

ARCHIE LEE: Your buck-toothed cousin named Bunny, didn't he hit on a new way of using oil-waste?

BABY DOLL: He did an' he didn't.

ARCHIE LEE: That statement don't make sense.

BABY DOLL: Well, you know Bunny. He hits on something and ropes in a few stockholders and then it blows up and the stockholders all go to court. And also he says that his wife's got female trouble.

ARCHIE LEE: They've all got something because they're not mental giants but they've got enough sense to know the old lady is going to break down pretty soon and none of 'em wants it to be while she's on their hands.

BABY DOLL: That is about the size of it.

ARCHIE LEE: And I'm stuck with her?

BABY DOLL: Don't holler.

ARCHIE LEE: I'm nominated the goat!

BABY DOLL: Don't holler, don't holler! [AUNT ROSE *sings faintly by rose-bush.*]

ARCHIE LEE: Then pass the old lady on to one of them others.

BABY DOLL: Which one, Archie Lee?

ARCHIE LEE: Eeny-meeny-miney-mo.—Mo gets her.

BABY DOLL: Which is "Mo"?

ARCHIE LEE: Not me! [*Moving slowly and cautiously around the rose-bush with her scissors,* AUNT ROSE *sings to herself. Intersperses lines of the hymn with dialogue on porch. A blue dusk is gathering in the yard but a pool of clear light remains upon the rose-bush.* ARCHIE LEE, *with religious awe.*] Some of them get these lingering types of diseases and have to be given morphine, and they tell me that morphine is just as high as a cat's back.

BABY DOLL: Some of them hang on forever, taking morphine.

ARCHIE LEE: And quantities of it!

BABY DOLL: Yes, they take quantities of it!

ARCHIE LEE: Suppose the old lady broke a hip-bone or something, something that called for morphine!

BABY DOLL: The rest of the folks would have to pitch in and help us.

ARCHIE LEE: Try and extract a dime from your brother Jim! Or Susie or Tom or Bunny! They're all tight as drums, they squeeze ev'ry nickel until th' buffalo bleeds!

BABY DOLL: They don't have much and what they have they hold onto.

ARCHIE LEE: Well, if she does, if she breaks down an' dies on us here, I'm giving you fair warning—— [*Lurches heavily to his feet and spits over edge of porch.*] I'll have her burned up and her ashes put in an old Coca-cola bottle—— [*Flops down again.*] Unless your folks kick in with the price of a coffin! [AUNT ROSE *has clipped a few roses. Now she wanders toward the front of the cottage with them.*] Here she comes back. Now tell her.

BABY DOLL: Tell her what?

ARCHIE LEE: That she's out-stayed her welcome.

AUNT ROSE [*Still at some distance*]: I want you children to look.

ARCHIE LEE: You going to tell her?

AUNT ROSE: I want you children to look at these poems of nature!

ARCHIE LEE: Or do I have to tell her?

BABY DOLL: You hush up and I'll tell her.

ARCHIE LEE: Then tell her right now, and no more pussy-footing.

AUNT ROSE [*Now close to the porch*]: Look at them, look at them, children, they're poems of nature! [*But the "Children" stare unresponsively, not at the flowers but at* AUNT ROSE'S *face with its extravagant brightness. She laughs uncertainly and turns to* ARCHIE LEE *for a more direct appeal.*] Archie Lee, aren't they, aren't they just poems of nature? [*He grunts and gets up, and as he passes* BABY DOLL'S *chair he gives it a kick to remind her.* BABY DOLL *clears her throat.*]

BABY DOLL [*Uneasily*]: Yes, they are poems of nature, Aunt Rose, there is no doubt about it, they are. And, Aunt Rose—while we are talking—step over here for a minute so I can speak to you. [AUNT ROSE *had started away from the porch, as if with a premonition of danger. She stops, her back to the porch, and the fear is visible in her face. It is a familiar fear, one that is graven into her very bones, but which she has never become inured to.*]

AUNT ROSE: What is it, honey? [*She turns around slowly.*] I know you children are feeling upset about something. It don't take a Gypsy with cards to figure that out. You an' Archie Lee both are upset about something. I think you were both unsatisfied with your supper. Isn't that it, Baby Doll? The greens didn't boil long enough. Don't you think I know that? [*She looks from* BABY DOLL'S *face to* ARCHIE LEE'S *back with a hesitant laugh.*] I played a fool trick with my stove, I thought it was lighted and all that time it was . . .

BABY DOLL: Aunt Rose, won't you set down so we can talk comfortably?

AUNT ROSE [*With a note of hysteria*]: I don't want to set down, I don't want to set down, I can talk on my feet! I tell you, getting up an' down is more trouble than it's worth! Now what is it, honey? As soon as I've put these in water, I'm going to light up my stove an' cook you two children some Eggs Birmingham. Archie Lee, Son, you hear that?

ARCHIE LEE [*Roughly, his back still turned*]: I don't want Eggs Birmingham.

BABY DOLL: He don't want Eggs Birmingham and neither do I. But while we are talking, Aunt Rose—well—Archie Lee's wondered and I've been wondering, too . . .

AUNT ROSE: About what, Baby Doll?

BABY DOLL: Well, as to whether or not you've—made any plans.

AUNT ROSE: Plans?

BABY DOLL: Yes, plans.

AUNT ROSE: What kind of plans, Baby Doll?

BABY DOLL: Why, plans for the future, Aunt Rose.

AUNT ROSE: Oh! Future! No—no, when an old maid gets to be nearly a hundred years old, the future don't seem to require much planning for, honey. Many's a time I've wondered but I've never doubted. . . . [*Her voice dies out and there is a strain of music as she faces away from the porch.*] I'm not forgotten by Jesus! No, my Sweet Savior has not forgotten about me! The time isn't known to me or to you, Baby Doll, but it's known by Him and when it comes He will call me. A wind'll come down and lift me an' take me away! The way that it will the roses when they're like I am. . . . [*The music dies out and she turns back to the tribunal on the front porch.*]

BABY DOLL [*Clearing her throat again*]: That's all very well, Aunt Rose, to trust in Jesus, but we've got to remember that Jesus only helps those that—well—help themselves!

AUNT ROSE: Oh, I know that, Baby Doll! [*She laughs.*] Why, I learned that in my cradle, I reckon I must have learned that before I was born. Now when have I ever been helpless? I could count my sick days, the days that I haven't been up and around, on my fingers! My Sweet Savior has kept me healthy an' active, active an' healthy, yes, I do pride myself on it, my age hasn't made me a burden! And when the time comes that I have to lean on His shoulder, I—— [ARCHIE LEE *turns about roughly.*]

ARCHIE LEE: All this talk about Jesus an' greens didn't boil an' so forth has got nothing at all to do with the situation! Now look here, Aunt Rose——

100

BABY DOLL [*Getting up*]: Archie Lee, will you hold your tongue for a minute?

ARCHIE LEE: Then you talk up! And plain! What's there to be so pussy-footing about?

BABY DOLL: There's ways and there's ways of talking anything over!

ARCHIE LEE: Well, talk it over and get off the subject of Jesus! There's Susie, there's Jim, there's Tom and Jane and there's Bunny! And if none of them suits her, there's homes in the county will take her! Just let her decide on which one she is ready to visit. First thing in the morning I'll pile her things in the car and drive her out to whichever one's she's decided! Now ain't that a simple procedure compared to all of this pussy-footing around? Aunt Rose has got sense. She's counted the rooms in this house! She knows that I'm nervous, she knows that I've got work to do and a workingman's got to be fed! And his house is his house and he wants it the way that he wants it! Well, Jesus Almighty, if that's not a plain, fair and square way of settling the matter, I'll wash my hands clean and leave you two women to talk it over yourselves! Yes, I'll—be God damned if—! [*He rushes in and slams the screen door. There is a long pause in which* BABY DOLL *looks uncomfortably at nothing, and* AUNT ROSE *stares at the screen door.*]

AUNT ROSE [*Finally*]: I thought you children were satisfied with my cooking. [*A blue dusk has gathered in the yard.* AUNT ROSE *moves away from the porch and there is a strain of music. The music is drowned out by the cat-like whine of the wind turning suddenly angry.* BABY DOLL *gets up from her wicker chair.*]

BABY DOLL: Archie Lee, Archie Lee, you help me in with these chairs before they blow over! [*She drags her chair to the screen door.*] It looks and sounds like a twister! Hold that screen open for me! Pull in that chair! Now this one! We better get down in the cellar! [*As an afterthought.*] Aunt Rose, come in here so we can shut this door! [AUNT ROSE *shakes her head slightly. Then she looks toward the sky, above and beyond the proscenium, where something portentous is forming.* BABY DOLL *back in the house.*] Call Aunt Rose in!

ARCHIE LEE [*Near the door*]: The stubborn old thing won't budge. [*The door slams shut. The whine of the angry cat turns into a distant roar and the roar approaches. But* AUNT ROSE *remains in the yard, her face still somberly but quietly thoughtful. The loose gray calico of her dress begins to whip and tug at the skeleton lines of her figure. She looks wonderingly at the sky, then back at the house beginning to shrink into darkness, then back at the sky from which the darkness is coming, at each with the same unflinching but troubled expression. Nieces and nephews and cousins, like pages of an album, are rapidly turned through her mind, some of them loved as children but none of them really her children and all of them curiously unneedful of the devotion that she had offered so freely, as if she had always carried an armful of roses that no one had ever offered a vase to receive. The flimsy gray scarf is whipped away from her shoulders. She makes an awkward gesture and sinks to her knees. Her arms let go of the roses. She reaches vaguely after them. One or two she catches. The rest blow away. She struggles back to her feet. The blue dusk deepens to purple and the purple to black and the roar comes on with the force of a locomotive as* AUNT ROSE's *figure is still pushed toward the rose-bush.*]

THE CURTAIN FALLS

How "Bigger" Was Born

RICHARD WRIGHT

I am not so pretentious as to imagine that it is possible for me to account completely for my own book, *Native Son*. But I am going to try to account for as much of it as I can, the sources of it, the material that went into it, and my own years' long changing attitude toward that material.

In a fundamental sense, an imaginative novel represents the merging of two extremes; it is an intensely intimate expression on the part of a consciousness couched in terms of the most objective and commonly known events. It is at once something private and public by its very nature and texture. Confounding the author who is trying to lay his cards on the table is the dogging knowledge that his imagination is a kind of community medium of exchange: what he has read, felt, thought, seen, and remembered is translated into extensions as impersonal as a worn dollar bill.

The more closely the author thinks of why he wrote, the more he comes to regard his imagination as a kind of self-generating cement which glued his facts together, and his emotions as a kind of dark and obscure designer of those facts. Always there is something that is just beyond the tip of the tongue that could explain it all. Usually, he ends up by discussing something far afield, an act which incites skepticism and suspicion in those anxious for a straight-out explanation.

Yet the author is eager to explain. But the moment he makes the attempt his words falter, for he is confronted and defied by the inexplicable array of his own emotions. Emotions are subjective and he can communicate them only when he clothes them in objective guise; and how can he ever be so arrogant as to know when he is dressing up the right emotion in the right Sunday suit? He is always left with the uneasy notion that maybe *any* objective drapery is as good as *any* other for any emotion.

And the moment he does dress up an emotion, his mind is confronted with the riddle of that "dressed up" emotion, and he is left peering with eager dismay back into the dim reaches of his own incommunicable life.

103

Field Workers, Thomas Hart Benton

Reluctantly, he comes to the conclusion that to account for his book is to account for his life, and he knows that that is impossible. Yet, some curious, wayward motive urges him to supply the answer, for there is the feeling that his dignity as a living being is challenged by something within him that is not understood.

So, at the outset, I say frankly that there are phases of *Native Son* which I shall make no attempt to account for. There are meanings in my book of which I was not aware until they literally spilled out upon the paper. I shall sketch the outline of how I *consciously* came into possession of the materials that went into *Native Son*, but there will be many things I shall omit, not because I want to, but simply because I don't know them.

The birth of Bigger Thomas goes back to my childhood, and there was not just one Bigger, but many of them, more than I could count and more than you suspect. But let me start with the first Bigger, whom I shall call Bigger No. 1.

When I was a bareheaded, barefoot kid in Jackson, Mississippi, there was a boy who terrorized me and all of the boys I played with. If we were playing games, he would saunter up and snatch from us our balls, bats, spinning tops, and marbles. We would stand around pounting, sniffling, trying to keep back our tears, begging for our playthings. But Bigger would refuse. We never demanded that he give them back; we were afraid, and Bigger was bad. We had seen him clout boys when he was angry and we did not want to run that risk. We never recovered our toys unless we flattered him and made him feel that he was superior to us. Then, perhaps, if he felt like it, he condescended, threw them at us and then gave each of us a swift kick in the bargain, just to make us feel his utter contempt.

That was the way Bigger No. 1 lived. His life was a continuous challenge to others. At all times he *took* his way, right or wrong, and those who contradicted him had him to fight. And never was he happier than when he had someone cornered and at his mercy; it seemed that the deepest meaning of his squalid life was in him at such times.

I don't know what the fate of Bigger No. 1 was. His swaggering personality is swallowed up somewhere in the amnesia of my childhood. But I suspect that his end was violent. Anyway, he left a marked impression upon me; maybe it was because I longed secretly to be like him and was afraid. I don't know.

If I had known only one Bigger I would not have written *Native Son*.

Let me call the next one Bigger No. 2; he was about seventeen and tougher than the first Bigger. Since I, too, had grown older, I was a little less afraid of him. And the hardness of this Bigger No. 2 was not directed toward me or the other Negroes, but toward the whites who ruled the South. He bought clothes and food on credit and would not pay for them. He lived in the dingy shacks of the white landlords and refused to pay rent. Of course, he had no money, but neither did we. We did without the necessities of life and starved ourselves, but he never would. When we asked him why he acted as he did, he would tell us (as though we were little children in a kindergarten) that the white folks had everything and he had nothing. Further, he would tell us that we were fools not to get what we wanted while we were alive in this world. We would listen and silently agree. We longed to believe and act as he did, but we were afraid. We were Southern Negroes and we were hungry and we wanted to live, but we were more willing to tighten our belts than risk conflict. Bigger No. 2 wanted to live and he did; he was in prison the last time I heard from him.

There was Bigger No. 3, whom the white folks called a "bad nigger." He carried his life in his hands in a literal fashion. I once worked as a ticket-taker in a Negro movie house (all movie houses in Dixie are Jim Crow; there are movies for whites and movies for blacks), and many times Bigger No. 3 came to the door and gave my arm a hard pinch and walked into the theater. Resentfully and silently, I'd nurse my bruised arm. Presently, the proprietor would come over and ask how things were going. I'd point into the darkened theater and say: "Bigger's in there." "Did he pay?" the proprietor would ask. "No, sir," I'd answer. The proprietor would pull down the corners of his lips and speak through his teeth: "We'll kill that goddamn nigger one of these days." And the episode would end right there. But later on Bigger No. 3 was killed during the days of Prohibition: while delivering liquor to a customer he was shot through the back by a white cop.

And then there was Bigger No. 4, whose only law was death. The Jim Crow laws of the South were not for him. But as he laughed and cursed and broke them, he knew that some day he'd have to pay for his freedom. His rebellious spirit made him violate all the taboos and consequently he always oscillated between moods of intense elation and depression. He was never happier than when he had outwitted some foolish custom, and he was never more melancholy than when brooding over the impossibility of his ever

106

being free. He had no job, for he regarded digging ditches for fifty cents a day as slavery. "I can't live on that," he would say, Ofttimes I'd find him reading a book; he would stop and in a joking, wistful, and cynical manner ape the antics of the white folks. Generally, he'd end his mimicry in a depressed state and say: "The white folks won't let us do nothing." Bigger No. 4 was sent to the asylum for the insane.

Then there was Bigger No. 5, who always rode the Jim Crow streetcars without paying and sat wherever he pleased. I remember one morning his getting into a streetcar (all streetcars in Dixie are divided into two sections: one section is for whites and is labeled—FOR WHITES; the other section is for Negroes and is labeled—FOR COLORED) and sitting in the white section. The conductor went to him and said: "Come on, nigger. Move over where you belong. Can't you read?" Bigger answered: "Naw, I can't read." The conductor flared up: "Get out of that seat!" Bigger took out his knife, opened it, held it nonchalantly in his hand, and replied: "Make me." The conductor turned red, blinked, clenched his fists, and walked away, stammering: "The goddamn scum of the earth!" A small angry conference of white men took place in the front of the car and the Negroes sitting in the Jim Crow section overheard: "That's that Bigger Thomas nigger and you'd better leave 'im alone." The Negroes experienced an intense flash of pride and the streetcar moved on its journey without incident. I don't know what happened to Bigger No. 5. But I can guess.

The Bigger Thomases were the only Negroes I know of who consistently violated the Jim Crow laws of the South and got away with it, at least for a sweet brief spell. Eventually, the whites who restricted their lives made them pay a terrible price. They were shot, hanged, maimed, lynched, and generally hounded until they were either dead or their spirits broken.

There were many variations to this behavioristic pattern. Later on I encountered other Bigger Thomases who did not react to the locked-in Black Belts with this same extremity and violence. But before I use Bigger Thomas as a springboard for the examination of milder types, I'd better indicate more precisely the nature of the environment that produced these men, or the reader will be left with the impression that they were essentially and organically bad.

In Dixie there are two worlds, the white world and the black world, and they are physically separated. There are white schools and black schools, white churches and black churches, white businesses and black businesses, white graveyards and black graveyards, and, for all I know, a white God and a black God. . . .

The separation was accomplished after the Civil War by the terror of the Ku Klux Klan, which swept the newly freed Negro through arson, pillage, and death out of the United States Senate, the House of Representatives, the many state legislatures, and out of the public, social, and economic life of the South. The motive for this assault was simple and urgent. The imperialistic tug of history had torn the Negro from his African home and had placed him ironically upon the most fertile plantation areas of the South; and, when the Negro was freed, he outnumbered the whites in many of these fertile areas. Hence, a fierce and bitter struggle took place to keep the ballot from the Negro, for had he had a chance to vote, he would have automatically controlled the richest lands of the South and with them the social, political, and economic destiny of a third of the Republic. Though the South is politically a part of America, the problem that faced her was peculiar and the struggle between the whites and the blacks after the Civil War was in essence a struggle for power, ranging over thirteen states and involving the lives of tens of millions of people.

But keeping the ballot from the Negro was not enough to hold him in check; disfranchisement had to be supplemented by a whole panoply of rules, taboos, and penalties designed not only to insure peace (complete submission), but to guarantee that no real threat would ever arise. Had the Negro lived upon a common territory, separate from the bulk of the white population, this program of oppression might not have assumed such a brutal and violent form. But this war took place between people who were neighbors, whose homes adjoined, whose farms had common boundaries. Guns and disfranchisement, therefore, were not enough to make the black neighbor keep his distance. The white neighbor decided to limit the amount of education his black neighbor could receive; decided to keep him off the police force and out of the local national guards; to segregate him residentially; to Jim Crow him in public places; to restrict his participation in the professions and jobs; and to build up a vast, dense ideology of racial superiority that would justify any act of violence taken against him to defend white dominance; and further, to condition him to hope for little and to receive that little without rebelling.

But, because the blacks were so *close* to the very civilization which sought to keep them out, because they could not *help* but react in some way to its incentives and prizes, and because the very tissue of their consciousness received its tone and timbre from the strivings of that dominant civilization, oppression spawned among them a myriad variety of reactions, reaching from outright blind rebellion to a sweet, other-worldly submissiveness.

In the main, this delicately balanced state of affairs has not greatly altered since the Civil War, save in those parts of the South which have been industrialized or urbanized. So volatile and tense are these relations that if a Negro rebels against rule and taboo, he is lynched and the reason for the lynching is usually called "rape," that catchword which has garnered such vile connotations that it can raise a mob anywhere in the South pretty quickly, even today.

Now for the variations in the Bigger Thomas pattern. Some of the Negroes living under these conditions got religion, felt that Jesus would redeem the void of living, felt that the more bitter life was in the present the happier it would be in the hereafter. Others, clinging still to that brief glimpse of post-Civil War freedom, employed a thousand ruses and stratagems of struggle to win their rights. Still others projected their hurts and longings into more naïve and mundane forms—blues, jazz, swing—and, without intellectual guidance, tried to build up a compensatory nourishment for themselves. Many labored under hot suns and then killed the restless ache with alcohol. Then there were those who strove for an education, and when they got it, enjoyed the financial fruits of it in the style of their bourgeois oppressors. Usually they went hand in hand with the powerful whites and helped to keep their groaning brothers in line, for that was the safest course of action. Those who did this called themselves "leaders." To give you an idea of how completely these "leaders" worked with those who oppressed, I can tell you that I lived the first seventeen years of my life in the South without so much as hearing of or seeing one act of rebellion from *any* Negro, save the Bigger Thomases.

But why did Bigger revolt? No explanation based upon a hard and fast rule of conduct can be given. But there were always two factors psychologically dominant in his personality. First, through some quirk of circumstance, he had become estranged from the religion and the folk culture of his race. Second, he was trying to react to and answer the call of the dominant civilization whose glitter came to him through the newspapers, magazines, radios, movies, and the mere imposing sight and sound of daily American life. In many respects his emergence as a distinct type was inevitable.

As I grew older, I became familiar with the Bigger Thomas conditioning and its numerous shadings no matter where I saw it in Negro life. It was not, as I have already said, as blatant or extreme as in the originals; but it was there, nevertheless, like an undeveloped negative.

Sometimes, in areas far removed from Mississippi, I'd hear a Negro say: "I wish I didn't have to live this way. I feel like I want to burst." Then the anger would pass; he would go back to his job and try to eke out a few pennies to support his wife and children.

Sometimes I'd hear a Negro say: "God, I wish I had a flag and a country of my own." But that mood would soon vanish and he would go his way placidly enough.

Sometimes I'd hear a Negro ex-soldier say: "What in hell did I fight in the war for? They segregated me even when I was offering my life for my country." But he, too, like the others, would soon forget, would become caught up in the tense grind of struggling for bread.

I've even heard Negroes, in moments of anger and bitterness, praise what Japan is doing in China, not because they believed in oppression (being objects of oppression themselves), but because they would suddenly sense how empty their lives were when looking at the dark faces of Japanese generals in the rotogravure supplements of the Sunday newspapers. They would dream of what it would be like to live in a country where they could forget their color and play a responsible role in the vital processes of the nation's life.

I've even heard Negroes say that maybe Hitler and Mussolini are all right; that maybe Stalin is all right. They did not say this out of any intellectual comprehension of the forces at work in the world, but because they felt that these men "did things," a phrase which is charged with more meaning than the mere words imply. There was in the back of their minds, when they said this, a wild and intense longing (wild and intense because it was suppressed!) to belong, to be identified, to feel that they were alive as other people were, to be caught up forgetfully and exultingly in the swing of events, to feel the clean, deep, organic satisfaction of doing a job in common with others.

It was not until I went to live in Chicago that I first thought seriously of writing of Bigger Thomas. Two items of my experience combined to make me aware of Bigger as a meaningful and prophetic symbol. First, being free of the daily pressure of the Dixie environment, I was able to come into possession of my own feelings. Second, my contact with the labor movement and its ideology made me see Bigger clearly and feel what he meant.

I made the discovery that Bigger Thomas was not black all the time; he was white, too, and there were literally millions of him, everywhere. The extension of my sense of the personality of Bigger was the pivot of my life; it altered the complexion of my existence. I became conscious, at first dimly, and then later on with increasing clarity and conviction, of a vast, muddied pool of human life in America. It was as though I had put on a pair of spectacles whose power was that of an x-ray enabling me to see deeper into the lives of men. Whenever I picked up a newspaper, I'd no longer feel that I was reading of the doings of whites alone (Negroes are rarely mentioned in the press unless they've committed some crime!), but of a complex struggle for life going on in my country, a struggle in which I was involved. I sensed, too, that the Southern scheme of oppression was but an appendage of a far vaster and in many respects more ruthless and impersonal commodity-profit machine.

Trade-union struggles and issues began to grow meaningful to me. The flow of goods across the seas, buoying and depressing the wages of men, held a fascination. The pronouncements of foreign governments, their policies, plans, and acts were calculated and weighed in relation to the lives of people about me. I was literally overwhelmed when, in reading the works of Russian revolutionists, I came across descriptions of the "holiday energies of the masses," "the locomotives of history," "the conditions prerequisite for revolution," and so forth. I approached all of these new revelations in the light of Bigger Thomas, his hopes, fears, and despairs; and I began to feel far-flung kinships, and sense, with fright and abashment, the possibilities of *alliances* between the American Negro and other people possessing a kindred consciousness.

As my mind extended in this general and abstract manner, it was fed with even more vivid and concrete examples of the lives of Bigger Thomas. The urban environment of Chicago, affording a more stimulating life, made the Negro Bigger Thomases react more violently than even in the South. More than ever I began to see and understand the environmental factors which made for this extreme conduct. It was not that Chicago segregated

111

Negroes more than the South, but that Chicago had more to offer, that Chicago's physical aspect—noisy, crowded, filled with the sense of power and fulfillment—did so much more to dazzle the mind with a taunting sense of possible achievement that the segregation it did impose brought forth from Bigger a reaction more obstreperous than in the South.

So the concrete picture and the abstract linkages of relationships fed each other, each making the other more meaningful and affording my emotions an opportunity to react to them with success and understanding. The process was like a swinging pendulum, each to and fro motion throwing up its tiny bit of meaning and significance, each stroke helping to develop the dim negative which had been implanted in my mind in the South.

During this period the shadings and nuances which were filling in Bigger's picture came, not so much from Negro life, as from the lives of whites I met and grew to know. I began to sense that they had their own kind of Bigger Thomas behavioristic pattern which grew out of a more subtle and broader frustration. The waves of recurring crime, the silly fads and crazes, the quicksilver changes in public taste, the hysteria and fears— all of these had long been mysteries to me. But now I looked back at them and felt the pinch and pressure of the environment that gave them their pitch and peculiar kind of being. I began to feel with my mind the inner tensions of the people I met. I don't mean to say that I think that environment *makes* consciousness (I suppose God makes that, if there is a God), but I do say that I felt and still feel that the environment supplies the instrumentalities through which the organism expresses itself, and if that environment is warped or tranquil, the mode and manner of behavior will be affected toward deadlocking tensions or orderly fulfillment and satisfaction. . . .

I don't know if *Native Son* is a good book or a bad book. And I don't know if the book I'm working on now will be a good book or a bad book. And I really don't care. The mere writing of it will be more fun and a deeper satisfaction than any praise or blame from anybody. . . .

The Alligator

BEATRICE RAVENAL

He roars in the swamp.
For two hundred years he has clamored in Spring;
He is fourteen feet long, and his track scars the earth in the
      night-time,
His voice scars the air.
Oak-boughs have furred their forks, are in velvet;
Jessamine crackle their fire-new sparks;
The grass is full of a nameless wildness of color, or flowers in
      solution.
The glass-blower birds twist their brittle imaginings over the
      multiplied colors of water.

But the counterpoint of the Spring—
Exacerbate, resonant,
Raw like beginnings of worlds,
Cry of the mud made flesh, made articular, personal,
Midnight assailing the morning, myopic sound, blinded by
      sun,—
Roars from the swamp.
A thing in itself,
Not only alive, but the very existence of death would be news
      to it.
Will—
Will without inflection,
Making us shudder, ashamed of our own triviality—
The bull alligator roars in the swamp.

The Bitterness

This is queer country.
One does not walk nor climb for a view;
It comes right up to the porch, like a hound to be patted.
Under our hog-back
The swamp, inchoate creature, fumbles its passage, still nearer;
Puffing a vapor of flowers before it.

This week there are ponds in the wood, vertiginous skies
          underfoot,
Pondering heaven.
Next week in the pashing mud of the footpath
Fish may be gasping, baffled in semi-solids.
The negroes will eat them.

This is queer country.
Thick-blooded compulsive sound,
Like scum in the branch, chokes, mantles the morning.

Sangarrah! . . . Sangarrah! . . . Sangarrah!

Two hundred years back—
And the medicine-man of the Yemassee
Sat in the thick of the swamp, on the ridge where the cypresses
          flung
Their elfin stockade.
Wrinkled his chest as the cast-off skin of the blacksnake,
The hide of his cheeks hung square and ridged as the hide
Of the grown alligator.
A young alligator squirmed on his naked knees
While he muttered its lesson.

That was strong medicine.   Over the old man's eyes
    Drooped the holy beloved crest of the swan-plumes;
Otter-skin straps cut under his arms

114

From the breastplate of conch-shells.
Fawn-trotters fell from his boot-tops; the white beloved mantle
Lined with raw scarlet, hung on the gum-tree, along with the
      ocelot quiver
And locust-weed bow.
He had fasted, drinking the dark button snake-root. He
      shuddered,
Calling the secret name, the name of the Manneyto,
Y-O-He,
Never known by the people.
On the infant saurian, long-lived, ruled into patterns, his hands
Moved, taking the shape of a sharp-curved arrow;
He spoke, teaching its lesson, calling its name;
"Nanneb-Chunchaba,
Fish-like-a-Mountain,
Remember!

"By the day-sun and the night-sun
By the new beloved fire of the corn-feast;
By the Arrow of Lightning, that came from the storm,
From the Spirit of Fire to the ancient chief of the Yemassee—
Totem of Yemassee!
Let our voice be remembered.

"We go from the hunting-grounds of our fathers.
The lands that we took, fighting north through the man-eating
      Westoes,
Fall from our hands.
In the hills of our dead, in the powdering flesh that conceived
      us,
    Shall the white man plant corn.

"The trails where we fought with the fierce Tuscarora
Will call us in vain;

The Bitterness

No pictures of skillful canoemen will green Isundiga paint clear
       in his waters.

We shall be cut from the land as the medicine-man cuts the
       totem
From the arm of the outcast.

"From the sky they cannot cut our totem!

"My name too shall vanish.
When the drums and the music for three days are silent
And men praise me under the peach-trees,
My over-wise spirit
Shall root itself here, as the oak-tree takes hold.
Who will wait for me? Which of the spirits
That have made of my body a lodge, that have twisted my
       sinews
As women twist withes for their baskets, will claim habitation,
That have spoken their wisdom
Out of my mouth?
I shall hide from them all, as the war-chiefs
Cover their lives with the tree-tops,
Leaving them safe when they go on the war-path.
I shall sleep in this place.
In the new days,
The days when our voice shall be silent,
Speak for the Yemassee!
Nanneb-Chunchaba, you, little Fish-like-a-Mountain,
Shout through the forest the terrible war-cry of Yemassee!

"Sangarrah! . . . Sangarrah-me! . . . Sangarrah-me!
Shout! I shall hear you!
Sangarrah! . . ."

116

For two hundred years—
Will, without inflection—
The bull alligator
Roars from the swamp
In the Spring.

The Faith

Since the first Pilgrim landing at Plymouth, ours has been a nation "under God," and religion took on a special dimension in the antebellum South, where it became not only a means of spiritual growth, but an excellent framework for supporting an aristocratic society. Most of the slaves were illiterate. Their only education came from the Scriptures, from which they learned at least what their masters wished them to know—the importance of human suffering in achieving eternal life after death. If they bore their earthly lot with meekness and patience, they, too, would be welcomed into the heavenly host. And to help them along the way was a gentle Jesus, Himself of humble birth, who taught them how to bear persecution.

This hope of their religion was their salvation—and their masters' also; it helped keep the slaves somewhat content and in their place. Church attendance was encouraged, and the masters' families set the example. They went to church also, but not to the same church, or even the same denomination. The masters usually chose the formality of Episcopalianism, the American counterpart of the Church of England. Black churches were Pentecostally oriented.

In supporting religion plantation owners set the tone for more than their own slaves. Persons in all classes were drawn to the hope of future glory, and churches of all kinds ranging from high to fundamentalist filled the land. Church affiliation became in itself a way of attaining status. But until recent years southern blacks and whites attended separate churches, even when they were of the same denomination.

This is not to say that Southerners are more religious than other Americans, but that here religion was reinforced by the prevailing

119

social and economic structures. Religion—or at least its forms—is still a viable force in the South. Almost every public meeting, social gathering, and sports event begins with prayer; and any who scoff at this custom are regarded with some suspicion.

The Creation

A Negro Sermon

JAMES WELDON JOHNSON

And God stepped out on space,
And He looked around and said,
"I'm lonely—
I'll make me a world."

And as far as the eye of God could see
Darkness covered everything,
Blacker than a hundred midnights
Down in a cypress swamp.

Then God smiled,
And the light broke,
And the darkness rolled up on one side,
And the light stood shining on the other,
And God said, *"That's good!"*

Then God reached out and took the light in His hands,
And God rolled the light around in His hands,
Until He made the sun;
And He set that sun a-blazing in the heavens.
And the light that was left from making the sun
God gathered up in a shining ball
And flung against the darkness,
Spangling the night with the moon and stars.

121

Then down between
The darkness and the light
He hurled the world;
And God said, *"That's good!"*

Then God himself stepped down—
And the sun was on His right hand,
And the moon was on His left;
The stars were clustered about His head,
And the earth was under His feet.
And God walked, and where He trod
His footsteps hollowed the valleys out
And bulged the mountains up.

Then He stopped and looked and saw
That the earth was hot and barren.
So God stepped over to the edge of the world
And He spat out the seven seas;
He batted His eyes, and the lightnings flashed;
He clapped His hands, and the thunders rolled;
And the waters above the earth came down,
The cooling waters came down.

Then the green grass sprouted,
And the little red flowers blossomed,
The pine-tree pointed his finger to the sky,
And the oak spread out his arms;
The lakes cuddled down in the hollows of the ground,
And the rivers ran down to the sea;
And God smiled again,
And the rainbow appeared,
And curled itself around His shoulder.

The Faith

Then God raised His arm and He waved His hand
Over the sea and over the land,
And He said, *"Bring forth! Bring forth!"*
And quicker than God could drop His hand,
Fishes and fowls
And beasts and birds
Swam the rivers and the seas,
Roamed the forests and the woods,
And split the air with their wings,
And God said, *"That's good!"*

Then God walked around
And God looked around
On all that He had made.
He looked at His sun,
And He looked at His moon,
And He looked at His little stars;
He looked on His world
With all its living things,
And God said, *"I'm lonely still."*

Then God sat down
On the side of a hill where He could think;
By a deep, wide river He sat down;
With His head in His hands,
God thought and thought,
Till He thought, *"I'll make me a man!"*

Up from the bed of the river
God scooped the clay;
And by the bank of the river
He kneeled Him down;

124

And there the great God Almighty,
Who lit the sun and fixed it in the sky,
Who flung the stars to the most far corner of the night,
Who rounded the earth in the middle of His hand—
This Great God,
Like a mammy bending over her baby,
Kneeled down in the dust
Toiling over a lump of clay
Till He shaped it in His own image;
Then into it He blew the breath of life,
And man became a living soul.
Amen. Amen.

Sister Lou

STERLING A. BROWN

Honey
When de man
Calls out de las' train
You're gonna ride,
Tell him howdy.

Gather up yo' basket
An' yo' knittin' an' yo' things,
An' go on up an' visit
Wid frien' Jesus fo' a spell.

Show Marfa
How to make yo' greengrape jellies,
An' give po' Lazarus
A passel of them Golden Biscuits.

Scald some meal
Fo' some rightdown good spoonbread
Fo' li'l box-plunkin' David.

An' sit aroun'
An' tell them Hebrew Chillen
All yo' stories. . . .

Honey
Don't be feared of them pearly gates,
Don't go 'round to de back,
No mo' dataway
Not evah no mo'.

Let Michael tote yo' burden
An' yo' pocketbook an' evah thing
'Cept yo' Bible,
While Gabriel blows somp'n
Solemn but loudsome
On dat horn of his'n.

Honey
Go straight on to de Big House,
An' speak to yo' God
Widout no fear an' tremblin'.

Then sit down
An' pass de time of day awhile.

Give a good talkin' to
To yo' favorite 'postle Peter,
An' rub the po' head
Of mixed-up Judas,
An' joke awhile wid Jonah.

Then, when you gits de chance,
Always rememberin' yo' raisin',
Let 'em know youse tired
Jest a mite tired.

Jesus will find yo' bed fo' you
Won't no servant evah bother wid yo' room.

The Faith

Jesus will lead you
To a room wid windows
Openin' on cherry trees an' plum trees
Bloomin' everlastin'.

An' dat will be yours
Fo' keeps.
Den take yo' time. . . .
Honey, take yo' blessed time.

Atlanta Exposition Address

BOOKER T. WASHINGTON

Mr. President and Gentlemen of the Board of Directors and Citizens: One third of the population of the South is of the Negro race. No enterprise seeking the material, civil, or moral welfare of this section can disregard this element of our population and reach the highest success. I but convey to you, Mr. President and Directors, the sentiment of the masses of my race when I say that in no way have the value and manhood of the American Negro been more fittingly and generously recognized than by the managers of this magnificent exposition at every stage of its progress. It is a recognition that will do more to cement the friendship of the two races than any occurrence since the dawn of our freedom.

Not only this, but the opportunity here afforded will awaken among us a new era of industrial progress. Ignorant and inexperienced, it is not strange that in the first years of our new life we began at the top instead of at the bottom; that a seat in Congress or the State Legislature was more sought than real estate or industrial skill; that the political convention or stump speaking had more attraction than starting a dairy farm or truck garden.

A ship lost at sea for many days suddenly sighted a friendly vessel. From the mast of the unfortunate vessel was seen a signal: "Water, water; we die of thirst!" The answer from the friendly vessel at once came back: "Cast down your bucket where you are." A second time the signal, "Water, water; send us water!" ran up from the distressed vessel, and was answered: "Cast down your bucket where you are." And a third and fourth signal for water was answered, "Cast down your bucket where you are." The captain of the distressed vessel, at last heeding the injunction, cast down his bucket, and it came up full of fresh, sparkling water from the mouth of the Amazon River. To those of my race who depend upon bettering their condition in a foreign land, or who underestimate the importance of cultivating friendly relations with the Southern white man who is their next-door neighbor, I would say: "Cast down your bucket where you are"—cast it down in making

129

friends, in every manly way, of the people of all races by whom we are surrounded.

Cast it down in agriculture, mechanics, in commerce, in domestic service, and in the professions. And in this connection it is well to bear in mind
that whatever other sins the South may be called to bear, when it comes to
business, pure and simple, it is in the South that the Negro is given a man's
chance in the commercial world, and in nothing is this Exposition more eloquent than in emphasizing this chance. Our greatest danger is that in the
great leap from slavery to freedom we may overlook the fact that the masses
of us are to live by the productions of our hands, and fail to keep in mind
that we shall prosper in proportion as we learn to dignify and glorify common labor, and put brains and skill into the common occupations of life;
shall prosper in proportion as we learn to draw the line between the superfi-
cial and the substantial, the ornamental gew-gaws of life and the useful. No
race can prosper till it learns that there is as much dignity in tilling a field as
in writing a poem. It is at the bottom of life we must begin, and not at the
top. Nor should we permit our grievances to overshadow our opportunities.

To those of the white race who look to the incoming of those of foreign
birth and strange tongue and habits for the prosperity of the South, were I
permitted, I would repeat what I say to my own race, "Cast down your
bucket where you are." Cast it down among the eight million Negroes
whose habits you know, whose fidelity and love you have tested in days
when to have proved treacherous meant the ruin of your firesides. Cast
down your bucket among these people who have without strikes and labor
wars tilled your fields, cleared your forests, builded your railroads and cities, brought forth treasures from the bowels of the earth, and helped make
possible this magnificent representation of the progress of the South. Cast-
ing down your bucket among my people, helping and encouraging them as
you are doing on these grounds, and, with education of head, hand, and
heart, you will find that they will buy your surplus land, make blossom the
waste places in your fields, and run your factories. While doing this, you
can be sure in the future, as in the past, that you and your families will be
surrounded by the most patient, faithful, law-abiding, and unresentful people that the world has seen. As we have proved our loyalty to you in the
past, in nursing your children, watching by the sick bed of your mothers
and fathers, and often following them with tear-dimmed eyes to their

130

graves, so in the future, in our humble way, we shall stand by you with a devotion that no foreigner can approach, ready to lay down our lives, if need be, in defense of yours, interlacing our industrial, commercial, civil, and religious life with yours in a way that shall make the interests of both races one. In all things that are purely social we can be as separate as the fingers, yet one as the hand in all things essential to mutual progress.

There is no defense or security for any of us except in the highest intelligence and development of all. If anywhere there are efforts tending to curtail the fullest growth of the Negro, let these efforts be turned into stimulating, encouraging, and making him the most useful and intelligent citizen. Effort or means so invested will pay a thousand per cent interest. These efforts will be twice blessed—"Blessing him that gives and him that takes."

There is no escape through law of man or God from the inevitable:

> "The laws of changeless justice bind
> Oppressor with oppressed;
> And close as sin and suffering joined
> We march to fate abreast."

Nearly sixteen millions of hands will aid you in pulling the load upward, or they will pull, against you, the load downward. We shall constitute one third and more of the ignorance and crime of the South, or one third its intelligence and progress; we shall contribute one third to the business and industrial prosperity of the South, or we shall prove a veritable body of death, stagnating, depressing, retarding every effort to advance the body politic.

Gentlemen of the Exposition, as we present to you our humble effort at an exhibition of our progress, you must not expect overmuch. Starting thirty years ago with ownership here and there in a few quilts and pumpkins and chickens (gathered from miscellaneous sources), remember, the path that has led from these to the inventions and production of agricultural implements, buggies, steam engines, newspapers, books, statuary, carving, paintings, the management of drugstores and banks, has not been trodden without contact with thorns and thistles. While we take pride in what we exhibit as a result of our independent efforts, we do not for a moment forget that our part in this exhibition would fall far short of your expectations but for

131

the constant help that has come to our educational life, not only from the Southern states, but especially from Northern philanthropists, who have made their gifts a constant stream of blessing and encouragement.

The wisest among my race understand that the agitation of questions of social equality is the extremest folly, and that progress in the enjoyment of all the privileges that will come to us must be the result of severe and constant struggle rather than of artificial forcing. No race that has anything to contribute to the markets of the world is long, in any degree, ostracized. It is important and right that all privileges of the law be ours, but it is vastly more important that we be prepared for the exercise of those privileges. The opportunity to earn a dollar in a factory just now is worth infinitely more than the opportunity to spend a dollar in an opera house.

In conclusion, may I repeat that nothing in thirty years has given us more hope and encouragement, and drawn us so near to you of the white race, as this opportunity offered by the Exposition; and here bending, as it were, over the altar that represents the results of the struggles of your race and mine, both starting practically empty-handed three decades ago, I pledge that, in your effort to work out the great and intricate problem which God has laid at the doors of the South, you shall have at all times the patient, sympathetic help of my race; only let this be constantly in mind, that while, from representations in these buildings of the product of field, of forest, of mine, of factory, letters, and art, much good will come, yet far above and beyond material benefits will be that higher good, that, let us pray God, will come in a blotting out of sectional differences and racial animosities and suspicions, in a determination to administer absolute justice, in a willing obedience among all classes to the mandates of law. This, coupled with our material prosperity, will bring into our beloved South a new heaven and a new earth.

The River

FLANNERY O'CONNOR

The child stood glum and limp in the middle of the dark living room while his father pulled him into a plaid coat. His right arm was hung in the sleeve but the father buttoned the coat anyway and pushed him forward toward a pale spotted hand that stuck through the half-open door.

"He ain't fixed right," a loud voice said from the hall.

"Well then for Christ's sake fix him," the father muttered. "It's six o'clock in the morning." He was in his bathrobe and barefooted. When he got the child to the door and tried to shut it, he found her looming in it, a speckled skeleton in a long pea-green coat and felt helmet.

"And his and my carfare," she said. "It'll be twict we have to ride the car."

He went in the bedroom again to get the money and when he came back, she and the boy were both standing in the middle of the room. She was taking stock. "I couldn't smell those dead cigarette butts long if I was ever to come sit with you," she said, shaking him down in his coat.

"Here's the change," the father said. He went to the door and opened it wide and waited.

After she had counted the money she slipped it somewhere inside her coat and walked over to a watercolor hanging near the phonograph. "I know what time it is," she said, peering closely at the black lines crossing into broken planes of violent color. "I ought to. My shift goes on at 10 P.M. and don't get off till 5 and it takes me one hour to ride the Vine Street car."

"Oh, I see," he said. "Well, we'll expect him back tonight, about eight or nine?"

"Maybe later," she said. "We're going to the river to a healing. This particular preacher don't get around this way often. I wouldn't have paid for that," she said, nodding at the painting, "I would have drew it myself."

"All right, Mrs. Connin, we'll see you then," he said drumming on the door.

A toneless voice called from the bedroom, "Bring me an ice-pack."

"Too bad his mamma's sick," Mrs. Connin said. "What's her trouble?"

"We don't know," he muttered.

"We'll ask the preacher to pray for her. He's healed a lot of folks. The Reverend Bevel Summers. Maybe she ought to see him sometime."

"Maybe so," he said. "We'll see you tonight," and he disappeared into the bedroom and left them to go.

The little boy stared at her silently, his nose and eyes running. He was four or five. He had a long face and bulging chin and half-shut eyes set far apart. He seemed mute and patient, like an old sheep waiting to be let out.

"You'll like this preacher," she said. "The Reverend Bevel Summers. You ought to hear him sing."

The bedroom door opened suddenly and the father stuck his head out and said, "Good-by, old man. Have a good time."

"Good-by," the little boy said and jumped as if he had been shot.

Mrs. Connin gave the watercolor another look. Then they went out into the hall and rang for the elevator. "I wouldn't have drew it," she said.

Outside the gray morning was blocked off on either side by the unlit empty buildings. "It's going to fair up later," she said, "but this is the last time we'll be able to have any preaching at the river this year. Wipe your nose, Sugar Boy."

He began rubbing his sleeve across it but she stopped him. "That ain't nice," she said. "Where's your handkerchief?"

He put his hands in his pockets and pretended to look for it while she waited. "Some people don't care how they send one off," she murmured to her reflection in the coffee shop window. "You pervide." She took a red and blue flowered handkerchief out of her pocket and stooped down and began to work on his nose. "Now blow," she said and he blew. "You can borry it. Put it in your pocket."

He folded it up and put it in his pocket carefully and they walked on to the corner and leaned against the side of a closed drugstore to wait for the car. Mrs. Connin turned up her coat collar so that it met her hat in the back. Her eyelids began to droop and she looked as if she might go to sleep against the wall. The little boy put a slight pressure on her hand.

"What's your name?" she asked in a drowsy voice. "I don't know but only your last name. I should have found out your first name."

Raftsmen Playing Cards, George Caleb Bingham

His name was Harry Ashfield and he had never thought at any time before of changing it. "Bevel," he said.

Mrs. Connin raised herself from the wall. "Why ain't that a coincident!" she said. "I told you that's the name of this preacher!"

"Bevel," he repeated.

She stood looking down at him as if he had become a marvel to her. "I'll have to see you meet him today," she said. "He's no ordinary preacher. He's a healer. He couldn't do nothing for Mr. Connin though. Mr. Connin didn't have the faith but he said he would try anything once. He had this griping in his gut."

The trolley appeared as a yellow spot at the end of the deserted street.

"He's gone to the government hospital now," she said, "and they taken one-third of his stomach. I tell him he better thank Jesus for what he's got left but he says he ain't thanking nobody. Well I declare," she murmured, "Bevel!"

They walked out to the tracks to wait. "Will he heal me?" Bevel asked.

"What you got?"

"I'm hungry," he decided finally.

"Didn't you have your breakfast?"

"I didn't have time to be hungry yet then," he said.

"Well when we get home we'll both have us something," she said. "I'm ready myself."

They got in the car and sat down a few seats behind the driver and Mrs. Connin took Bevel on her knees. "Now you be a good boy," she said, "and let me get some sleep. Just don't get off my lap." She lay her head back and as he watched, gradually her eyes closed and her mouth fell open to show a few long scattered teeth, some gold and some darker than her face; she began to whistle and blow like a musical skeleton. There was no one in the car but themselves and the driver and when he saw she was asleep, he took out the flowered handkerchief and unfolded it and examined it carefully. Then he folded it up again and unzipped a place in the innerlining of his coat and hid it in there and shortly he went to sleep himself.

Her house was a half-mile from the end of the car line, set back a little from the road. It was tan paper brick with a porch across the front of it and a tin top. On the porch there were three little boys of different sizes with identical speckled faces and one tall girl who had her hair up in so many aluminum curlers that it glared like the roof. The three boys followed them inside and closed in on Bevel. They looked at him silently, not smiling.

"That's Bevel," Mrs. Connin said, taking off her coat. "It's a coincident he's named the same as the preacher. These boys are J. C., Spivey, and Sinclair, and that's Sarah Mildred on the porch. Take off that coat and hang it on the bed post, Bevel."

The three boys watched him while he unbuttoned the coat and took it off. Then they watched him hang it on the bed post and then they stood, watching the coat. They turned abruptly and went out the door and had a conference on the porch.

Bevel stood looking around him at the room. It was part kitchen and part bedroom. The entire house was two rooms and two porches. Close to his foot the tail of a light-colored dog moved up and down between two floor boards as he scratched his back on the underside of the house. Bevel jumped on it but the hound was experienced and had already withdrawn when his feet hit the spot.

The walls were filled with pictures and calendars. There were two round photographs of an old man and woman with collapsed mouths and another picture of a man whose eyebrows dashed out of two bushes of hair and clashed in a heap on the bridge of his nose; the rest of his face stuck out like a bare cliff to fall from. "That's Mr. Connin," Mrs. Connin said, standing back from the stove for a second to admire the face with him, "but it don't favor him any more." Bevel turned from Mr. Connin to a colored picture over the bed of a man wearing a white sheet. He had long hair and a gold circle around his head and he was sawing on a board while some children stood watching him. He was going to ask who that was when the three boys came in again and motioned for him to follow them. He thought of crawling under the bed and hanging onto one of the legs but the three boys only stood there, speckled and silent, waiting, and after a second he followed them at a little distance out on the porch and around the corner of the house. They started off through a field of rough yellow weeds to the hog pen, a five-foot boarded square full of shoats, which they intended to ease him over into. When they reached it, they turned and waited silently, leaning against the side.

He was coming very slowly, deliberately bumping his feet together as if he had trouble walking. Once he had been beaten up in the park by some strange boys when his sitter forgot him, but he hadn't known anything was going to happen that time until it was over. He began to smell a strong odor of garbage and to hear the noises of a wild animal. He stopped a few feet from the pen and waited, pale but dogged.

The three boys didn't move. Something seemed to have happened to them. They stared over his head as if they saw something coming behind him but he was afraid to turn his own head and look. Their speckles were pale and their eyes were still and gray as glass. Only their ears twitched slightly. Nothing happened. Finally, the one in the middle said, "She'd kill us," and turned, dejected and hacked, and climbed up on the pen and hung over, staring in.

Bevel sat down on the ground, dazed with relief, and grinned up at them.

The one sitting on the pen glanced at him severely. "Hey you," he said after a second, "if you can't climb up and see these pigs you can lift that bottom board off and look in thataway." He appeared to offer this as a kindness.

Bevel had never seen a real pig but he had seen a pig in a book and knew they were small fat pink animals with curly tails and round grinning faces and bow ties. He leaned forward and pulled eagerly at the board.

"Pull harder," the littlest boy said. "It's nice and rotten. Just lift out thet nail."

He eased a long reddish nail out of the soft wood.

"Now you can lift up the board and put your face to the . . ." a quiet voice began.

He had already done it and another face, gray, wet and sour, was pushing into his, knocking him down and back as it scraped out under the plank. Something snorted over him and charged back again, rolling him over and pushing him up from behind and then sending him forward, screaming through the yellow field, while it bounded behind.

The three Connins watched from where they were. The one sitting on the pen held the loose board back with his gangling foot. Their stern faces didn't brighten any but they seemed to become less taut, as if some great need had been partly satisfied. "Maw ain't going to like him lettin' out thet hawg," the smallest one said.

Mrs. Connin was on the back porch and caught Bevel up as he reached the steps. The hog ran under the house and subsided, panting, but the child screamed for five minutes. When she had finally calmed him down, she gave him his breakfast and let him sit on her lap while he ate it. The shoat

138

climbed the two steps onto the back porch and stood outside the screen door, looking in with his head lowered sullenly. He was long-legged and humpbacked and part of one of his ears had been bitten off.

"Git away!" Mrs. Connin shouted. "That one yonder favors Mr. Paradise that has the gas station," she said. "You'll see him today at the healing. He's got the cancer over his ear. He always comes to show he ain't been healed."

The shoat stood squinting a few seconds longer and then moved off slowly. "I don't want to see him," Bevel said.

They walked to the river, Mrs. Connin in front with him and the three boys strung out behind and Sarah Mildred, the tall girl, at the end to holler if one of them ran out on the road. They looked like the skeleton of an old boat with two pointed ends, sailing slowly on the edge of the highway. The white Sunday sun followed at a little distance, climbing fast through a scum of gray cloud as if it meant to overtake them. Bevel walked on the outside edge, holding Mrs. Connin's hand and looking down into the orange and purple gulley that dropped off from the concrete.

It occurred to him that he was lucky this time that they had found Mrs. Connin who would take you away for the day instead of an ordinary sitter who only sat where you lived or went to the park. You found out more when you left where you lived. He had found out already this morning that he had been made by a carpenter named Jesus Christ. Before he had thought it had been a doctor named Sladewall, a fat man with a yellow mustache who gave him shots and thought his name was Herbert, but this must have been a joke. They joked a lot where he lived. If he had thought about it before, he would have thought Jesus Christ was a word like "oh" or "damn" or "God," or maybe somebody who had cheated them out of something sometime. When he had asked Mrs. Connin who the man in the sheet in the picture over her bed was, she had looked at him a while with her mouth open. Then she had said, "That's Jesus," and she had kept on looking at him.

In a few minutes she had got up and got a book out of the other room. "See here," she said, turning over the cover, "this belonged to my great grandmamma. I wouldn't part with it for nothing on earth." She ran her finger under some brown writing on a spotted page. "Emma Stevens Oakley, 1832," she said. "Ain't that something to have? and every word of it the gospel truth." She turned the next page and read him the name: "The Life of Jesus Christ for Readers Under Twelve." Then she read him the book.

It was a small book, pale brown on the outside with gold edges and a smell like old putty. It was full of pictures, one of the carpenter driving a crowd of pigs out of a man. They were real pigs, gray and sour-looking, and Mrs. Connin said Jesus had driven them all out of this one man. When she finished reading, she let him sit on the floor and look at the pictures again.

Just before they left for the healing, he had managed to get the book inside his innerlining without her seeing him. Now it made his coat hang down a little farther on one side than the other. His mind was dreamy and serene as they walked along and when they turned off the highway onto a long red clay road winding between banks of honeysuckle, he began to make wild leaps and pull forward on her hand as if he wanted to dash off and snatch the sun which was rolling away ahead of them now.

They walked on the dirt road for a while and then they crossed a field stippled with purple weeds and entered the shadows of a wood where the ground was covered with thick pine needles. He had never been in woods before and he walked carefully, looking from side to side as if he were entering a strange country. They moved along a bridle path that twisted downhill through crackling red leaves, and once, catching at a branch to keep himself from slipping, he looked into two frozen green-gold eyes enclosed in the darkness of a tree hole. At the bottom of the hill, the woods opened suddenly onto a pasture dotted here and there with black and white cows and sloping down, tier after tier, to a broad orange stream where the reflection of the sun was set like a diamond.

There were people standing on the near bank in a group, singing. Long tables were set up behind them and a few cars and trucks were parked in a road that came up by the river. They crossed the pasture, hurrying, because Mrs. Connin, using her hand for a shed over her eyes, saw the preacher already standing out in the water. She dropped her basket on one of the tables and pushed the three boys in front of her into the knot of people so that they wouldn't linger by the food. She kept Bevel by the hand and eased her way up to the front.

The preacher was standing about ten feet out in the stream where the water came up to his knees. He was a tall youth in khaki trousers that he had rolled up higher than the water. He had on a blue shirt and a red scarf around his neck but no hat and his light-colored hair was cut in sideburns that curved into the hollows of his cheeks. His face was all bone and red light reflected from the river. He looked as if he might have been nineteen years old. He was singing in a high twangy voice, above the singing on the bank, and he kept his hands behind him and his head tilted back.

He ended the hymn on a high note and stood silent, looking down at the water and shifting his feet in it. Then he looked up at the people on the bank. They stood close together, waiting; their faces were solemn but expectant and every eye was on him. He shifted his feet again.

"Maybe I know why you come," he said in the twangy voice, "maybe I don't.

"If you ain't come for Jesus, you ain't come for me. If you just come to see can you leave your pain in the river, you ain't come for Jesus. You can't leave your pain in the river," he said. "I never told nobody that." He stopped and looked down at his knees.

"I seen you cure a woman oncet!" a sudden high voice shouted from the hump of people. "Seen that woman git up and walk out straight where she had limped in!"

The preacher lifted one foot and then the other. He seemed almost but not quite to smile. "You might as well go home if that's what you come for," he said.

Then he lifted his head and arms and shouted, "Listen to what I got to say, you people! There ain't but one river and that's the River of Life, made out of Jesus' Blood. That's the river you have to lay your pain in, in the River of Faith, in the River of Life, in the River of Love, in the rich red river of Jesus' Blood, you people!"

His voice grew soft and musical. "All the rivers come from that one River and go back to it like it was the ocean sea and if you believe, you can lay your pain in that River and get rid of it because that's the River that was made to carry sin. It's a River full of pain itself, pain itself, moving toward the Kingdom of Christ, to be washed away, slow, you people, slow as this here old red water river round my feet.

"Listen," he sang, "I read in Mark about an unclean man, I read in Luke about a blind man, I read in John about a dead man! Oh you people hear! The same blood that makes this River red, made that leper clean, made that blind man stare, made that dead man leap! You people with

141

trouble," he cried, "lay it in that River of Blood, lay it in that River of Pain, and watch it move away toward the Kingdom of Christ."

While he preached, Bevel's eyes followed drowsily the slow circles of two silent birds revolving high in the air. Across the river there was a low red and gold grove of sassafras with hills of dark blue trees behind it and an occasional pine jutting over the skyline. Behind, in the distance, the city rose like a cluster of warts on the side of the mountain. The birds revolved downward and dropped lightly in the top of the highest pine and sat hunch-shouldered as if they were supporting the sky.

"If it's this River of Life you want to lay your pain in, then come up," the preacher said, "and lay your sorrow here. But don't be thinking this is the last of it because this old red river don't end here. This old red suffering stream goes on, you people, slow to the Kingdom of Christ. This old red river is good to Baptize in, good to lay your faith in, good to lay your pain in, but it ain't this muddy water here that saves you. I been all up and down this river this week," he said. "Tuesday I was in Fortune Lake, next day in Ideal, Friday me and my wife drove to Lulawillow to see a sick man there. Them people didn't see no healing," he said and his face burned redder for a second. "I never said they would."

While he was talking a fluttering figure had begun to move forward with a kind of butterfly movement—an old woman with flapping arms whose head wobbled as if it might fall off any second. She managed to lower herself at the edge of the bank and let her arms churn in the water. Then she bent farther and pushed her face down in it and raised herself up finally, streaming wet; and still flapping, she turned a time or two in a blind circle until someone reached out and pulled her back into the group.

"She's been that way for thirteen years," a rough voice shouted. "Pass the hat and give this kid his money. That's what he's here for." The shout, directed out to the boy in the river, came from a huge old man who sat like a humped stone on the bumper of a long ancient gray automobile. He had on a gray hat that was turned down over one ear and up over the other to expose a purple bulge on his left temple. He sat bent forward with his hands hanging between his knees and his small eyes half closed.

Bevel stared at him once and then moved into the folds of Mrs. Connin's coat and hid himself.

The boy in the river glanced at the old man quickly and raised his fist.

142

"Believe Jesus or the devil!" he cried. "Testify to one or the other!"

"I know from my own self-experience," a woman's mysterious voice called from the knot of people, "I know from it that this preacher can heal. My eyes have been opened! I testify to Jesus!"

The preacher lifted his arms quickly and began to repeat all that he had said before about the River and the Kingdom of Christ and the old man sat on the bumper, fixing him with a narrow squint. From time to time Bevel stared at him again from around Mrs. Connin.

A man in overalls and a brown coat leaned forward and dipped his hand in the water quickly and shook it and leaned back, and a woman held a baby over the edge of the bank and splashed its feet with water. One man moved a little distance away and sat down on the bank and took off his shoes and waded out into the stream; he stood there for a few minutes with his face tilted as far back as it would go, then he waded back and put on his shoes. All this time, the preacher sang and did not appear to watch what went on.

As soon as he stopped singing, Mrs. Connin lifted Bevel up and said, "Listen here, preacher, I got a boy from town today that I'm keeping. His mamma's sick and he wants you to pray for her. And this is a coincident—his name is Bevel! Bevel," she said, turning to look at the people behind her, "same as his. Ain't that a coincident, though?"

There were some murmurs and Bevel turned and grinned over her shoulder at the faces looking at him. "Bevel," he said in a loud jaunty voice.

"Listen," Mrs. Connin said, "have you ever been Baptized, Bevel?"

He only grinned.

"I suspect he ain't ever been Baptized," Mrs. Connin said, raising her eyebrows at the preacher.

"Swang him over here," the preacher said and took a stride forward and caught him.

He held him in the crook of his arm and looked at the grinning face. Bevel rolled his eyes in a comical way and thrust his face forward, close to the preacher's. "My name is Bevvvuuuuul," he said in a loud deep voice and let the tip of his tongue slide across his mouth.

The preacher didn't smile. His bony face was rigid and his narrow gray eyes reflected the almost colorless sky. There was a loud laugh from the old

143

man sitting on the car bumper and Bevel grasped the back of the preacher's collar and held it tightly. The grin had already disappeared from his face. He had the sudden feeling that this was not a joke. Where he lived everything was a joke. From the preacher's face, he knew immediately that nothing the preacher said or did was a joke. "My mother named me that," he said quickly.

"Have you ever been Baptized?" the preacher asked.

"What's that?" he murmured.

"If I Baptize you," the preacher said, "you'll be able to go to the Kingdom of Christ. You'll be washed in the river of suffering, son, and you'll go by the deep river of life. Do you want that?"

"Yes," the child said, and thought, I won't go back to the apartment then, I'll go under the river.

"You won't be the same again," the preacher said. "You'll count." Then he turned his face to the people and began to preach and Bevel looked over his shoulder at the pieces of the white sun scattered in the river. Suddenly the preacher said, "All right, I'm going to Baptize you now," and without more warning, he tightened his hold and swung him upside down and plunged his head into the water. He held him under while he said the words of Baptism and then he jerked him up again and looked sternly at the gasping child. Bevel's eyes were dark and dilated. "You count now," the preacher said. "You didn't even count before."

The little boy was too shocked to cry. He spit out the muddy water and rubbed his wet sleeve into his eyes and over his face.

"Don't forget his mamma," Mrs. Connin called. "He wants you to pray for his mamma. She's sick."

"Lord," the preacher said, "we pray for somebody in affliction who isn't here to testify. Is your mother sick in the hospital?" he asked. "Is she in pain?"

The child stared at him. "She hasn't got up yet," he said in a high dazed voice. "She has a hangover." The air was so quiet he could hear the broken pieces of the sun knocking the water.

The preacher looked angry and startled. The red drained out of his face and the sky appeared to darken in his eyes. There was a loud guffaw from the bank and Mr. Paradise shouted, "Haw! Cure the afflicted woman with the hangover!" and began to beat his knee with his fist.

144

"He's had a long day," Mrs. Connin said, standing with him in the door of the apartment and looking sharply into the room where the party was going on. "I reckon it's past his regular bedtime." One of Bevel's eyes was closed and the other half closed; his nose was running and he kept his mouth open and breathed through it. The damp plaid coat dragged down on one side.

That would be her, Mrs. Connin decided, in the black britches—long black satin britches and barefoot sandals and red toenails. She was lying on half the sofa, with her knees crossed in the air and her head propped on the arm. She didn't get up.

"Hello Harry," she said. "Did you have a big day?" She had a long pale face, smooth and blank, and straight sweet-potato-colored hair, pulled back.

The father went off to get the money. There were two other couples. One of the men, blond with little violet-blue eyes, leaned out of his chair and said, "Well Harry, old man, have a big day?"

"His name ain't Harry. It's Bevel," Mrs. Connin said.

"His name is Harry," *she* said from the sofa. "Whoever heard of anybody named Bevel?"

The little boy had seemed to be going to sleep on his feet, his head drooping farther and farther forward; he pulled it back suddenly and opened one eye; the other was stuck.

"He told me this morning his name was Bevel," Mrs. Connin said in a shocked voice. "The same as our preacher. We been all day at a preaching and healing at the river. He said his name was Bevel, the same as the preacher's. That's what he told me."

"Bevel!" his mother said. "My God! what a name."

"This preacher is name Bevel and there's no better preacher around," Mrs. Connin said. "And furthermore," she added in a defiant tone, "he Baptized this child this morning!"

His mother sat straight up. "Well the nerve!" she muttered.

"Furthermore," Mrs. Connin said, "he's a healer and he prayed for you to be healed."

"Healed!" she almost shouted. "Healed of what for Christ's sake?"

"Of your affliction," Mrs. Connin said icily.

The father had returned with the money and was standing near Mrs. Connin waiting to give it to her. His eyes were lined with red threads. "Go

145

on, go on," he said, "I want to hear more about her affliction. The exact nature of it has escaped . . ." He waved the bill and his voice trailed off. "Healing by prayer is mighty inexpensive," he murmured.

Mrs. Connin stood a second, staring into the room, with a skeleton's appearance of seeing everything. Then, without taking the money, she turned and shut the door behind her. The father swung around, smiling vaguely, and shrugged. The rest of them were looking at Harry. The little boy began to shamble toward the bedroom.

"Come here, Harry," his mother said. He automatically shifted his direction toward her without opening his eyes any farther. "Tell me what happened today," she said when he reached her. She began to pull off his coat.

"I don't know," he muttered.

"Yes you do know," she said, feeling the coat heavier on one side. She unzipped the innerlining and caught the book and a dirty handkerchief as they fell out. "Where did you get these?"

"I don't know," he said and grabbed for them. "They're mine. She gave them to me."

She threw the handkerchief down and held the book too high for him to reach and began to read it, her face after a second assuming an exaggerated comical expression. The others moved around and looked at it over her shoulder. "My God," somebody said.

One of the men peered at it sharply from behind a thick pair of glasses. "That's valuable," he said. "That's a collector's item," and he took it away from the rest of them and retired to another chair.

"Don't let George go off with that," his girl said.

"I tell you it's valuable," George said. "1832."

Bevel shifted his direction again toward the room where he slept. He shut the door behind him and moved slowly in the darkness to the bed and sat down and took off his shoes and got under the cover. After a minute a shaft of light let in the tall silhouette of his mother. She tiptoed lightly cross the room and sat down on the edge of his bed. "What did that dolt of a preacher say about me?" she whispered. "What lies have you been telling today, honey?"

He shut his eye and heard her voice from a long way away, as if he were under the river and she on top of it. She shook his shoulder. "Harry," she said, leaning down and putting her mouth to his ear, "tell me what he said."

She pulled him into a sitting position and he felt as if he had been drawn up from under the river. "Tell me," she whispered and her bitter breath covered his face.

He saw the pale oval close to him in the dark. "He said I'm not the same now," he muttered. "I count."

After a second, she lowered him by his shirt front onto the pillow. She hung over him an instant and brushed her lips against his forehead. Then she got up and moved away, swaying her hips lightly through the shaft of light.

He didn't wake up early but the apartment was still dark and close when he did. For a while he lay there, picking his nose and eyes. Then he sat up in bed and looked out the window. The sun came in palely, stained gray by the glass. Across the street at the Empire Hotel, a colored cleaning woman was looking down from an upper window, resting her face on her folded arms. He got up and put on his shoes and went to the bathroom and then into the front room. He ate two crackers spread with anchovy paste, that he found on the coffee table, and drank some ginger ale left in a bottle and looked around for his book but it was not there.

The apartment was silent except for the faint humming of the refrigerator. He went into the kitchen and found some raisin bread heels and spread a half jar of peanut butter between them and climbed up on the tall kitchen stool and sat chewing the sandwich slowly, wiping his nose every now and then on his shoulder. When he finished he found some chocolate milk and drank that. He would rather have had the ginger ale he saw but they left the bottle openers where he couldn't reach them. He studied what was left in the refrigerator for a while—some shriveled vegetables that she had forgot were there and a lot of brown oranges that she bought and didn't squeeze; there were three or four kinds of cheese and something fishy in a paper bag; the rest was a pork bone. He left the refrigerator door open and wandered back in to the dark living room and sat down on the sofa.

He decided they would be out cold until one o'clock and that they would all have to go to a restaurant for lunch. He wasn't high enough for the table yet and the waiter would bring a highchair and he was too big for a highchair. He sat in the middle of the sofa, kicking it with his heels. Then he got up and wandered around the room, looking into the ashtrays at the

147

butts as if this might be a habit. In his own room he had picture books and blocks but they were for the most part torn up; he found the way to get new ones was to tear up the ones he had. There was very little to do at any time but eat; however, he was not a fat boy.

He decided he would empty a few ashtrays on the floor. If he only emptied a few, she would think they had fallen. He emptied two, rubbing the ashes carefully into the rug with his finger. Then he lay on the floor for a while, studying his feet which he held up in the air. His shoes were still damp and he began to think about the river.

Very slowly, his expression changed as if he were gradually seeing appear what he didn't know he'd been looking for. Then all of a sudden he knew what he wanted to do.

He got up and tiptoed into their bedroom and stood in the dim light there, looking for her pocketbook. His glance passed her long pale arm hanging off the edge of the bed down to the floor, and across the white mound his father made, and past the crowded bureau, until it rested on the pocketbook hung on the back of a chair. He took a car-token out of it and half a package of Life Savers. Then he left the apartment and caught the car at the corner. He hadn't taken a suitcase because there was nothing from there he wanted to keep.

He got off the car at the end of the line and started down the road he and Mrs. Connin had taken the day before. He knew there wouldn't be anybody at her house because the three boys and the girl went to school and Mrs. Connin had told him she went out to clean. He passed her yard and walked on the way they had gone to the river. The paper brick houses were far apart and after a while the dirt place to walk on ended and he had to walk on the edge of the highway. The sun was pale yellow and high and hot.

He passed a shack with an orange gas pump in front of it but he didn't see the old man looking out at nothing in particular from the doorway. Mr. Paradise was having an orange drink. He finished it slowly, squinting over the bottle at the small plaid-coated figure disappearing down the road. Then he set the empty bottle on a bench and, still squinting, wiped his sleeve over his mouth. He went in the shack and picked out a peppermint stick, a foot long and two inches thick, from the candy shelf, and stuck it in his hip pocket. Then he got in his car and drove slowly down the highway after the boy.

The Great Smoky Mountains, North Carolina

The Faith

By the time Bevel came to the field speckled with purple weeds, he was dusty and sweating and he crossed it at a trot to get into the woods as fast as he could. Once inside, he wandered from tree to tree, trying to find the path they had taken yesterday. Finally he found a line worn in the pine needles and followed it until he saw the steep trail twisting down through the trees.

Mr. Paradise had left his automobile back some way on the road and had walked to the place where he was accustomed to sit almost every day, holding an unbaited fishline in the water while he stared at the river passing in front of him. Anyone looking at him from a distance would have seen an old boulder half hidden in the bushes.

Bevel didn't see him at all. He only saw the river, shimmering reddish yellow, and bounded into it with his shoes and his coat on and took a gulp. He swallowed some and spit the rest out and then he stood there in water up to his chest and looked around him. The sky was a clear pale blue, all in one piece—except for the hole the sun made—and fringed around the bottom with treetops. His coat floated to the surface and surrounded him like a strange gay lily pad and he stood grinning in the sun. He intended not to fool with preachers any more but to Baptize himself and to keep on going this time until he found the Kingdom of Christ in the river. He didn't mean to waste any more time. He put his head under the water at once and pushed forward.

In a second he began to gasp and sputter and his head reappeared on the surface; he started under again and the same thing happened. The river wouldn't have him. He tried again and came up, choking. This was the way it had been when the preacher held him under—he had had to fight with something that pushed him back in the face. He stopped and thought suddenly: it's another joke, it's just another joke! He thought how far he had come for nothing and he began to hit and splash and kick the filthy river. His feet were already treading on nothing. He gave one low cry of pain and indignation. Then he heard a shout and turned his head and saw something like a giant pig bounding after him, shaking a red and white club and shouting. He plunged under once and this time, the waiting current caught him like a long gentle hand and pulled him swiftly forward and down. For an instant he was overcome with surprise: then since he was moving quickly and knew that he was getting somewhere, all his fury and fear left him.

150

Mr. Paradise's head appeared from time to time on the surface of the water. Finally, far downstream, the old man rose like some ancient water monster and stood empty-handed, staring with his dull eyes as far down the river line as he could see.

Maestro De Emaus

MERCEDES GARCÍA TUDURÍ DE COYA

Sabría que eras Tú porque en la senda
por donde Te acercaras brotarían
los lirios; y la brisa, de repente,
de música y de olor se lienaría.

Porque al mirarte, todas las palomas
a tu paso su vuelo detendrían,
por ver la luz dorada de la tarde
coronar tu cabeza pensativa.

Sabría que eras Tú, por esa forma
de saciarse mi sed en tu agua viva,
si me dieras a cambio de mi cántaro
un agua que la sed por siempre extinga.

Y al verte en nuestra mesa, silencioso,
ya ni una duda quedaría a mi afán:
isabría que eras Tú por la manera
de unir las manos y partir el pan! . . .

Lord of Emaus

MERCEDES GARCÍA TUDURÍ DE COYA
Translated by **MARIAN SMITH**

I shall know that it is You, for along Your path
As You draw near, the lilies
Will wax into bloom, and the breeze will suddenly
Be filled with music and sweet scent.

Glimpsing You, the doves in the air
Will pause in their flight at Your footfall,
And wonder at the golden light of the evening
Crowning Your pensive head.

I shall know that it is You by Your act
Of quenching my thirst with the living fountain,
When You give me, in exchange for my vessel,
Water that will slake my thirst forever.

And, seeing You silent at our table,
The last doubt will vanish from my longing,
As I watch Your hands join together
And your way of breaking the bread.

The Good Life

The pursuit of happiness as a natural and noble end of human existence is explicitly stated in our Declaration of Independence, and no part of America offers a more ideal setting for this purpose. The relatively warm climate, the natural beauty and variety of the terrain, the exotic vegetation seem an open invitation to enjoy "the good life" to be found in the simple pleasures of nature. Sidney Lanier captures this sentiment in his sumptuous "Marshes of Glynn." His poem sparkles with its profusion of images, its intricate maze of rhymes and meters, the lushness of sentences that wind on and about. This copious style is as southern in feeling as the copiousness of the southern seascape it paints. No bleak coastline here or bitter cold to discipline the mind to starkness or haste; instead there is extravagant vegetation, ". . . beautiful-braided and woven/ With intricate shades of . . . vines," kudzu, sandy beaches, and the warm sea.

But warm climes and natural beauty alone do not account for the charm of southern life. The tempo of daily living is as slow and easy-going as the rhythms of southern speech patterns. Except in athletics and during other moments of dramatic urgency, nothing and nobody—even in business matters—seems to move faster than is comfortable or natural. There is a luxurious sense of serenity which grows out of this subtle reassurance that there is plenty of time for everything.

The small-town lifestyle disseminates an air of sociability and neighborliness. Except for very special occasions, manners and dress are informal and easy-going. There is an earnest preoccupation with the personal pleasures of daily life—good food and drink, resting

155

and amusing oneself, love and laughter—and lesiure to enjoy them all.

In this aspect of southern tradition, there have never been any class distinctions. By tacit agreement such facets of "The Good Life" are every Southerner's birthright.

The Marshes of Glynn

SIDNEY LANIER

Glooms of the live oaks, beautiful-braided and woven
With intricate shades of the vines that myriad-cloven
Clamber the forks of the multiform boughs—
    Emerald twilights—
    Virginal shy lights,
Wrought of the leaves to allure to the whisper of vows,
When lovers pace timidly down through the green colonnades
Of the dim sweet woods, of the dear dark woods,
    Of the heavenly woods and glades,
That run to the radiant marginal sand-beach within
    The wide sea-marshes of Glynn—
Beautiful glooms, soft dusks in the noonday fire—
Wildwood privacies, closets of lone desire,
Chamber from chamber parted with wavering arras of leaves—
Cells for the passionate pleasure of prayer for the soul that
       grieves,
Pure with a sense of the passing of saints through the wood,
Cool for the dutiful weighing of ill with good—

O braided dusks of the oak and woven shades of the vine,
While the riotous noonday sun of the June day long did shine
Ye held me fast in your heart and I held you fast in mine;
But now when the noon is no more, and riot is rest,
And the sun is await at the ponderous gate of the West,
And the slant yellow beam down the wood-aisle doth seem
Like a lane into heaven that leads from a dream—
Ay, now, when my soul all day hath drunken the soul of the
       oak,

The Marshes of Glynn, South Carolina

And my heart is at ease from men, and the wearisome sound of
    the stroke
  Of the scythe of time, and the trowel of trade is low,
  And belief overmasters doubt, and I know that I know,
  And my spirit is grown to a lordly great compass within,
That the length and the breadth and the sweep of the marshes
    of Glynn
Will work me no fear like the fear they have wrought me of
    yore
When length was fatigue, and when breadth was but bitterness
    sore,
And when terror and shrinking and dreary unnamable pain
Drew over me out of the merciless miles of the plain—

Oh, now, unafraid, I am fain to face
  The vast sweet visage of space.
To the edge of the wood I am drawn, I am drawn,
Where the gray beach glimmering runs, as a belt of the dawn,
    For a mete and a mark
    To the forest-dark—
      So:
Affable live oak, bending low—
Thus—with your favor—soft, with a reverent hand,
(Not lightly touching your person, Lord of the land!)
Bending your beauty aside, with a step I stand
On the firm-packed sand,
    Free
By a world of marsh that borders a world of sea.

  Sinuous southward and sinuous northward the shimmering
    band
  Of the sand-beach fastens the fringe of the marsh to the
    folds of the land.

The Good Life

Inward and outward to northward and southward the beach-
    lines linger and curl
As a silver-wrought garment that clings to and follows the firm
    sweet limbs of a girl.
Vanishing, swerving, evermore curving again into sight,
Softly the sand-beach wavers away to a dim gray looping of
    light.
And what if behind me to westward the wall of the woods
    stands high?
The world lies east: how ample, the marsh and the sea and the
    sky!
A league and a league of marsh-grass, waist-high, broad in the
    blade,
Green, and all of a height, and unflecked with a light or a
    shade,
Stretch leisurely off, in a pleasant plain,
To the terminal blue of the main.
Oh, what is abroad in the marsh and the terminal sea?
    Somehow my soul seems suddenly free
From the weighing of fate and the sad discussion of sin,
By the length and the breadth and the sweep of the marshes of
    Glynn.

Ye marshes, how candid and simple and nothing withholding
    and free
Ye publish yourselves to the sky and offer yourselves to the
    sea!
Tolerant plains, that suffer the sea and the rains and the sun,
Ye spread and span like the catholic man who hath mightily
    won
God out of knowledge and good out of infinite pain
And sight out of blindness and purity out of a stain.

As the marsh-hen secretly builds on the watery sod,
Behold I will build me a nest on the greatness of God:

I will fly in the greatness of God as the marsh-hen flies
In the freedom that fills all the space 'twixt the marsh and the
      skies:
By so many roots as the marsh-grass sends in the sod
I will heartily lay me a-hold on the greatness of God:
Oh, like to the greatness of God is the greatness within
The range of the marshes, the liberal marshes of Glynn.

And the sea lends large, as the marsh: lo, out of his plenty the
       sea
Pours fast: full soon the time of the flood-tide must be:
Look how the grace of the sea doth go
About and about through the intricate channels that flow
    Here and there,
        Everywhere,
Till his waters have flooded the uttermost creeks and the low-
      lying lanes,
And the marsh is meshed with a million veins,
That like as with rosy and silvery essences flow
    In the rose-and-silver evening glow.
        Farewell, my lord Sun!
The creeks overflow: a thousand rivulets run
'Twixt the roots of the sod; the blades of the marsh-grass stir;
Passeth a hurrying sound of wings that westward whir;
Passeth, and all is still; and the currents cease to run;
And the sea and the marsh are one.

How still the plains of the waters be!
The tide is in his ecstasy;
The tide is at his highest height;
    And it is night.

And now from the Vast of the Lord will the waters of sleep
Roll in on the souls of men,
But who will reveal to our waking ken

The Good Life

The forms that swim and the shapes that creep
    Under the waters of sleep?
And I would I could know what swimmeth below when the
        tide comes in
On the length and the breadth of the marvelous marshes of
        Glynn.

Daybreak in Alabama

LANGSTON HUGHES

When I get to be a composer
I'm gonna write me some music about
Daybreak in Alabama.
And I'm gonna put the purtiest songs in it
Rising out of the ground like a swamp mist
And falling out of heaven like soft dew.
I'm gonna put some tall tall trees in it
And the scent of pine needles
And the smell of red clay after rain
And long red necks
And poppy colored faces
And big brown arms
And the field daisy eyes
Of black and white black white black people
And I'm gonna put white hands
And black hands and brown and yellow hands
And red clay earth hands in it
Touching everybody with kind fingers
And touching each other natural as dew
In that dawn of music when I
Get to be a composer
And write about daybreak
In Alabama.

Lily Daw and
the Three Ladies

EUDORA WELTY

Mrs. Watts and Mrs. Carson were both in the post office in Victory when the letter came from the Ellisville Institute for the Feeble-Minded of Mississippi. Aimee Slocum, with her hand still full of mail, ran out in front and handed it straight to Mrs. Watts, and they all three read it together. Mrs. Watts held it taut between her pink hands, and Mrs. Carson underscored each line slowly with her thimbled finger. Everybody else in the post office wondered what was up now.

"What will Lily say," beamed Mrs. Carson at last, "when we tell her we're sending her to Ellisville!"

"She'll be tickled to death," said Mrs. Watts, and added in a guttural voice to a deaf lady, "Lily Daw's getting in at Ellisville!"

"Don't you all dare go off and tell Lily without me!" called Aimee Slocum, trotting back to finish putting up the mail.

"Do you suppose they'll look after her down there?" Mrs. Carson began to carry on a conversation with a group of Baptist ladies waiting in the post office. She was the Baptist preacher's wife.

"I've always heard it was lovely down there, but crowded," said one.

"Lily lets people walk over her so," said another.

"Last night at the tent show—" said another, and then popped her hand over her mouth.

"Don't mind me, I know there are such things in the world," said Mrs. Carson, looking down and fingering the tape measure which hung over her bosom.

"Oh, Mrs. Carson. Well, anyway, last night at the tent show, why, the man was just before making Lily buy a ticket to get in."

"A ticket!"

"Till my husband went up and explained she wasn't bright, and so did everybody else."

The ladies all clucked their tongues.

165

"Oh, it was a very nice show," said the lady who had gone. "And Lily acted so nice. She was a perfect lady—just set in her seat and stared."

"Oh, she can be a lady—she can be," said Mrs. Carson, shaking her head and turning her eyes up. "That's just what breaks your heart."

"Yes'm, she kept her eyes on—what's that thing makes all the commotion?—the xylophone," said the lady. "Didn't turn her head to the right or to the left the whole time. Set in front of me."

"The point is, what did she do after the show?" asked Mrs. Watts practically. "Lily has gotten so she is very mature for her age."

"Oh, Etta!" protested Mrs. Carson, looking at her wildly for a moment.

"And that's how come we are sending her to Ellisville," finished Mrs. Watts.

"I'm ready, you all," said Aimee Slocum, running out with white powder all over her face. "Mail's up. I don't know how good it's up."

"Well, of course, I do hope it's for the best," said several of the other ladies. They did not go at once to take their mail out of their boxes; they felt a little left out.

The three women stood at the foot of the water tank.

"To find Lily is a different thing," said Aimee Slocum.

"Where in the wide world do you suppose she'd be?" It was Mrs. Watts who was carrying the letter.

"I don't see a sign of her either on this side of the street or on the other side," Mrs. Carson declared as they walked along.

Ed Newton was stringing Redbird school tablets on the wire across the store.

"If you're after Lily, she come in here while ago and tole me she was fixin' to git married," he said.

"Ed Newton!" cried the ladies all together, clutching one another. Mrs. Watts began to fan herself at once with the letter from Ellisville. She wore widow's black, and the least thing made her hot.

"Why she is not. She's going to Ellisville, Ed," said Mrs. Carson gently. "Mrs. Watts and I and Aimee Slocum are paying her way out of our own pockets. Besides, the boys of Victory are on their honor. Lily's not going to get married, that's just an idea she's got in her head."

"More power to you, ladies," said Ed Newton, spanking himself with a tablet.

When they came to the bridge over the railroad tracks, there was Estelle Mabers, sitting on a rail. She was slowly drinking an orange Ne-Hi.

"Have you seen Lily?" they asked her.

"I'm supposed to be out here watching for her now," said the Mabers girl, as though she weren't there yet. "But for Jewel—Jewel says Lily come in the store while ago and picked out a two-ninety-eight hat and wore it off. Jewel wants to swap her something else for it."

"Oh, Estelle, Lily says she's going to get married!" cried Aimee Slocum.

"Well, I declare," said Estelle; she never understood anything.

Loralee Adkins came riding by in her Willys-Knight, tooting the horn to find out what they were talking about.

Aimee threw up her hands and ran out into the street. "Loralee, Loralee, you got to ride us up to Lily Daws'. She's up yonder fixing to get married!"

"Hop in, my land!"

"Well, that just goes to show you right now," said Mrs. Watts, groaning as she was helped into the back seat. "What we've got to do is persuade Lily it will be nicer to go to Ellisville."

"Just to think!"

While they rode around the corner Mrs. Carson was going on in her sad voice, sad as the soft noises in the hen house at twilight. "We buried Lily's poor defenseless mother. We gave Lily all her food and kindling and every stitch she had on. Sent her to Sunday school to learn the Lord's teachings, had her baptized a Baptist. And when her old father commenced beating her and tried to cut her head off with the butcher knife, why, we went and took her away from him and gave her a place to stay."

The paintless frame house with all the weather vanes was three stories high in places and had yellow and violet stained-glass windows in front and gingerbread around the porch. It leaned steeply to one side, toward the railroad, and the front steps were gone. The car full of ladies drew up under the cedar tree.

"Now Lily's almost grown up," Mrs. Carson continued. "In fact, she's grown," she concluded, getting out.

"Talking about getting married," said Mrs. Watts disgustedly. "Thanks, Loralee, you run on home."

They climbed over the dusty zinnias onto the porch and walked through the open door without knocking.

"There certainly is always a funny smell in this house. I say it every time I come," said Aimee Slocum.

Lily was there, in the dark of the hall, kneeling on the floor by a small open trunk.

When she saw them she put a zinnia in her mouth, and held still.

"Hello, Lily," said Mrs. Carson reproachfully.

"Hello," said Lily. In a minute she gave a suck on the zinnia stem that sounded exactly like a jay brid. There she sat, wearing a petticoat for a dress, one of the things Mrs. Carson kept after her about. Her milky-yellow hair streamed freely down from under a new hat. You could see the wavy scar on her throat if you knew it was there.

Mrs. Carson and Mrs. Watts, the two fattest, sat in the double rocker. Aimee Slocum sat on the wire chair donated from the drugstore that burned.

"Well, what are you doing, Lily?" asked Mrs. Watts, who led the rocking.

Lily smiled.

The trunk was old and lined with yellow and brown paper, with an asterisk pattern showing in darker circles and rings. Mutely the ladies indicated to each other that they did not know where in the world it had come from. It was empty except for two bars of soap and a green washcloth, which Lily was now trying to arrange in the bottom.

"Go on and tell us what you're doing, Lily," said Aimee Slocum.

"Packing, silly," said Lily.

"Where are you going?"

"Going to get married, and I bet you wish you was me now," said Lily. But shyness overcame her suddenly, and she popped the zinnia back into her mouth.

"Talk to me, dear," said Mrs. Carson. "Tell old Mrs. Carson why you want to get married."

"No," said Lily, after a moment's hesitation.

"Well, we've thought of something that will be so much nicer," said Mrs. Carson. "Why don't you go to Ellisville!"

"Won't that be lovely?" said Mrs. Watts. "Goodness, yes."

"It's a lovely place," said Aimee Slocum uncertainly.

"You've got bumps on your face," said Lily.

"Aimee, dear, you stay out of this, if you don't mind," said Mrs. Carson anxiously. "I don't know what it is comes over Lily when you come around her."

Lily stared at Aimee Slocum meditatively.

"There! Wouldn't you like to go to Ellisville now?" asked Mrs. Carson.

"No'm," said Lily.

"Why not?" All the ladies leaned down toward her in impressive astonishment.

" 'Cause I'm goin' to get married," said Lily.

"Well, and who are you going to marry, dear?" asked Mrs. Watts. She knew how to pin people down and make them deny what they'd already said.

Lily bit her lip and began to smile. She reached into the trunk and held up both cakes of soap and wagged them.

"Tell us," challenged Mrs. Watts. "Who you're going to marry, now."

"A man last night."

There was a gasp from each lady. The possible reality of a lover descended suddenly like a summer hail over their heads. Mrs. Watts stood up and balanced herself.

"One of those show fellows! A musician!" she cried.

Lily looked up in admiration.

"Did he—did he do anything to you?" In the long run, it was still only Mrs. Watts who could take charge.

"Oh, yes'm," said Lily. She patted the cakes of soap fastidiously with the tips of her small fingers and tucked them in with the washcloth.

"What?" demanded Aimee Slocum, rising up and tottering before her scream. "What?" she called out in the hall.

"Don't ask her what," said Mrs. Carson, coming up behind. "Tell me, Lily—just yes or no—are you the same as you were?"

"He had a red coat," said Lily graciously. "He took little sticks and went *ping-pong! ding-dong!*"

"Oh, I think I'm going to faint," said Aimee Slocum, but they said, "No, you're not."

"The xylophone!" cried Mrs. Watts. "The xylophone player! Why, the coward, he ought to be run out of town on a rail!"

"Out of town? He is out of town, by now," cried Aimee. "Can't you read?—the sign in the café—Victory on the ninth, Como on the tenth? He's in Como. Como!"

"All right! We'll bring him back!" cried Mrs. Watts. "He can't get away from me!"

"Hush," said Mrs. Carson. "I don't think it's any use following that line of reasoning at all. It's better in the long run for him to be gone out of our lives for good and all. That kind of a man. He was after Lily's body alone and he wouldn't ever in this world make the poor little thing happy, even if we went out and forced him to marry her like he ought—at the point of a gun."

"Still—" began Aimee, her eyes widening.

"Shut up," said Mrs. Watts. "Mrs. Carson, you're right, I expect."

"This is my hope chest—see?" said Lily politely in the pause that followed. "You haven't even looked at it. I've already got soap and a washrag. And I have my hat—on. What are you all going to give me?"

"Lily," said Mrs. Watts, starting over, "we'll give you lots of gorgeous things if you'll only go to Ellisville instead of getting married."

"What will you give me?" asked Lily.

"I'll give you a pair of hemstitched pillowcases," said Mrs. Carson.

"I'll give you a big caramel cake," said Mrs. Watts.

"I'll give you a souvenir from Jackson—a little toy bank," said Aimee Slocum. "Now will you go?"

"No," said Lily.

"I'll give you a pretty little Bible with your name on it in real gold," said Mrs. Carson.

"What if I was to give you a pink crêpe de Chine brassière with adjustable shoulder straps?" asked Mrs. Watts grimly.

"Oh, Etta."

"Well, she needs it," said Mrs. Watts. "What would they think if she ran all over Ellisville in a petticoat looking like a Fiji?"

"I wish *I* could go to Ellisville," said Aimee Slocum luringly.

"What will they have for me down there?" asked Lily softly.

"Oh! lots of things. You'll have baskets to weave, I expect. . . ." Mrs. Carson looked vaguely at the others.

"Oh, yes indeed, they will let you make all sorts of baskets," said Mrs. Watts; then her voice too trailed off.

"No'm, I'd rather get married," said Lily.

"Lily Daw! Now that's just plain stubbornness!" cried Mrs. Watts. "You almost said you'd go and then you took it back!"

"We've all asked God, Lily," said Mrs. Carson finally, "and God seemed to tell us—Mr. Carson, too—that the place where you ought to be, so as to be happy, was Ellisville."

Lily looked reverent, but still stubborn.

"We've really just got to get her there—now!" screamed Aimee Slocum all at once. "Suppose—! She can't stay here!"

"Oh, no, no, no," said Mrs. Carson hurriedly. "We mustn't think that."

They sat sunken in despair.

"Could I take my hope chest—to go to Ellisville?" asked Lily shyly, looking at them sidewise.

"Why, yes," said Mrs. Carson blankly.

Silently they rose once more to their feet.

"Oh, if I could just take my hope chest!"

"All the time it was just her hope chest," Aimee whispered.

Mrs. Watts struck her palms together. "It's settled!"

"Praise the fathers," murmured Mrs. Carson.

Lily looked up at them, and her eyes gleamed. She cocked her head and spoke out in a proud imitation of someone—someone utterly unknown.

"O.K.—Toots!"

The ladies had been nodding and smiling and backing away toward the door.

"I think I'd better stay," said Mrs. Carson, stopping in her tracks. "Where—where could she have learned that terrible expression?"

"Pack up," said Mrs. Watts. "Lily Daw is leaving for Ellisville on Number One."

In the station the train was puffing. Nearly everyone in Victory was hanging around waiting for it to leave. The Victory Civic Band had assembled without any orders and was scattered through the crowd. Ed Newton gave false signals to start on his bass horn. A crate full of baby chickens got loose on the platform. Everybody wanted to see Lily all dressed up, but Mrs. Carson and Mrs. Watts had sneaked her into the train from the other side of the tracks.

The two ladies were going to travel as far as Jackson to help Lily change trains and be sure she went in the right direction.

Lily sat between them on the plush seat with her hair combed and pinned up into a knot under a small blue hat which was Jewel's exchange for the pretty one. She wore a traveling dress made out of part of Mrs. Watt's last summer's mourning. Pink straps glowed through. She had a purse and a Bible and a warm cake in a box, all in her lap.

Aimee Slocum had been getting the outgoing mail stamped and bundled. She stood in the aisle of the coach now, tears shaking from her eyes.

"Good-bye, Lily," she said. She was the one who felt things.

"Good-bye, silly," said Lily.

"Oh, dear, I hope they get our telegram to meet her in Ellisville!" Aimee cried sorrowfully, as she thought how far away it was. "And it was so hard to get it all in ten words, too."

"Get off, Aimee, before the train starts and you break your neck," said Mrs. Watts, all settled and waving her dressy fan gaily. "I declare, it's so hot, as soon as we get a few miles out of town I'm going to slip my corset down."

"Oh, Lily, don't cry down there. Just be good, and do what they tell you—it's all because they love you." Aimee drew her mouth down. She was backing away, down the aisle.

Lily laughed. She pointed across Mrs. Carson's bosom out the window toward a man. He had stepped off the train and just stood there, by himself. He was a stranger and wore a cap.

"Look," she said, laughing softly through her fingers.

"Don't—look," said Mrs. Carson very distinctly, as if, out of all she had ever spoken, she would impress these two solemn words upon Lily's soft little brain. She added, "Don't look at anything till you get to Ellisville."

Outside, Aimee Slocum was crying so hard she almost ran into the stranger. He wore a cap and was short and seemed to have on perfume, if such a thing could be.

"Could you tell me, madam," he said, "where a little lady lives in this burg name of Miss Lily Daw?" He lifted his cap—and he had red hair.

"What do you want to know for?" Aimee asked before she knew it.

"Talk louder," said the stranger. He almost whispered, himself.

"She's gone away—she's gone to Ellisville!"

"Gone?"

"Gone to Ellisville!"

"Well, I like that!" The man stuck out his bottom lip and puffed till his hair jumped.

"What business did you have with Lily?" cried Aimee suddenly.

"We was only going to get married, that's all," said the man.

Aimee Slocum started to scream in front of all those people. She almost pointed to the long black box she saw lying on the ground at the man's feet. Then she jumped back in fright.

"The xylophone! The xylophone!" she cried, looking back and forth from the man to the hissing train. Which was more terrible? The bell began to ring hollowly, and the man was talking.

"Did you say Ellisville? That in the state of Mississippi?" Like lightning he had pulled out a red notebook entitled, "Permanent Facts & Data." He wrote down something. "I don't hear well."

Aimee nodded her head up and down, and circled around him.

Under "Ellis-Ville Miss" he was drawing a line; now he was flicking it with two little marks. "Maybe she didn't say she would. Maybe she said she wouldn't." He suddenly laughed very loudly, after the way he had whispered. Aimee jumped back. "Women!—Well, if we play anywheres near Ellisville, Miss., in the future I may look her up and I may not," he said.

The bass horn sounded the true signal for the band to begin. White steam rushed out of the engine. Usually the train stopped for only a minute in Victory, but the engineer knew Lily from waving at her, and he knew this was her big day.

"Wait!" Aimee Slocum did scream. "Wait, mister! I can get her for you. Wait, Mister Engineer! Don't go!"

Then there she was back on the train, screaming in Mrs. Carson's and Mrs. Watts's faces.

"The xylophone player! The xylophone player to marry her! Yonder he is!"

"Nonsense," murmured Mrs. Watts, peering over the others to look where Aimee pointed. "If he's there I don't see him. Where is he? You're looking at One-Eye Beasley."

"The little man with the cap—no, with the red hair! Hurry!"

"Is that really him?" Mrs. Carson asked Mrs. Watts in wonder. "Mercy! He's small, isn't he?"

"Never saw him before in my life!" cried Mrs. Watts. But suddenly she shut up her fan.

"Come on! This is a train we're on!" cried Aimee Slocum. Her nerves were all unstrung.

"All right, don't have a conniption fit, girl," said Mrs. Watts. "Come on," she said thickly to Mrs. Carson.

"Where are we going now?" asked Lily as they struggled down the aisle.

"We're taking you to get married," said Mrs. Watts. "Mrs. Carson, you'd better phone up your husband right there in the station."

"But I don't want to git married," said Lily, beginning to whimper. "I'm going to Ellisville."

"Hush, and we'll all have some ice-cream cones later," whispered Mrs. Carson.

Just as they climbed down the steps at the back end of the train, the band went into "Independence March."

The xylophone player was still there, patting his foot. He came up and said, "Hello, Toots. What's up—tricks?" and kissed Lily with a smack, after which she hung her head.

"So you're the young man we've heard so much about," said Mrs. Watts. Her smile was brilliant. "Here's your little Lily."

"What say?" asked the xylophone player.

"My husband happens to be the Baptist preacher of Victory," said Mrs. Carson in a loud, clear voice. "Isn't that lucky? I can get him here in five minutes: I know exactly where he is."

They were in a circle around the xylophone player, all going into the white waiting room.

"Oh, I feel just like crying, at a time like this," said Aimee Slocum. She looked back and saw the train moving slowly away, going under the bridge at Main Street. Then it disappeared around the curve.

"Oh, the hope chest!" Aimee cried in a stricken voice.

"And whom have we the pleasure of addressing?" Mrs. Watts was shouting, while Mrs. Carson was ringing up the telephone.

The band went on playing. Some of the people thought Lily was on the train, and some swore she wasn't. Everybody cheered, though, and a straw hat was thrown into the telephone wires.

Aunt Lympy's Interference

KATE CHOPIN

The day was warm, and Melitte, cleaning her room, strayed often to the south window that looked out toward the Annibelles' place. She was a slender young body of eighteen with skirts that escaped the ground and a pink-sprigged shirt-waist. She had the beauty that belongs to youth—the freshness, the dewiness—with healthy brown hair that gleamed and honest brown eyes that could be earnest as well as merry.

Looking toward the Annibelles' place, Melitte could see but a speck of the imposing white house through the trees. Men were at work in the field, head and shoulders above the cotton. She could occasionally hear them laugh or shout. The air came in little broken waves from the south, bringing the hot, sweet scent of flowers and sometimes the good smell of the plowed earth.

Melitte always cleaned her room thoroughly on Saturday, because it was her only free day; of late she had been conducting a small school which stood down the road at the far end of the Annibelle place.

Almost every morning, as she trudged to school, she saw Victor Annibelle mending the fence; always mending it, but why so much nailing and bracing were required, no one but himself knew. The spectacle of the young man so persistently at work was one to distress Melitte in the goodness of her soul.

"My! but you have trouble with yo' fence, Victor," she called out to him in passing.

His good-looking face changed from a healthy brown to the color of one of his own cotton blooms; and never a phrase could his wits find till she was out of ear-shot; for Melitte never stopped to talk. She would but fling him a pleasant word, turning her face to him framed, buried, in a fluted pink sun-bonnet.

He had not always been so diffident—when they were youngsters, for instance, and he lent her his pony, or came over to thrash the pecan-tree for her. Now it was different. Since he had been long away from home and had returned at twenty-two, she gave herself the airs and graces of a young lady.

He did not dare to call her "Melitte," he was ashamed to call her "Miss," so he called her nothing, and hardly spoke to her.

Sometimes Victor went over to visit in the evenings, when he would be amiably entertained by Melitte, her brother, her brother's wife, her two little nieces and one little nephew. On Saturdays the young man was apparently less concerned about the condition of his fences, and passed frequently up and down the road on his white horse.

Melitte thought it was perhaps he, calling upon some pretext, when the little tot of a nephew wabbled in to say that some one wanted to see her on the front gallery. She gave a flurried glance at the mirror and divested her head of the dust-cloth.

"It's Aunt Lympy!" exclaimed the two small nieces, who had followed in the wake of the toddling infant.

"She won't say w'at she wants, *ti tante*," pursued one of them. "She don't look pleased, an' she sittin' down proud as a queen in the big chair."

There, in fact, Melitte found Aunt Lympy, proud and unbending in all the glory of a flowered "challie" and a black grenadine shawl edged with a purple satin quilling; she was light-colored. Two heavy bands of jet-black hair showed beneath her bandanna and covered her ears down to the gold hoop earrings.

"W'y, Aunt Lympy!" cried the girl, cordially, extending both hands. "Didn't I hear you were in Alexandria?"

"Tha's true, ma' Melitte." Aunt Lympy spoke slowly and with emphasis. "I ben in Alexandria nussin' Judge Morse's wife. She well now, an' I ben sence Chuseday in town. Look like Severin git 'long well 'idout me an' I ant hurry to go home." Her dusky eyes glowed far from cheerfully.

"I yeard some'in' yonda in town," the woman went on, "what I don' wan' to b'lieve. An' I say to myse'f, 'Olympe, you don' listen to no sich tale tell you go axen ma' Melitte.'"

"Something you heard about me, Aunt Lympy?" Melitte's eyes were wide.

"I don' wan' to spick about befo' de chillun," said Aunt Lympy.

"I yeard yonda in town, ma' Melitte," she went on after the children had gone, "I yeard you was turn school-titcher! Dat ant true?"

176

The question in her eyes was almost pathetic.

"Oh!" exclaimed Melitte; an utterance that expressed relief, surprise, amusement, commiseration, affirmation.

"Den it's true," Aunt Lympy almost whispered; "a De Broussard turn school-titcher!" The shame of it crushed her into silence.

Melitte felt the inutility of trying to dislodge the old family servant's deep-rooted prejudices. All her effort was directed toward convincing Aunt Lympy of her complete self-satisfaction in this new undertaking.

But Aunt Lympy did not listen. She had money in her reticule, if that would do any good. Melitte gently thrust it away. She changed the subject, and kindly offered the woman a bit of refreshment. But Aunt Lympy would not eat, drink, unbend, nor lend herself to the subterfuge of small talk. She said good-by, with solemnity, as we part from those in sore affliction. When she had mounted into her ramshackle open buggy the old vehicle looked someway like a throne.

Scarcely a week after Aunt Lympy's visit Melitte was amazed by receiving a letter from her uncle, Gervais Leplain, of New Orleans. The tone of the letter was sad, self-condemnatory, reminiscent. A flood of tender recollection of his dead sister seemed to have suddenly overflowed his heart and glided from the point of his pen.

He was asking Melitte to come to them there in New Orleans and be as one of his own daughters, who were quite as eager to call her "sister" as he was desirous of subscribing himself always henceforward, her father. He sent her a sum of money to supply her immediate wants, and informed her that he and one of his daughters would come for her in person at an early date.

Never a word was said of a certain missive dictated and sent to him by Aunt Lympy, every line of which was either a stinging rebuke or an appeal to the memory of his dead sister, whose child was tasting the bitter dregs of poverty. Melitte would never have recognized the overdrawn picture of herself.

From the very first there seemed to be no question about her accepting the offer of her uncle. She had literally not time to lift her voice in protest, before relatives, friends, acquaintances throughout the country raised a very clamor of congratulation. What luck! What a chance! To form one of the Gervais Leplain household!

177

Perhaps Melitte did not know that they lived in the most sumptuous style in la rue Esplanade, with a cottage across the lake; and they travelled—they spent summers at the North! Melitte would see the great, the big, the beautiful world! They already pictured little Melitte gowned *en Parisienne;* they saw her name figuring in the society columns of the Sunday papers! as attending balls, dinners, luncheons and card parties.

The whole proceeding had apparently stunned Merlitte. She sat with folded hands; except that she put the money carefully aside to return to her uncle. She would in no way get it confounded with her own small hoard; that was something precious and apart, not to be contaminated by gift-money.

"Have you written to yo' uncle to thank him, Melitte?" asked the sister-in-law.

Melitte shook her head. "No; not yet."

"But, Melitte!"

"Yes; I know."

"Do you want yo' brother to write?"

"No! Oh, no!"

"Then don't put it off a day longer, Melitte. Such rudeness! W'at will yo' Uncle Gervais an' yo' cousins think!"

Even the babies that loved her were bitten with this feverish ambition for Melitte's worldly advancement. " 'Taint you, *ti tante,* that's goin' to wear a sunbonnet any mo', or calico dresses, or an apron, or feed the chickens!"

"Then you want *ti tante* to go away an' leave you all?"

They were not ready to answer, but hung their heads in meditative silence, which lasted until the full meaning of *ti tante's* question had penetrated the inner consciousness of the little man, whereupon he began to howl, loud and deep and long.

Even the curé, happy to see the end of a family estrangement, took Melitte's acceptance wholly for granted. He visited her and discoursed at length and with vivid imagination upon the perils and fascinations of "the city's" life, presenting impartially, however, its advantages, which he hoped she would use to the betterment of her moral and intellectual faculties. He recommended to her a confessor at the cathedral who had traveled with him from France so many years ago.

"It's time you were dismissing an' closing up that school of yo's, Melitte," advised her sister-in-law, puzzled and disturbed, as Melitte was preparing to leave for the schoolhouse.

She did not answer. She seemed to have been growing sullen and ill-humored since her great piece of good luck; but perhaps she did not hear, with the pink sunbonnet covering her pink ears.

Melitte was sensible of a strong attachment for the things about her—the dear, familiar things. She did not fully realize that her surroundings were poor and pinched. The thought of entering a different existence troubled her.

Why was every one, with single voice, telling her to "go"? Was it that no one cared? She did not believe this, but chose to nourish the fancy. It furnished her a pretext for tears.

Why should she not go, and live in ease, free from responsibility and care? Why should she stay where no soul had said, "I can't bear to have you go, Melitte?"

If they had only said, "I shall miss you, Melitte," it would have been something—but no! Even Aunt Lympy, who had nursed her as a baby, and in whose affection she had always trusted—even she had made her appearance and spent a whole day upon the scene, radiant, dispensing compliments, self-satisfied, as one who feels that all things are going well in her royal possessions.

"Oh, I'll go! I will go!" Melitte was saying a little hysterically to herself as she walked. The familiar road was a brown and green blur, for the tears in her eyes.

Victor Annibelle was not mending his fence that morning; but there he was, leaning over it as Melitte came along. He had hardly expected she would come, and at that hour he should have been back in the swamp with the men who were hired to cut timber; but the timber could wait, and the men could wait, and so could the work. It did not matter. There would be days enough to work when Melitte was gone.

She did not look at him; her head was down and she walked steadily on, carrying her bag of books. In a moment he was over the fence; he did not take the time to walk around to the gate; and with a few long strides he had joined her.

"Good morning, Melitte." She gave a little start, for she had not heard him approaching.

"Oh—good morning. How is it you are not at work this morning?"

"I'm going a little later. An' how is it you are at work, Melitte? I didn't expect to see you passing by again."

"Then you were going to let me leave without coming to say good-by?" she returned with an attempt at sprightliness.

And he, after a long moment's hesitation, "Yes, I believe I was. W'en do you go?"

"When do you go! When do you go!" There it was again! Even he was urging her. It was the last straw.

"Who said I was going?" She spoke with quick exasperation. It was warm, and he would have lingered beneath the trees that here and there flung a pleasant shade, but she led him a pace through the sun.

"Who said?" he repeated after her. "W'y, I don't know—everybody. You are going, of co'se?"

"Yes."

She walked slowly and then fast in her agitation, wondering why he did not leave her instead of remaining there at her side in silence.

"Oh, I can't bear to have you go, Melitte!"

They were so near the school it seemed perfectly natural that she should hurry forward to join the little group that was there waiting for her under a tree. He made no effort to follow her. He expected no reply; the expression that had escaped him was so much a part of his unspoken thought, he was hardly conscious of having uttered it.

But the few spoken words, trifling as they seemed, possessed a power to warm and brighten greater than that of the sun and the moon. What mattered now to Melitte if the hours were heavy and languid; if the children were slow and dull! Even when they asked, "W'en are you going, Miss Melitte?" she only laughed and said there was plenty of time to think of it. And were they so anxious to be rid of her? she wanted to know. She some way felt that it would not be so very hard to go now. In the afternoon, when she had dismissed the scholars, she lingered a while in the schoolroom. When she went to close the window, Victor Annibelle came up and stood outside with his elbows on the sill.

"Oh!" she said, with a start, "why are you not working this hour of the day?" She was conscious of reiteration and a sad lack of imagination or invention to shape her utterances. But the question suited his intention well enough.

180

Orleans Street, New Orleans, Louisiana

"I haven't worked all day," he told her. "I haven't gone twenty paces from this schoolhouse since you came into it this morning." Every particle of diffidence that had hampered his intercourse with her during the past few months had vanished.

"I'm a selfish brute," he blurted, "but I reckon it's instinct fo' a man to fight fo' his happiness just as he would fight fo' his life."

"I mus' be going, Victor. Please move yo' arms an' let me close the window."

"No, I won't move my arms till I say w'at I came here to say." And seeing that she was about to withdraw, he seized her hand and held it. "If you go away, Melitte—if you go I—oh! I don't want you to go. Since morning—I don't know w'y—something you said—or some way, I have felt that maybe you cared a little; that you might stay if I begged you. Would you, Melitte—would you?"

"I believe I would, Victor. Oh—never mind my hand; don't you see I must shut the window?"

So after all Melitte did not go to the city to become a *grande dame*. Why? Simply because Victor Annibelle asked her not to. The old people when they heard it shrugged their shoulders and tried to remember that they, too, had been young once; which is, sometimes, a very hard thing for old people to remember. Some of the younger ones thought she was right, and many of them believed she was wrong to sacrifice so brilliant an opportunity to shine and become a woman of fashion.

Aunt Lympy was not altogether dissatisfied; she felt that her interference had not been wholly in vain.

A Tree. A Rock. A Cloud

CARSON McCULLERS

It was raining that morning, and still very dark. When the boy reached the streetcar café he had almost finished his route and he went in for a cup of coffee. The place was an all-night café owned by a bitter and stingy man called Leo. After the raw, empty street the café seemed friendly and bright: along the counter there were a couple of soldiers, three spinners from the cotton mill, and in a corner a man who sat hunched over with his nose and half his face down in a beer mug. The boy wore a helmet such as aviators wear. When he went into the café he unbuckled the chin strap and raised the right flap up over his pink little ear; often as he drank his coffee someone would speak to him in a friendly way. But this morning Leo did not look into his face and none of the men were talking. He paid and was leaving the café when a voice called out to him:

'Son! Hey Son!'

He turned back and the man in the corner was crooking his finger and nodding at him. He had brought his face out of the beer mug and he seemed suddenly very happy. The man was long and pale, with a big nose and faded orange hair.

'Hey Son!'

The boy went toward him. He was an undersized boy of about twelve, with one shoulder drawn higher than the other because of the weight of the paper sack. His face was shallow, freckled, and his eyes were round child eyes.

'Yeah Mister?'

The man laid one hand on the paper boy's shoulders, then grasped the boy's chin and turned his face slowly from one side to the other. The boy shrank back uneasily.

'Say! What's the big idea?'

The boy's voice was shrill; inside the café it was suddenly very quiet.

The man said slowly: 'I love you.'

All along the counter the men laughed. The boy, who had scowled and sidled away, did not know what to do. He looked over the counter at Leo, and Leo watched him with a weary, brittle jeer. The boy tried to laugh also. But the man was serious and sad.

'I did not mean to tease you, Son,' he said. 'Sit down and have a beer with me. There is something I have to explain.'

Cautiously, out of the corner of his eye, the paper boy questioned the men along the counter to see what he should do. But they had gone back to their beer or their breakfast and did not notice him. Leo put a cup of coffee on the counter and a little jug of cream.

'He is a minor,' Leo said.

The paper boy slid himself up onto the stool. His ear beneath the up-turned flap of the helmet was very small and red. The man was nodding at him soberly. 'It is important,' he said. Then he reached in his hip pocket and brought out something which he held up in the palm of his hand for the boy to see.

'Look very carefully,' he said.

The boy stared, but there was nothing to look at very carefully. The man held in his big, grimy palm a photograph. It was the face of a woman, but blurred, so that only the hat and the dress she was wearing stood out clearly.

'See?' the man asked.

The boy nodded and the man placed another picture in his palm. The woman was standing on a beach in a bathing suit. The suit made her stomach very big, and that was the main thing you noticed.

'Got a good look?' He leaned over closer and finally asked: 'You ever seen her before?'

The boy sat motionless, staring slantwise at the man. 'Not so I know of.'

'Very well.' The man blew on the photographs and put them back into his pocket. 'That was my wife.'

'Dead?' the boy asked.

Slowly the man shook his head. He pursed his lips as though about to whistle and answered in a long-drawn way: 'Nuuu—' he said. 'I will explain.'

The beer on the counter before the man was in a large brown mug. He did not pick it up to drink. Instead he bent down and, putting his face over the rim, he rested there for a moment. Then with both hands he tilted the mug and sipped.

'Some night you'll go to sleep with your big nose in a mug and drown,' said Leo. 'Prominent transient drowns in beer. That would be a cute death.'

The paper boy tried to signal to Leo. While the man was not looking he screwed up his face and worked his mouth to question soundlessly: 'Drunk?' But Leo only raised his eyebrows and turned away to put some pink strips of bacon on the grill. The man pushed the mug away from him, straightened himself, and folded his loose crooked hands on the counter. His face was sad as he looked at the paper boy. He did not blink, but from time to time the lids closed down with delicate gravity over his pale green eyes. It was nearing dawn and the boy shifted the weight of the paper sack.

'I am talking about love,' the man said. 'With me it is a science.'

The boy half slid down from the stool. But the man raised his forefinger, and there was something about him that held the boy and would not let him go away.

'Twelve years ago I married the woman in the photograph. She was my wife for one year, nine months, three days, and two nights. I loved her. Yes . . .' He tightened his blurred, rambling voice and said again: 'I loved her. I thought also that she loved me. I was a railroad engineer. She had all home comforts and luxuries. It never crept into my brain that she was not satisfied. But do you know what happened?'

'Mgneeow!' said Leo.

The man did not take his eyes from the boy's face. 'She left me. I came in one night and the house was empty and she was gone. She left me.'

'With a fellow?' the boy asked.

Gently the man placed his palm down on the counter. 'Why naturally, Son. A woman does not run off like that alone.'

The café was quiet, the soft rain black and endless in the street outside. Leo pressed down the frying bacon with the prongs of his long fork. 'So you have been chasing the floozie for eleven years. You frazzled old rascal!'

For the first time the man glanced at Leo. 'Please don't be vulgar. Besides, I was not speaking to you.' He turned back to the boy and said in a trusting and secretive undertone: 'Let's not pay any attention to him. O.K.?'

The paper boy nodded doubtfully.

'It was like this,' the man continued. 'I am a person who feels many things. All my life one thing after another has impressed me. Moonlight. The leg of a pretty girl. One thing after another. But the point is that when I had enjoyed anything there was a peculiar sensation as though it was laying around loose in me. Nothing seemed to finish itself up or fit in with the other things. Women? I had my portion of them. The same. Afterwards laying around loose in me. I was a man who had never loved.'

Very slowly he closed his eyelids, and the gesture was like a curtain drawn at the end of a scene in a play. When he spoke again his voice was excited and the words came fast—the lobes of his large, loose ears seemed to tremble.

'Then I met this woman. I was fifty-one years old and she always said she was thirty. I met her at a filling station and we were married within three days. And do you know what it was like? I just can't tell you. All I had ever felt was gathered together around this woman. Nothing lay around loose in me any more but was finished up by her.'

The man stopped suddenly and stroked his long nose. His voice sank down to a steady and reproachful undertone: 'I'm not explaining this right. What happened was this. There were these beautiful feelings and loose little pleasures inside me. And this woman was something like an assembly line for my soul. I run these little pieces of myself through her and I come out complete. Now do you follow me?'

'What was her name?' the boy asked.

'Oh,' he said. 'I called her Dodo. But that is immaterial.'

'Did you try to make her come back?'

The man did not seem to hear. 'Under the circumstances you can imagine how I felt when she left me.'

Leo took the bacon from the grill and folded two strips of it between a bun. He had a gray face, with slitted eyes, and a pinched nose saddled by faint blue shadows. One of the mill workers signaled for more coffee and Leo poured it. He did not give refills on coffee free. The spinner ate breakfast there every morning, but the better Leo knew his customers the stingier he treated them. He nibbled his own bun as though he grudged it to himself.

'And you never got hold of her again?'

The boy did not know what to think of the man, and his child's face was uncertain with mingled curiosity and doubt. He was new on the paper route; it was still strange to him to be out in the town in the black, queer early morning.

'Yes,' the man said. 'I took a number of steps to get her back. I went around trying to locate her. I went to Tulsa where she had folks. And to

Mobile. I went to every town she had ever mentioned to me, and I hunted down every man she had formerly been connected with. Tulsa, Atlanta, Chicago, Cheehaw, Memphis. . . . For the better part of two years I chased around the country trying to lay hold of her.'

'But the pair of them had vanished from the face of the earth!' said Leo.

'Don't listen to him,' the man said confidentially. 'And also just forget those two years. They are not important. What matters is that around the third year a curious thing begun to happen to me.'

'What?' the boy asked.

The man leaned down and tilted his mug to take a sip of beer. But as he hovered over the mug his nostrils fluttered slightly; he sniffed the staleness of the beer and did not drink. 'Love is a curious thing to begin with. At first I thought only of getting her back. It was a kind of mania. But then as time went on I tried to remember her. But do you know what happened?'

'No,' the boy said.

'When I laid myself down on a bed and tried to think about her my mind became a blank. I couldn't see her. I would take out her pictures and look. No good. Nothing doing. A blank. Can you imagine it?'

'Say Mac!' Leo called down the counter. 'Can you imagine this bozo's mind a blank!'

Slowly, as though fanning away flies, the man waved his hand. His green eyes were concentrated and fixed on the shallow little face of the paper boy.

'But a sudden piece of glass on a sidewalk. Or a nickel tune in a music box. A shadow on a wall at night. And I would remember. It might happen in a street and I would cry or bang my head against a lamppost. You follow me?'

'A piece of glass . . .' the boy said.

'Anything. I would walk around and I had no power of how and when to remember her. You think you can put up a kind of shield. But remembering don't come to a man face forward—it corners around sideways. I was at the mercy of everything I saw and heard. Suddenly instead of me combing the countryside to find her she begun to chase me around in my very soul. *She* chasing *me,* mind you! And in my soul.'

The boy asked finally: 'What part of the country were you in then?'

'Ooh,' the man groaned. 'I was a sick mortal. It was like smallpox. I confess, Son, that I boozed. I fornicated. I committed any sin that suddenly appealed to me. I am loath to confess it but I will do so. When I recall that period it is all curdled in my mind, it was so terrible.'

The man leaned his head down and tapped his forehead on the counter. For a few seconds he stayed bowed over in this position, the back of his stringy neck covered with orange furze, his hands with their long warped fingers held palm to palm in an attitude of prayer. Then the man straightened himself; he was smiling and suddenly his face was bright and tremulous and old.

'It was in the fifth year that it happened,' he said. 'And with it I started my science.'

Leo's mouth jerked with a pale, quick grin. 'Well none of we boys are getting any younger,' he said. Then with sudden anger he balled up a dishcloth he was holding and threw it down hard on the floor. 'You draggle-tailed old Romeo!'

'What happened?' the boy asked.

The old man's voice was high and clear: 'Peace,' he answered.

'Huh?'

'It is hard to explain scientifically, Son,' he said. 'I guess the logical explanation is that she and I had fleed around from each other for so long that finally we just got tangled up together and lay down and quit. Peace. A queer and beautiful blankness. It was spring in Portland and the rain came every afternoon. All evening I just stayed there on my bed in the dark. And that is how the science come to me.'

The windows in the streetcar were pale blue with light. The two soldiers paid for their beers and opened the door—one of the soldiers combed his hair and wiped off his muddy puttees before they went outside. The three mill workers bent silently over their breakfasts. Leo's clock was ticking on the wall.

'It is this. And listen carefully. I meditated on love and reasoned it out. I realized what is wrong with us. Men fall in love for the first time. And what do they fall in love with?'

The boy's soft mouth was partly open and he did not answer.

'A woman,' the old man said. 'Without science, with nothing to go by, they undertake the most dangerous and sacred experience in God's earth. They fall in love with a woman. Is that correct, Son?'

'Yeah,' the boy said faintly.

188

'They start at the wrong end of love. They begin at the climax. Can you wonder it is so miserable? Do you know how men should love?'

The old man reached over and grasped the boy by the collar of his leather jacket. He gave him a gentle little shake and his green eyes gazed down unblinking and grave.

'Son, do you know how love should be begun?'

The boy sat small and listening and still. Slowly he shook his head. The old man leaned closer and whispered:

'A tree. A rock. A cloud.'

It was still raining outside in the street: a mild, gray, endless rain. The mill whistle blew for the six o'clock shift and the three spinners paid and went away. There was no one in the café but Leo, the old man, and the little paper boy.

'The weather was like this in Portland,' he said. 'At the time my science was begun. I meditated and I started very cautious. I would pick up something from the street and take it home with me. I bought a goldfish and I concentrated on the goldfish and I loved it. I graduated from one thing to another. Day by day I was getting this technique. On the road from Portland to San Diego——'

'Aw shut up!' screamed Leo suddenly. 'Shut up! Shut up!'

The old man still held the collar of the boy's jacket; he was trembling and his face was earnest and bright and wild. 'For six years now I have gone around by myself and built up my science. And now I am a master. Son. I can love anything. No longer do I have to think about it even. I see a street full of people and a beautiful light comes in me. I watch a bird in the sky. Or I meet a traveler on the road. Everything, Son. And anybody. All stranger and all loved! Do you realize what a science like mine can mean?'

The boy held himself stiffly, his hands curled tight around the counter edge. Finally he asked: 'Did you ever really find that lady?'

'What? What say, Son?'

'I mean,' the boy asked timidly. 'Have you fallen in love with a woman again?'

The old man loosened his grasp on the boy's collar. He turned away and for the first time his green eyes had a vague and scattered look. He lifted the mug from the counter, drank down the yellow beer. His head was shaking slowly from side to side. Then finally he answered: 'No, Son. You see

Mangroves in the Florida Everglades

that is the last step in my science. I go cautious. And I am not quite ready yet.'

'Well!' said Leo. 'Well well well!'

The old man stood in the open doorway. 'Remember,' he said. Framed there in the gray damp light of the early morning he looked shrunken and seedy and frail. But his smile was bright. 'Remember I love you,' he said with a last nod. And the door closed quietly behind him.

The boy did not speak for a long time. He pulled down the bangs on his forehead and slid his grimy little forefinger around the rim of his empty cup. Then without looking at Leo he finally asked:

'Was he drunk?'

'No,' said Leo shortly.

The boy raised his clear voice higher. 'Then was he a dope fiend?'

'No.'

The boy looked up at Leo, and his flat little face was desperate, his voice urgent and shrill. 'Was he crazy? Do you think he was a lunatic?' The paper boy's voice dropped suddenly with doubt. 'Leo? Or not?'

But Leo would not answer him. Leo had run a night café for fourteen years, and he held himself to be a critic of craziness. There were the town characters and also the transients who roamed in from the night. He knew the manias of all of them. But he did not want to satisfy the questions of the waiting child. He tightened his pale face and was silent.

So the boy pulled down the right flap of his helmet and as he turned to leave he made the only comment that seemed safe to him, the only remark that could not be laughed down and despised:

'He sure has done a lot of traveling.'

Little Exercise at Four A.M.

ELIZABETH BISHOP

Think of the storm roaming the sky uneasily
like a dog looking for a place to sleep in,
listen to it growling.

Think how they must look now, the mangrove keys
lying out there unresponsive to the lightning
in dark, coarse-fibred families,

where occasionally a heron may undo his head,
shake up his feathers, make an uncertain comment
when the surrounding water shines.

Think of the boulevard and the little palm trees
all stuck in rows, suddenly revealed
as fistfuls of limp fish-skeletons.

It is raining there. The boulevard
and its broken sidewalks with weeds in every crack,
are relieved to be wet, the sea to be freshened.

Now the storm goes away again in a series
of small, badly lit battle-scenes,
each in 'Another part of the field.'

Think of someone sleeping in the bottom of a row-boat
tied to a mangrove root or the pile of a bridge;
think of him as uninjured, barely disturbed.

192

The New South

The New South has come about mainly as a result of recent legislation which has forced, as far as laws can, equality between races. These laws were national in scope but southern in focus because of the concentration of American blacks in this region.

The movement for black equality is not new, of course. Perhaps it began as early as the first slave ship that arrived in the New World, but it met with no measureable success until the War between the States abolished slavery. This victory was short-lived, however, for it was thwarted by Jim Crow laws—some legalized and some only traditionally sanctioned—which forced blacks, at least in the South, into a total segregation they had never known before: separate schools, churches, movie houses, and so on.

As the years passed, blacks began to distinguish themselves—Booker T. Washington, George Washington Carver, W. E. B. DuBois. More became famous in the arts—especially in music and theater—in sports, and in two world wars. A more liberal racial attitude began to grow in the North, but not as soon in the South.

Beginning with the Civil Rights movement in the late 1950s, the Jim Crow laws have been whittled away by national laws and Supreme Court rulings reinforced by the withholding of federal subsidies and other financial benefits from all schools, government offices, and businesses that fail to comply. In the South today blacks are no longer required to sit in the back of the bus, to use only facilities such as drinking fountains and rest rooms and entrances marked "Colored." The old signs are all gone.

Certain other factors have contributed to the image of the New

South, though none so importantly as the changes in race relations. Northern corporations have rediscovered the potential of the South, and a number of southern ones have grown or sprung into existence. Small towns become larger and larger, and cities and megalopolises grow apace. In short, the South is becoming more urbanized, although small-town ways and leisurely tempos still prevail. The liberal spirit of the times—E.R.A., new attitudes toward religion, sex, marriage, "success"—has come in conflict with all traditional American values, not only southern ones. And television, that great common denominator of popular tastes, has broadened—or flattened, depending upon one's point of view—our provinciality.

This New South is reflected by recent writers. There are echoes of the old southern themes, but not the preoccupation with them which marked the literature of the past. Their regional heritage serves the new writers as background only—locus, flavor, sometimes subject matter; but *southernness* is no longer the center of their creativity. Southern writers, if by that term one implies a certain literary tradition, have been superseded in the last twenty years by a prominent group of new writers whose backgrounds are southern, but whose concerns are catholic rather than regional in scope.

right on: white america

SONIA SANCHEZ

this country might have
been a pio
       neer land
once.
  but.   there ain't
no mo
      indians   blowing
custer's mind
      with a different
image of america.
            this country
might have
      needed shoot/
outs/ daily/
       once.
           but there ain't
no mo real/ white/   allmerican
            bad/ guys.
just.
   u & me.
      blk/ and un/ armed.

"In the North, the Negro had better educational facilities"
from *The Migration of the Negro,* by Jacob Lawrence

Old Men Dream Dreams, Young Men See Visions

JOHN WILLIAM CORRINGTON

I tried to remember if I had ever felt better. No, I had not ever felt better. And I could remember. I was only fifteen. And I was driving alone in my father's 1941 Ford to pick up Helena.

It was the first time I had ever had the car alone. That was a victory. My mother had fenced, thrust, and parried with my father, who said I was too young, too wild, too inexperienced to take a girl out in a car. Later, he said. How much later, my mother asked. Be reasonable, my father said. That's right, my mother answered. Be reasonable. The girl expects him. In the car. Do you want to shame him? He can be degraded, humiliated and dishonored as far as I'm concerned, my father told her. My mother gave him a distant wintry smile, one of her specialties. Like an advocate cross-examining an unacknowledged embezzler or black marketeer. Be reasonable, she said with smooth earth-scouring irony.

—All right, my father shouted, turning to me at last, admitting that I was party to the contest—indeed, the plaintiff vindicated.—Take it. Take the goddamned thing. Go out. Wreck it. Cost me my job. Kill yourself.

And then he tossed me the keys.

I parked in front of Helena's. She lived off Creswell Avenue in a nice part of town with solid houses and large pleasant lawns. We had met at one of those teen-age dances sponsored by parents who took great stock in supervised activities. They were awful, except that you could meet girls. The day after, I had walked from Jesuit High over to the girls' school to catch her as classes finished in the afternoon. It was a long walk—no, it was a run, because she got out at the same time I did and they would expect her home within an hour. Her parents were very strict, she had told me at the dance.

So when she came upon me as she walked up Kings Highway, she smiled with delight, and wordlessly we walked past Fairfield, past Line Avenue and down the shallow hill that ran alongside Byrd High School, where the Protestants went, and where eventually I would go when the Jesuits determined that I was bound to end badly, indeed, already bore a bad name. We reached Creswell and slowed down. I took her hand. We stopped at the little bayou where the street dipped, where water stood several feet deep in the road after a heavy rain. We looked down at the brown water and she asked me what kind of fish might live in there. Before I could answer, she realized that we had walked a block past her house. She grinned and lowered her eyes as if admitting to an indiscretion. I shrugged and did not admit knowing all the time that we had passed that fatal street, ransoming ten precious minutes more by my pretense.

We met and walked so almost every day unless the weather was very bad and her mother drove to the school to pick her up. At last, one day, Helena asked me to come home with her to meet her mother. It was a beautifully furnished house, done in what I know now to have been good unobtrusive taste, though strongly feminine. Today I would put such a furnished house down as the work of a moderately talented interior decorator. But in 1949, I doubt that it was. People in Shreveport then had more substantial vices. They had not yet come to the contrefaction of sophistication.

As I waited for Helena to find her mother back in the unknown regions of the house, I stood caught up in a net of feelings that I had never experienced before. I saw Helena's round, bright, unremarkable face, her quick excited smile. I conjured her body, her slender legs and ankles. Sexuality was the least of it. That part was good and without complications because it was no more than an imagining, a vague aura that played around the person of every girl I met without settling into a realizable conception. Because then it seemed that an actual expression of unconcealed desire would surely smash itself and me against an invisible but real obstacle as unsettling as the sound barrier. No, it was something else that made me raise my arms and spread them as I smiled into a gold-framed mirror there in the foyer. I loved someone. It was a feeling composed and balanced between heights and depths that flared through me, leaving me exultant and ready for new things in the midst of a profound and indeterminate sadness. I looked at myself quizzically, arms akimbo, hair badly finger-combed. Was it the one or the other? Neither my own emotional history nor the mind that Jesuits had already forged in me had warned of ambivalence. It was disquieting and

198

thrilling, somehow better than certainty. It was a victory taken from the flood of moments I lived but could not order. But even as I studied the physical shape of love in my face, I saw in the mirror, watching me from the parlor, a small face, serious, almost suffering, the face of a tiny Cassandra mute and miserable. For just an instant I thought insanely that it was Helena creeping up behind me on her knees. I was hot with embarrassment, chilled by something less personal, more sinister, as if a shard of some tomorrow had fallen inexplicably into the present. But the tiny disturbed copy of Helena's face vanished and I stood alone again fumbling a dog-eared Latin reader filled with the doings of Caesar.

Helena's mother was neat, attractive. The very picture of an efficient mother and housewife. Her eyes were dark, her face unlined in that metastatic poise of a woman who had passed forty by chronology but remains for months or a year as she must have been at thirty. She met me graciously, prepared Cokes for the three of us, and introduced me to Helena's small sister. I recognized the wraith in the foyer mirror. She did indeed look like Helena. Only without the smile, without the capacity to be excited and filled by a moment. I tousled her hair patronizingly, seeing in her eyes even as I did so a look that might have meant either *I know what you're really like*—or *help*.

It was a few days later that I asked Helena for a date. I had had a few dates before: humiliating affairs where my father drove me to the girl's house, took us to a movie, then came back and took us home afterward. But this would be different. This would be my first real date. And with someone I loved.

When I reached her house it was already dark. The air was chill. It was November, and the wind swept across my face as I opened the old car's door. Her porch light burned beyond the trees like an altar candle and I moved from the car toward it, key in my hand like power, into the circle of weak light close to Helena. When I rang, it was her mother who opened the door. Even entranced by the current of my triumphs and the size of coming pleasure, I noticed that her smile was forced. Had she had a tiring day? Or had she heard ill of me somewhere? That was possible. I had already the first stirrings of a bad name in certain Shreveport circles. But I forgot her expression as she introduced me to her husband, Helena's father.

He stood up heavily, a short red-faced man without charm or presence. He had reddish hair and that odd parti-colored complexion of certain red-headed farmers I knew who were most sensitive to the sun and yet obliged by their calling to work under it always. He looked at me as if I had come to clean the drains and was for some reason he could not fathom intruding into his parlor.

He shook hands with me perfunctorily and began at once to give me instructions as to where Helena and I might go, where we couldn't go. He brushed aside an attempt by his wife to make conversation and continued, making certain that I knew the time Helena was to be home. Eleven o'clock. He asked me to repeat the time back to him. I did so automatically, paying little attention because as he spoke I could make out the rank smell of whiskey on his breath, as if every word he uttered were being propelled up from his spreading shirtfront by the borrowed force of alcohol. As he went on talking, he looked not at me but past me toward the door, as if the effort of actually seeing me was more than he could bear. I stood silent, glancing at his wife. She was gnawing at the corner of her lip and looking down the hall toward the back of the house. At the edge of the dark hall I thought I could see, dim and distant, the face of Helena's little sister.

Then Helena came. She was dressed in a pale red woolen suit, high heels, a piece of gold jewerly like a bird of paradise on her shoulder. Her father turned from me, studied her, and said nothing. There was a flurry of last words and we were outside walking toward the car. As soon as the door closed, our hands met and clasped. We said nothing because both of us were back in the foyer of her house, the tension, her father and mother, vanished, annulled, decomposed by the look that had passed between us as we saw each other. We had sensed the whole garden of possibilities into which we were about to step. She came from her room assuming a schoolboy awaited her, only to find a slightly nervous young man in a sports jacket standing before her father armed with the key to an ancient car. I had been waiting for a girl but a young woman came to meet me. What joined us then, a current of our spirits, was all the stronger because neither of us had ever felt it flow forth to meet its counterpart before.

We reached the car. As I slid under the wheel, I turned to Helena. She was looking at me and her hand moved to meet mine again. We sat for a long moment until, embarrassed by the weight of our feeling, we drew apart and I started the car. Helena noticed that the inner door handle on her side was missing.

—That's to keep you in, I tried to joke, suddenly ashamed of my father's old car, seeing for the first time its shabbiness, the dusty dashboard, the stained head lining.

—I don't want to get out. Except with you, Helena said, her eyes large, the beginning of a smile on her lips.

For a while we drove. I headed in toward the city, driving up Highland Avenue past Causey's Music Shop, where I had learned the wherewithal of my bad name. I played trumpet every so often in a road house across the Red River in Bossier Parish. It was called the Skyway Club and had bad name enough to splotch any number of fifteen-year-olds who could talk Earl Blessey, the band leader, into letting them limp through a chorus of "Blue Prelude" or "Georgia on my Mind." Before the Skyway Club and I were done with each other, I would have lost and gained things there enough to be worth any number of bad names.

We drove downtown and looked at the marquees of the Don and Strand theaters.

—What would you like to see, I asked Helena.

—I don't think I want to go to the movies, she said.

—What would you like to do?

—Could we . . . just go somewhere? And talk?

—Sure, I said. We could go to the Ming Tree over in Bossier . . . No, your father . . .

—Why don't we just go out to the lake?

As I turned the car, I reached for her shoulder and drew her close to me. The lake was where people went when they had no reason to waste time with football games or movies. They went there to be alone, to construct within their cars apartments, palaces, to be solitary and share one another for a few hours.

Cross Lake was cold and motionless, a bright sheet under the autumn stars. Around us, trees rustled in the light breeze. But we were warm and I lit a cigarette and listened to Helena talk. She told me that she was sorry about her father. I said it was nothing. He was only thinking of her. He didn't know me. No, she said, he was thinking of himself. He drank at night. He sat drinking in the parlor, talking to himself, cursing his wife and the children sometimes. Sometimes it was worse than that. She said she wanted me to know. Because if I were to think less of her . . .

—That's crazy, I said, turning her to face me. And we kissed.

It would not surprise me to find that moment, that kiss, the final indelible sensation last to fade from my mind as I lie dying. Not because I am sentimental. I have used and misused kisses and promises, truths and lies, honor and fraud and violence as the years moved on. That world where I knew Helena recedes from me more rapidly each day, each year, shifting red with the sting of its velocity, but never vanishing, its mass increasing in my soul toward infinity as, one who has managed the world as it is better than well, I am subtle enough to recover those fragments from the past which at the moment of their transaction were free from plan or prophecy or the well-deep cynicism of one who recognizes the piquancy of an apparently innocent moment precisely because he knows not only that it will not, cannot last, but because he has long before taken that fragility, that ephemeral certainty, into account in order to enjoy his instant all the more.

And so I remember that kiss. It was well-done. Our lips fused, moving together as if contained in them was the sum of our bodies. Without the conscious thought of sex we achieved a degree of sensuality unmatched in all the embraces I had still to seek or to endure.

—I love you, I told her.

—You can't mean it, she said.

We kissed again and then sat looking at the water, each of us touched beyond speech. We held ourselves close and sent our happiness, our exultation, out to move among the pines, over the water, toward the cold observant stars, keeping a time of their own. We sat that way for a long while.

In retrospect the appearances of banality are simple to determine. But the fact of it was not present between us that night. Banality presumes a certain self-consciousness, a kind of déjà vu, a realization explicit or implied that what one is doing has values other than those which seem. Or that certain values are missing. There must be a sly knowledge that the game in hand is not only not worth the candle, but hardly worth striking the match.

But Helena and I knew nothing then but each other and the shape of our victory. We were not repeating for the tenth or even the second time a ritual tarnished in its parts and lethally sure in its conclusion. We had for this moment conquered chance and youth, our fathers, the traps and distances laid for us. We were alone beside Cross Lake and no one on earth knew where we were. We belonged to ourselves, to each other. We did not know that neither of us, together or apart, would ever find this time and place, find each other like this again. It will always be exactly like this, we

202

would have thought. Had we thought. It was not banal. The rest of our lives might be so, but not tonight.

Tonight we told each other of our troubles and our hopes. We said, each in a different way, that our fathers made us unhappy. That one day we would leave Shreveport, journey to London and Paris, to the farthest places we could imagine. Only now, after tonight, we would go together. We talked about much more, words cascading over each other as we exchanged all that we had been and done apart, all we planned and wished for together. Until, amidst a moment of silence, a pause for breath, Helena looked at her watch.

—Oh God, she gasped, her face stricken.

—What?

—It's . . .

—We're going to be late . . . ?

—It's . . . almost four o'clock. In the morning.

We stared at each other. I lit a match and look at her watch. It was eight minutes to four. I closed my eyes. We were supposed to be home by eleven. Even my father would be aroused, knowing that I wasn't at the Skyway Club with Earl. I tried not to think about Helena's father but his squat body, his nearly angry face, rose in my mind again and again like a looped strip of film.

—O God, I do love you, Helena said.

We kissed again, touched, embraced. Her nylon-covered legs rose and touched my body. My hand found her breasts. None of this had we intended. The fruit of the tree in that garden we entered was the knowledge of time, of duration: time past, time lost. Even then, in those hysterical seconds, we were trying not so much to hasten passage from recognition to fulfillment as to claim what we might before it was too late, before we were separated and everything died.

But we stopped. We were not brave enough. We were too wise. We could not bring ourselves to wager what we had found against the sullen covenant of all our fathers. We kissed one last time hastily and I started the car, the beginning of an anguish inside me even as my heart beat insanely from her touch.

I cut the engine and coasted up in front of Helena's house. It seemed as if I had not seen it in centuries. Inside, many lights were on and I could see that the front door was a little ajar. Helena turned to me and touched my arm. I could see that there were tears on her cheeks, and the anguish grew.

—Go on, she said. Don't come up to the house with me. He'll be awful, really . . .

—No, I said without thought. I'm going to take you to the door. I was not frightened, only apprehensive. I had been in too many hassles to spook before the event. There was always time to flush, sometimes only a second or two but always time. Anyhow, I had that fifty-yard walk to make, I knew. My bad name did not include cowardice, at least not of the overt and measurable kind. More important, there would be nothing left if I drove away, left the field and Helena upon it to her father. Our triumph would dwindle to an absurdity. I was not yet old enough to weight those things against reality. What we had found in each other was real, I thought. And I was not a boy any longer. What you do not defend, you cannot keep: the oldest of all rules.

We walked toward the lights. Out of our world back into theirs. We did not walk hand in hand and later I would wonder how much of the future had been bent around that smallest of omissions. As we reached the door we could hear Helena's father. He was now very drunk and he was cursing and bullying her mother.

— . . . nice. Oh yes, Jesus son of God what do you reckon he's done . . . my baby. That little bastard. Telling her it's all right, taking off her . . . clothes . . .

I closed my eyes and blushed as if I were guilty of it all and more. Helena looked down at the concrete steps. Then she pushed open the door and stepped into the foyer to forestall any more of his raving.

—Hello, everybody, she said loudly, almost brightly, in that tone she used to greet me when we met after school each day.

Her father whirled about, his face red, thick, inarticulate with anger. Standing just behind Helena, I could not quite see the look that passed between them but it seemed to me that she nearly smiled, pale and upset as she was.

—Get to your room, her father spat out, swaying from side to side as he moved toward us. Toward me. No, don't say anything. I'll see to you later.

Helena's mother shook her head and signaled Helena to go, to leave it alone. But Helena wasn't ready.

—No, I want to say . . .

But her father pushed her out of the way roughly in order to face me. Her mother stepped forward behind him and took her from the foyer. She was beginning to cry.

—What did you do, he rasped. Where did you take her? What kind of dirt . . .

He clenched his fists in front of my face. I thought coldly that he could smash me to pieces easily. But for some reason the realization meant nothing.

—We talked, I said. —I'm sorry we . . .

—Talked? You liar . . . you . . .

Helena's mother, her face anxious, truly frightened, came back into the foyer. She touched her husband's arm. He shook her off. Now he was swaying, blinking.

—Nothing happened, I said, considering the immensity of that lie.

—I think you'd better go now, Bill, Helena's mother said, motioning me toward the door with her anxious eyes.

I started to say something more, but I could think of nothing more to say. Then I backed toward the door, too old by far in the ways of Caddo and Bossier Parishes to show my back to a drunk who held a score against me, a blood score. The occasions of my bad name had made me cautious. Before I reached the door, there in the gloom of the dark hallway I saw, dressed in a long nightgown, the figure of Helena's little sister. Her face was pinched and no larger than an orange, it seemed. Her eyes were wide with excitement and certainty.

As I stepped outside, Helena's father, who had followed me with his inflamed eyes, began to weep. He twisted his fists into his eyes, his shoulders quaking. He turned to his wife, who looked after me one last time and then gave her attention to her husband, who leaned against her like a child swallowed in the skirts of its mother. Behind, the little girl stood alone, one hand pressed against that duplicate of Helena's face.

—My little girl, her father sobbed, as if he knew Helena to be dead.— My baby . . .

I turned then and breathed deeply, walking slowly toward the black mass of my father's sequestered Ford. I stopped at the car door and looked back at Helena's house under two cedar trees, dwarfed by a sweep of sky pricked with distant stars. I breathed again, taking in the chill early-morning air like one who stares down from some great height at the place where his lover sleeps or the field where his enemy lies broken. Then, full of some large uncertain joy, I sat down in the old car and jammed the ignition key home.

The Other Way

SHIRLEY ANN GRAU

Sandra Lee was late. It was nearly five o'clock when she got off the school bus. She walked through the narrow alley along the side of her house and heard the hollow echo of her heels on the brick. The philodendrons which her grandmother insisted on growing in the six inches of soil by the high board fence brushed crinkled leaves against her face, and she ducked her head to avoid them.

I been doing this every day of my life, she thought, since I been old enough to walk. And how many times does that make it?

She liked to think of numbers. She always counted things. The walk now, it had two hundred and sixty-eight bricks. And then you were at the kitchen door. She climbed the worn wood steps, the ones her grandmother still scrubbed with brown soap every day, rain or shine, hot or cold. The way she had done ever since she was a young bride just moved into the house. The steps now were a silvery gray color, the veins of the wood standing up hard and clear, the surface rough and uneven like a washboard when you sat on it.

She went in, letting the screen bang shut behind her. She knew who would be there—the same people were always there each day when she came home from school. There was her mother, short and heavy, dark brown and frizzled-haired, with only light green eyes to show her white blood. She would be standing at the enamel-topped table under the window beginning to fix supper, staring out at the line of fluttering clothes that ran from the back porch to the back shed. There was her aunt Norris, sitting in her wheel chair, across her withered legs the endless balls of cord she used to crochet. She went very fast, the shiny little hook squirming about among the knotting thread. So fast that the finished product seemed to run smoothly off the tips of her black fingers. And there was the old lady, her grandmother. She would be at the wooden dining table, back in the dusky part of the room, reading the evening paper under the light of the overhead lamp, her gold-rimmed glasses sliding halfway down her nose. She had gotten those glasses from a lady she cooked for years ago, back when her children were still small; she found the glasses suited her fine and she had used them ever since. Now and then she would take them off, and stare at them, and you could tell that she was remembering back to those days when she was young.

Most likely too, they would be talking when Sandra Lee came in—the soft, muttered Cajun French. They always spoke it during the day when they were alone in the house. It was the only language her grandmother felt comfortable in. English came stiff and hard to her tongue, she said.

When Sandra Lee came, they stopped at once, for they would never speak French in front of her. She asked sometimes, but they only laughed and told her, "Layovers to catch meddlers, baby. No need for you to go talking the old folks' talk."

This was the same as every other evening. They stopped talking when they heard her foot on the step. They all looked up when she came through the door. Her mother asked: "How was school today?" and she answered, "Fine," and put her books down on the table beside her grandmother's paper.

Then her mother would tell her what to do: go to the grocery, or get the clothes in, or wash your hands and set the table.

Today her mother said: "I won't be needing any help. But you could put the hem in that dress I ripped for you this morning."

"Growing like a Jerusalem weed," Norris said, as her fingers went back to their contortions with the strip of steel and the cotton thread.

So Sandra Lee fetched the dress, and brought it back to the kitchen and threaded her needle and checked to see just how it was that her mother had basted the hem.

"Who'd you eat lunch with?" her mother asked.

"Some kids." She began sewing, quickly, deftly.

"Like who?"

"Well, Peggy, and Amelie."

"What they have for lunch?"

"I didn't look."

"Lunch now," her grandmother said. "It used to be called dinner. When I was cooking we'd have four or five courses and never think anything

208

of it. Excepting it was crawfish bisque. I guess I picked ten tons of crawfish in my day."

"If John and the boys got them," Norris said, "we could make some again this spring."

And then Sandra Lee said what she had been saving up to say all afternoon: "I'm not going back."

They stopped whatever they were doing. They all looked at her. She could feel them looking through her.

"I'm not going back to that school." She found she was speaking louder than she intended. "I'm going where I was last year."

In the little silence they could hear the rattle of dishes and the television set in the house next door.

Her mother said slowly: "What do I got to tell your father?"

Her grandmother said: "Jesus Lord!"

"I thought you liked it. I thought you was happy there," her mother said.

And Norris said: "Alberta's quitting, no?"

She knows everything, Sandra Lee thought. And she nodded.

"And you plain don't want to be the only little black chile in the school."

"God, God," her mother said, chopping onions on the wood board with a steady, practiced thumping.

Norris said: "Alberta's a silly little ass."

"She quit yesterday," Sandra Lee said. "She wasn't there today."

"Was they mean to you?" her grandmother said.

"Did somebody say something to you today?" her mother asked. "Was somebody mean to you?"

Sandra Lee shook her head and began stitching in the hem, slowly.

Norris smoothed the folds of her finished crochet work against her knee. "There's more than what you saying."

"I don't want to talk about it," Sandra Lee said.

Her grandmother cleared her throat and spat into her wad of tissue. "Since when do you come to be short of words?"

"Since now," Sandra Lee said.

Her grandmother's little beady black eyes glared at her. "No mocking in my house, miss."

Sandra Lee bit her lip and began stitching furiously.

"How do I got to tell your father?" her mother whispered to the paring knife in her hands.

Norris gave her wheel chair a quick little spin, the boards under the linoleum creaked, and she was at Sandra Lee's side. She pulled the sewing from her hands. "You began out by talking," she said, "now you finish up."

"I told you."

"Don't they eat lunch with you?" her mother asked faintly. "You said they eat with you."

"Sort of. But it isn't just lunch."

"How?" Norris said. "Tell us how."

"Well," Sandra Lee said, "if I go sit at a table that's empty they don't ever come and sit by me. But if I go sit with them, they talk to me and it's all right."

"Lord of mine!" her mother hissed her breath with relief. "What you expect them to do? They been going there for years and you just come. And what's it got to hurt you to go to their table and not them."

"Little jackass," Norris said bitterly.

And for a minute Sandra Lee wondered whether she meant her or her mother.

"We thought about nothing when we was young," her grandmother said suddenly, "beyond the color of our new shoes, and our men, and if there was going to be somebody to play the piano in the evenings."

"You just got to work harder," her mother said, "no reason you can't keep up. You won the scholarship."

"I'm keeping up," Sandra Lee said. "I don't have any trouble keeping up."

"You don't want to be the only one," Norris said softly. "Not the only black face all by yourself in all that white."

"I just don't want to go."

"My God," her mother said, "oh my God."

"*Tais-toi!*" Norris said, forgetting. "You are more foolish than your child."

Sandra Lee looked down at her empty hands folded across her lap.

"You are fixing to come running back to where you been," Norris asked. "No?"

"I don't belong there," Sandra Lee said, "that's all."

Norris snickered. "Where you belong, *chère?* Tell me."

"I don't know," Sandra Lee said miserably.

Norris snickered again. "You belong in Africa, maybe?" She held up the blue plaid dress. "You going back to Africa wearing this dress?"

Her mother chuckled and dropped the chopped onions into a frying pan.

"I'm just not going," Sandra Lee said.

"I won't, I won't, I won't," her grandmother mimicked.

"You going back," Norris said, "because there's no place else for you."

Sandra Lee bent her head and was surprised to see the splotches of water fall on her hands. She had not realized that she was crying.

"We won't say nothing about this," her mother said, "not to your father nor nobody else."

"I been trouble all my life." Norris looked at her withered legs. "From the day I was born, I been troubling others and there wasn't nothing to do about it."

"The Lord in his mercy," the grandmother said.

"But you now, you got two legs and a head on your shoulders, and you got no cause to be a burden."

"There's eight more months of school," Sandra Lee said, and she saw them stretch ahead like the shining curve of a railroad track, endless.

"You going tomorrow," Norris said as if she had not heard, "and all the days after. And when you come home in the evening, you are going to tell us what kind of a day you had, and what you did at lunchtime, and all that you learned."

Sandra Lee had turned her hands over and was studying the insides of them, the lines and hollows. Some people, she thought, they could tell what would happen to you from your hands, that the mark of the future was there, all spelled out, if you could just read it.

"And," Norris said, "you won't tell us no more of what you're thinking."

"No," her grandmother said. "No more."

The silence was thick and heavy until her mother said, "There's no milk for the morning, and I was forgetting about that."

"Yes'm," Sandra Lee said.

"My purse's on top the bureau."

Sandra Lee got up and walked toward the front of the house. She opened the purse and found a fifty-cent piece and, holding it in her hand, she went out the front door, the one that let directly onto the street.

The bricks gave out their gentle sound under her steps. The houses passed one after the other, misted and shaded by fear and misery. She felt the pressure of her people behind her, pushing her, cutting off her tears.

She got the milk. For a minute she thought about throwing the bottle down in the gutter and running off in the other direction. Instead she looked at the black and white spotted cat that ambled loose-limbed along the walk, hugging the shelter of the houses. And so the moment passed, and when she looked up again, the other way was gone. The street in front of her had only one opening and one way to it, and her feet put themselves on that path, and she walked home.

"How was school?" her mother asked.

Sandra Lee put the milk in the icebox and closed the door. "It was fine," she said.

Cherrylog Road

JAMES DICKEY

Off Highway 106
At Cherrylog Road I entered
The '34 Ford without wheels,
Smothered in kudzu,
With a seat pulled out to run
Corn whiskey down from the hills,

And then from the other side
Crept into an Essex
With a rumble seat of red leather
And then out again, aboard
A blue Chevrolet, releasing
The rust from its other color,

Reared up on three building blocks.
None had the same body heat;
I changed with them inward, toward
The weedy heart of the junkyard,
For I knew that Doris Holbrook
Would escape from her father at noon

And would come from the farm
To seek parts owned by the sun
Among the abandoned chassis,
Sitting in each in turn
As I did, leaning forward
As in a wild stock-car race

The New South

In the parking lot of the dead.
Time after time, I climbed in
And out the other side, like
An envoy or movie star
Met at the station by crickets.
A radiator cap raised its head,

Become a real toad or a kingsnake
As I neared the hub of the yard,
Passing through many states,
Many lives, to reach
Some grandmother's long Pierce-Arrow
Sending platters of blindness forth

From its nickel hubcaps
And spilling its tender upholstery
On sleepy roaches,
The glass panel in between
Lady and colored driver
Not all the way broken out,

The back-seat phone
Still on its hook.
I got in as though to exclaim,
"Let us go to the orphan asylum,
John; I have some old toys
For children who say their prayers."

I popped with sweat as I thought
I heard Doris Holbrook scrape
Like a mouse in the southern-state sun
That was eating the paint in blisters
From a hundred car tops and hoods.
She was tapping like code,

Loosening the screws,
Carrying off headlights,
Sparkplugs, bumpers,
Cracked mirrors and gear-knobs,
Getting ready, already,
To go back with something to show

Other than her lips' new trembling
I would hold to me soon, soon,
Where I sat in the ripped back seat
Talking over the interphone,
Praying for Doris Holbrook
To come from her father's farm

And to get back there
With no trace of me on her face
To be seen by her red-haired father
Who would change, in the squalling barn,
Her back's pale skin with a strop,
Then lay for me

In a bootlegger's roasting car
With a string-triggered 12-gauge shotgun
To blast the breath from the air.
Not cut by the jagged windshields,
Through the acres of wrecks she came
With a wrench in her hand,

Through dust where the blacksnake dies
Of boredom, and the beetle knows
The compost has no more life.
Someone outside would have seen
The oldest car's door inexplicably
Close from within;

The New South

I held her and held her and held her,
Convoyed at terrific speed
By the stalled, dreaming traffic around us,
So the blacksnake, stiff
With inaction, curved back
Into life, and hunted the mouse

With deadly overexcitement,
The beetles reclaimed their field
As we clung, glued together,
With the hooks of the seat springs
Working through to catch us red-handed
Amidst the gray breathless batting

That burst from the seat at our backs.
We left by separate doors
Into the changed, other bodies
Of cars, she down Cherrylog Road
And I to my motorcycle
Parked like the soul of the junkyard

Restored, a bicycle fleshed
With power, and tore off
Up Highway 106, continually
Drunk on the wind in my mouth,
Wringing the handlebar for speed,
Wild to be wreckage forever.

The Daughters of Blum

CHARLES WRIGHT

The daughters of Blum
Are growing older.
These chill winter days,
Locking their rooms, they
Seem to pause, checking,

Perhaps, for the lights,
The window curtain,
Or something they want
To remember that
Keeps slipping their minds.

You have seen them, how
They stand there, perplexed,
—And a little shocked—
As though they had spied,
Unexpectedly,

From one corner of
One eye, the lives they
Must have left somewhere
Once on a dresser—
Gloves waiting for hands.

Nikki-Rosa

NIKKI GIOVANNI

childhood remembrances are always a drag
if you're Black
you always remember things like living in Woodlawn
with no inside toilet
and if you become famous or something
they never talk about how happy you were to have
your mother
all to yourself and
how good the water felt when you get your bath
from one of those
big tubs that folk in chicago barbecue in
and somehow when you talk about home
it never gets across how much you
understood their feelings
as the whole family attended meetings about Hollydale
and even though you remember
your biographers never understand
your father's pain as he sells his stock
and another dream goes
and though you're poor it isn't poverty that
concerns you
and though they fought a lot
it isn't your father's drinking that makes any difference
but only that everybody is together and you
and your sister have happy birthdays and very good
Christmases
and I really hope no white person ever has cause

to write about me
because they never understand
Black love is Black wealth and they'll
probably talk about my hard childhood
and never understand that
all the while I was quite happy.

The Way We Went

WALLACE E. KNIGHT

We were at an artfully chosen spot about forty yards from the bridge and near the graveled driveway of a store, our suitcases side by side so that the sign on Fooey's—GOING TO—and on mine—CHARLESTON?—composed what we thought was a clever plea. From there we could see southbound cars coming for a full half mile. We knew we would have plenty of time to get up and stand attentively behind our suitcases, cupping cigarettes discreetly, so that any driver, having slowed down to take the sharp turn at the end of the bridge, would see us at our best, smiling and thumbing.

Fate, driving a pickup, had left us at Adrian, and so Fooey and I had looked the situation over and walked across the bridge and established our station where the grass was deep and pleasant. We sat and smoked. The sun was high. Four or five cars passed.

Before us the two stingy lanes of Route 4 curved marvelously around a hill to descend to French Creek and the bridge. We watched the point of the road's appearance hopefully.

And here came a car like a panther, alternately black and twinkling as its glass caught the sun, coming so fast its roar down the hill didn't reach us for a second. It started to brake and throw dust halfway down, touching the berm and swaying; momentarily it was hidden behind trees and a building, and then it was on the bridge, screeching, and Fooey and I jumped up slack-jawed and stuck our thumbs out.

The car had to slow down. It almost stopped, whipping sideways and spraying dust and gravel, and then it was by us and I glimpsed two faces, thrust up near the windshield.

I thought I saw sparks. The car skidded and crouched and stopped, and then shifted and started coming back, and a man hung out of the door yelling.

At such times there are things to be done. I grabbed my suitcase and jumped back, and Fooey reached for his and fell over it, onto the pavement,

220

kicking by the time he hit until he was standing up again with grit in his palms and bag retrieved. I caught the back of his jacket and jerked, and his heels came down on my toes. We swayed together, occupying nearly the same space.

Over the gunning of the engine came voices. They were shouting "Get in! Get in!" and so we got in fast, interlocked, and sprawled across the pin-striped back seat. The car started forward, and I twisted up and slammed the door.

Nobody said anything for a moment, and then the driver, pulling the car into high, raised his chin and tilted back toward us. "You fellows going to Charleston?"

"Yes, sir," said Fooey.

"Well, you're lucky because that's where we're going," said the driver. The speedometer needle climbed steadily to 80.

He was a plump man, thirty-five or forty, with a creased roll of fat across the back of his neck that a baseball cap leaned on, its bill pointing toward the sun visor. Brown hair stuck out all around it. I glimpsed, as he turned— he bounced around a lot, fixing his fingers on the steering wheel and shift-ing his weight—a long nose, lean for his round face. One ear was higher than the other.

"I'm Bruce Hammond," he said, straightening the car out of a gentle turn and accelerating to 95, which until that day was as fast as I'd ever seen a car go. He threw the words over his shoulder. "This is Merv York. How about you boys switching places and you"—indicating me—"pull your box over in front of your feet and leave the other one in the middle."

I slid over and squared my suitcase across my ankles, as instructed, and Fooey climbed across me and then sat back, looking ill.

"What's your name, son?" the driver said, apparently to both of us, jerk-ing his head again in our direction.

"Harold Fletcher," said Fooey. "I go to school in Buckhannon, and we were looking for a ride to Charleston to go home. For the weekend." He said this very fast, as if he were driving 95.

I told them my name and said we appreciated getting picked up and then I asked the question. "What are you driving so fast for?"

The driver laughed, and the other man—York—laughed too, cautiously, and then York said they liked to get where they were going so they could relax when they got there. He was a lean man, younger than Hammond, with dark, darting, humorless eyes.

"You're going to get a long weekend," he added. "You'll get lots of time to spend in Charleston."

"Hell, Merv, go ahead and tell them," said Hammond. "You tell them, and I'll get us going."

Already we had crossed over into Lewis County, flying up the valley of the right fork of the Buckhannon River. In a brand-new high-bodied Hudson sedan. Quick. With pinched-in sides, vestigial running boards, thunder.

So Merv told us. "We got this bet. We bet this car can get us from the front of the courthouse in Buckhannon to the front of the courthouse in Charleston in two hours flat. Got a hundred dollars each on it, and we took off at one o'clock sharp."

Two hours. I think it's 136 miles. And these guys were going through country where the creeks planned the roads, with towns and railroad tracks and one-way bridges and farmers everywhere driving wagons.

Fooey was pale, I noticed, and I think I was, too.

"Why did you pick us up?" I asked.

"You're ballast," said York, grinning.

And that's the way we went to Charleston once in the spring of 1947, through lovely country that few people know, relatively speaking, as the world is so large. We went out of Upshur County and across the southern neck of Lewis, past Ireland, which is a cluster of cottages in green, and into the watershed of the Little Kanawha, into Braxton County, to Falls Mills and Bulltown, out of the Kittanning coal country and into the Pittsburgh seams, across the Roanoke syncline and the Orlando anticline, through Wine Gap to Heaters and Flat Woods, and then down Granny Creek to Sutton Junction.

And there, as you may know but probably have never had the chance to know, runs the Elk, shallow and sometimes clear, snaking and straggling all the way to Charleston, past some other remarkable places.

"Fooey," I whispered, leaning toward him as we swept into another turn. I wanted to ask him how we could get out. I nudged his leg. He never heard me, or at least he didn't look at me. "Fooey," I whispered, "for God's sake, listen here." He didn't.

Fooey, who later got killed in a motorcycle wreck, was skinny, dark-haired, had acne scars, and customarily was quietly pleasant. 'We roomed in the same house in Buckhannon, and there we had found we were both from near Charleston, not near enough to know the same people but familiar with the neighborhoods and football teams and so forth. We had thumbed back together two earlier Fridays during the winter, and we'd meet at the Greyhound station Sunday afternoons and ride the bus to Buckhannon on the slower, surer road through Spencer and Weston.

He got his nickname from a movie—I've forgotten its name—in which there was a ship's doctor named Louie who was a drunk. Harold Fletcher wanted to be a doctor, and he liked beer, so we started calling him Louie. He spoonerized well, and so became Fooey Letcher, but eventually the Letcher had been dropped.

This process can be harsh. A sophomore girl whose name was Dorothy Snider—Dottie—was turned into Snotty Dider, and I think it affected her personality. Fooey didn't seem to mind being spoonerized, though.

We had been taking some bad turns, and York swiveled and stared back at us.

"Boys," he said, "you're going to have to help a little. Lean away from the curves. Lean uphill. This car's tall, and we got to keep her square." Hammond nodded without saying anything, and so did Fooey and I. We were back to 80 now, and Hammond had been straightening bends by easing over to the left when the road rolled left, touching the right berm when we turned right. He continued to bounce around and adjust his grip, and he'd mutter and even occasionally chuckle. He was pleased with the pace, I think.

I saw the Bulltown marker flash by, and saw the river and low field to the right. I had stopped here once while riding with an old couple from North Carolina, and we had read the brief statement of its history. Everyone should read markers.

Bulltown is notable only for a mistake.

There had been a man named Stroud who lived deep in the Glades of the Gauley. Once, in 1772, he came to Bulltown for salt, and got to know the Indians who lived there, a small band of displaced Delawares who were friendly and mild. When he went back south across the mountains to his home he found the bodies of his wife and children, scalped, and the trail of his livestock led back toward Bulltown.

So Stroud had taken off north again and as he trotted through the forest

224

he quit grieving and started hating. He gathered friends from Hacker's Creek and the Buckongehanon country and led them back to Bulltown. There, in a few moments, they killed everybody. John Cutright, who lived to be 105, past the Mexican War, said they scalped the Delawares and threw the bodies into the Little Kanawha. It's quite shallow, so the mess must have been around for some time.

A few days later the men learned that Stroud's family had been murdered by Shawnees, who had purposely left signs pointing toward Bulltown. Tricked, damn it, Stroud sank out of history. A Mrs. Cutright was the cook for our rooming house, an admirable woman who baked excellent pigs in a blanket, and she said John was her great-grandfather. Bulltown was named for Captain Bull, a chief. A rush of wind and we were past it.

Nobody was talking, but the car was filled with noise. Both vane windows were open a quarter inch, and wind whistled across them, low and powerful and at the same time with a persistent warble modulated by every sway. Bumps brought loud clicks as well as jolts; the shock absorbers weren't what they should have been. And there was a rattle up front that I took, after analysis, to be a loose horn button. The seats made noises, and the frame creaked, and I felt that my body was making noises too. And from outside came the almost constant cry of the tires.

I looked out of the window directly to the side and could see almost nothing, as trees and weeds and grass blended into a yellow-green smear occasionally interrupted by a mud smear or a house smear. Little else was identifiable. A bridge was a noise, rather than something seen.

I have never enjoyed the rides at amusement parks or fairs; I get sick. A park manager told me once, with professionalism leaning on every word, that there were riding families and nonriding families, and if this is true, I'm from a nonriding family. The Hudson was becoming a car on a roller coaster, swooping and fluttering and falling, and queasiness crept in beside my fear. So I started looking ahead, over the driver's shoulder.

We came to a railroad track, a quick dip to the right, skidded, straightened out, and flew ahead, the road smooth and fast, and were in Flat Woods, a town that hadn't pulled itself together but stood in its own wide fields, with just a school and a few stores and neat homes.

Flat Woods, according to collectors of things, is the geographical center of West Virginia. I'm not sure how such things are decided. If you draw a

225

line from the southernmost point in the state to its northern tip, and then
from the farthest east to farthest west, the intersection is somewhere near
Linden in Roane County, thirty miles east of Flat Woods. I never heard of
anybody at Linden getting excited about this, but at Flat Woods there
definitely is pride in centerness. If West Virginia didn't have such an irregu-
lar border, perhaps it would be easier to find the middle.

Flat Woods is where the Braxton County Monster visited in, I think,
1953 or 1954; actually, it was near Flat Woods. He was a great green giant
ten feet tall with a red face and a helmet that seemed to have horns, and he
landed on a forested hill and got out of his luminous spaceship to look
around. The odor was harsh and penetrating and persistent, and this was
vividly recalled by the woman and four boys who met him. They ran off,
and presumably so did the monster. Others smelled the stink, though, and
saw burned places.

If you think it is a small thing to be so visited, you're wrong. This
monster stopped no place else on earth, but stood above Flat Woods and
looked down toward Cedar Creek, and what visions he gained came from
here and no place else. "It's a damp place," he could have said, "dewy and
rather dark, but I made out many white oaks and shagbark hickories and
meadows lined with thorns and sumac, and a fair amount of cedar. There
was greenbrier pulling at my boots. The earth is beautiful."

Of course, this had not yet happened when Fooey and I and Bruce
Hammond and York raced through there in 1947. But it was going to happen.

McNutt's next on Route 4, and then Karl's Siding on the B&O. It's on
Granny Creek.

Hammond glanced back again. "You all watch this one," he said as we
arced down an easy hill. "Right up here we're going to bust or win. This is
where the trooper parks."

It was a flat statement, cold and reckless. We were coming to Sutton
Junction, where the highway joins the Elk at an angle leading off east to
Sutton itself, a placid, messy town. But here we had to turn acutely west.
Prudent people drove up beside the restaurant and filling station at the
junction, stopped, looked both ways, and eased off in low. We weren't
going to do that, I knew.

I saw the restaurant and a clutter of gasoline pumps and cars in front of
it. It seemed in the air flying at us. Hammond pumped the brake, jerking

us, jerking down from 90 to 60 and sliding us forward in our seats. Then he cut off the road—right off the road and into a backyard tangle of garbage cans and junk behind the station, making a dust cloud that must have billowed for minutes, and sending a big dog up and over a barbed-wire fence like a deer. We dipped and the Hudson's body banged down on its springs and my head hit the roof hard. Down again and up again, with the car turning sideways under me. And then we were going west, with the calm Elk to our left, picking up speed and going faster and faster.

"I didn't see him," said York.

"I didn't either," Hammond answered.

So presumably the state trooper was someplace else.

"I didn't see him either," said Fooey.

The next place is Gassaway—another place to look out for, with two traffic lights, a bad bridge, two sharp turns a block apart, and a clutter of slow people.

Henry Gassaway Davis is the man it was named for, a gloriously rich man who made his money from coal and timber and railroads, and who entertained Presidents, looked out for things in the Senate (1871–1883), and went to international conferences in behalf of the interests of the United States. When he was young he lived for a while in a boxcar, and later he built the Coal & Coke Railroad, 175 miles long, that opened this part of the world so that its wealth could pour out. When the Coal & Coke came here, Gassaway was born. When Henry Gassaway Davis was an old man, he gave every school in West Virginia a state flag. On the whole he lived a good life, as he gave people things to do. He took long rifles out of their hands and gave them green and red lanterns to swing, and you must remember that this had never been done here before. He destroyed a wilderness, which once was considered commendable.

He preferred to ride horseback.

Over the bridge, into town, through a green light, through a red light, quick right past the depot, quick left to keep from landing on the tracks—his tracks—and we were out in the country again.

"That was Gassaway," York told us. "It's easy from here on in."

That is not necessarily true. It has never been true, as the hills are old and ragged. Sometimes, I've been told, even the creeks here have gotten lost. A man at Frametown once told me, as if he believed it—and he frowned and left when I laughed—that he had found a place where a creek got confused and tried to run up a hill. It had gone up and run into a hole under an overhang, and then had turned around and come back. Water ran both ways, he said; leaves floated upstream and down. It sounded to me as if he found a spring.

But think of William Strange if you think that's odd, because Bruce Hammond now was getting us to Strange Creek. I saw the store beside the riverbank a little ahead, and the old steel bridge to the left, and the rush of the car smeared it away. I looked back at it momentarily.

William Strange had come here in 1795 to hunt and to map the ground. He was with a party that came up the Elk, and actually they shouldn't have had any trouble. In 1795 there were forty or more people living in Charleston, which had been chartered the year before; Kentucky already had become a state; and the last man to die at the hands of Indians in this region, hapless Shadrack Harmon, was four years buried.

But Strange got lost. He couldn't find his friends, and they couldn't find him. He got hungry, but he couldn't get anything to eat. Maybe he lost his powder. And so he did a very unusual thing. He carved a poem into a tree. It said, hauntingly, with rhythm and grace:

> Strange is my name
> And I'm on strange ground,
> And strange it is
> I can't be found.

Probably it was a beech, with even gray bark and a trunk large enough for such a message.

Several years later his rifle was found leaning there, and his bones were nearby.

I'm not skeptical, as it's better to believe that improbable things frequently occur than it is to demand the commonplace, but I do find William Strange's death inconsistent with the nature of the region, so rich in game and fish and Queen Anne's lace to eat. Perhaps he just sat out there and thought, "I've written four lines too good to leave . . ." Or perhaps sometimes the streams do run back and forth.

Strange Creek is where the big bend in the Elk comes. On to Villa Nova, which has a post office named Duck, by the county line, by Ira and Groves to Ivydale, long and narrow, past Standingrock, following closely the turns in the river to Clay Junction. The magisterial district to the north had

228

been Otter; to the south, Buffalo. Now we were in Henry District, man having come to conquer forests, and the fiercest barriers were behind.

Clay, seat of Clay County, is off Route 4 a mile or so; the road turns west from the river and runs up Lower Two Run toward Maysel and Laurel Creek. Lower Two is logically named; it is south of Upper Two. And so we went away from the valley of the Elk for a while, across the Handley syncline and the Hansford anticline and toward the Grassland syncline, along which the old oil field north of Bomont is located.

The character of the land changed as if Hammond were sweeping it away and substituting new sights by turning the Hudson's wheels. We went up and up, flashing past cottages set in nooks and stores held together with Nehi and Clabber Girl and SSS Tonic signs.

I tried to talk to York once, when he looked back.

"You guys live in Buckhannon?" I said tentatively.

"He does," said York, pointing to Hammond. "I live up at Lorentz."

"Do you all come this way a lot?" I asked.

"Not this way. We get to Sutton sometimes, but not down here. I haven't been here since I got drafted. It's too far."

"I can tell you some things about this road," Fooey broke in. "There's a God-awful turn up here a few miles, going down the hill to Procious. It just keeps turning. I'll tell you when we're coming to it."

Hammond had been sagging back a little, but now he bounced up again.

"Kid," he said, "you just hold your corner of the car down and I'll watch this corner. When we get to a turn I can't make I'll let you know."

I knew the turn Fooey meant. When we got there the tires started to scream, and they screamed, evenly and long, until we were through it. It wasn't bad. And we were back beside Elk River again.

In the next two miles we left Clay County and went into Kanawha County by King Shoals Run. Then we looped back into Clay County for a long bend, perhaps a thousand yards, and took off west once more. Behind us was farmland and riverland and tangled hills. Ahead was Clendenin, mainly on the other side of the river but still big enough to put cars in our path, and Falling Rock, Blue Creek, Elkview, Big Chimney—places where children and dogs played, trucks backed out, and buses and tank wagons and timber haulers crept.

"We're going to be coming to a lot of traffic," I said. "Have you figured on that?"

"Well, I figure on not stopping," Hammond answered after a pause. "Nothing's on the road here from noon until the school buses start out. And by the time they start, we'll be in Charleston."

I leaned up and got a quick look at York's wrist watch. It was 2:30 almost exactly.

When I looked ahead again there was a wall in front of us and Hammond was trying not to hit it. It was a dusty brown wall with red lights all over it and it was across half the road and towering over our windshield. I must have yelled, but I heard only the brakes and saw, like dust devils, two cars whip by us going east.

"Slow son of a bitch," York shouted. Hammond said something and then cut right, onto the narrow berm, and passed the truck on the right side. He whipped back into the roadway and Clendenin Bridge was before us. We sidestepped it. I looked back and saw the brown truck ponderously jackknifing just short of the abutment.

Fooey, who hadn't said anything since before Procious hill, started to speak now, very emphatically.

"You let me out of this goddamn car or I'll wreck it," he said. He threw himself against me. "We'll tip over on the next turn. Stop, or I'll throw your keys out!"

Behind his acne Fooey was white. He started to push me into the corner of the car, and then he began to bounce heavily, wildly.

"Boy," said York, swinging around lightly, "you're almost dead."

He looked straight at Fooey, but I felt the power of his gaze from my place deep in the corner.

"You're going to kill us all and lose my hundred dollars, and even if you live I'll kill you."

It was not a very logical thought, but it was effective. Fooey, as I did, had a vision of sundering steel and shattered glass, the car flipping over and over, and York rising from the wreckage and choking him and then all of us sinking into flame and going to hell together. Fooey shut up and slid over, and slowly, after more glowering, York turned around. We passed the refinery at Falling Rock and the high school and the funeral home at Elkview and the base of the chimney at Big Chimney, the chimney itself having been torn down long before.

Twenty till three. There was traffic: a bread truck, three cars, an RC delivery truck, and a stubby flatbed. We passed them all in one heroic rush, and then got caught behind an old Packard as other cars plugged the left lane. There was nothing to do except cut to 40 and fidget, which Hammond did. "Goddamn."

He started blowing the horn. He blew the car ahead of us off the road. Kids stared out of every window.

And so we went up the last hill and down, through Elk Forest, down and across railroad tracks with a bitter, skidding bounce, turned past a greenhouse, and roared on the straight stretch by the river—still the Elk, of course—toward the Charleston city limits. It was our last roar, and the needle reached 90. At ten till three.

I wasn't really scared anymore. I don't think Fooey was, either. We had begun anticipating an end to the ride, win or lose, and although I hadn't thought about getting out and saying thank you and watching the black Hudson drive off, I felt now this could happen.

Had I felt this at Flat Woods or Gassaway? I don't know. I don't think so. Gassaway was past, and consequently had become unreal. Strange Creek was not real, either—something imagined. And Villa Nova, where people sat waiting for the train on a bench at the end of the station, was so far away I'm not certain it ever existed. I've been there and watched the bustle, and they seemed like actual people, those who walked over and talked to the conductor, people from the other side of the Elk, but I know if you went there today they would not be there. Duck Post Office; a ridiculous name.

It was all a part of time's passage. Some passed there slowly, turning over rocks and looking under them for mussels. Some, such as we, passed fast.

To become a part of a place, one must cut marks into it. Henry Gassaway Davis did, and so did William Strange. So, for that matter, did the Braxton County Monster, scarring the stone exposed by wind on Cedar Creek, burning a message: "Come from far off. Left something to talk about. I was more here than Grover Cleveland, and, as Grover Cleveland lived, so too did I."

Dodge to the right, over tracks and a rise past homes crowded on narrow lots; this was Bigley Avenue, Charleston. And we got behind a bus.

There wasn't any room to pass, none at all. A row of parked cars was beside us, the bus in front, and cars passing swiftly to our left. Hammond nosed out and dipped back, three times, four times. The bus let people off

Miami Beach, Florida

and took others on, stopping in the street as there was no place to pull over.

"We've got time," York yelped. "Seven minutes." He turned around and looked at me. "Now, where's the courthouse?"

"You don't know where it is?" I gasped. "You've come all this way and you don't know where to stop?"

"Bruce, this kid's arguing with me," York yelled just as Hammond jerked the wheel, gunned out, and stopped the other lane so that every car for a block rocked and began honking. The bus stopped too, and its horn was high-pitched and excited as we dipped in front of it. York flipped up on his knees in the front seat, facing me, with his arms dangling as if he wanted to grab me.

"I am not," I shouted. "I just didn't think you wouldn't know."

Hammond started shouting now, an awful noise in the car with the windows up. "How far is it and how do we get there?"

I had to think and couldn't. I'm not good at giving directions anytime. Fooey giggled and didn't try to save me, but I realized later it was a scared giggle.

"Well, there are several ways—" I started.

"Lord God!" screeched York. "Point!"

I pointed straight ahead, down Bigley, felt like crying, and then collected myself. "Straight ahead to the next railroad tracks, and then turn left, over to Pennsylvania Avenue, and then right on down to Virginia Street. It's maybe a mile or so."

York deflated. He sank back to his seat and pointed for Hammond, who was shaking his head slowly from side to side. He seemed unaware that cars were all around us, moving slowly, and that we were dodging them with sometimes only inches to spare. As if in slow motion, but terribly fast, Hammond drove up to their bumpers, blew, gunned, braked.

They had expected a tall building with an enormous clock, a stone building at the very center of a round city, and consequently they hadn't asked if this were so. Buckhannon's courthouse doesn't have to be inquired about, nor does Clay's or Sutton's. Why should Charleston's?

Fooey's finger tips gouged my leg, and when I realized what it was I remembered he had been poking at me for a long time—for seconds. I looked irritably toward him. He mouthed words I couldn't hear, and then I heard.

"Take them over the Spring Street bridge," he said. "It's quicker."

Spring Street led to a part of town I didn't know much about, a tangle of warehouses and wholesale places and can-covered lots; and the bridge itself was narrow and old. I didn't want to go that way. It would be too easy to get mixed up and lost.

Why did Fooey do this, confusing me when I had enough trouble already? York turned around to Fooey, bright eyes narrow, and shouted:

"What did you say about a bridge?"

"Fooey, you gutless bastard," I shrieked, "They're not going to let you off at any bridge. We're going to win this thing if you'll shut up!"

York sneered and spun away, and Fooey and I looked at each other. Neither of us said anything. I tried to create an expression that indicated I'm sorry but I'll explain later, but I couldn't. Fooey's expression was shocked and awful.

Ten seconds and we crossed Spring Street, and I looked left, trying to take in the view photographically. I saw Spring Street bridge and it was empty. Not a car or a person on it. And Fooey saw it too.

Hammond sped on and I leaned forward and pointed the way across his shoulder. He cursed the cars. Space seemed to pluck at us. Hammond fought it, but nothing helped.

More cars crept into our way, more and more and more, and then there were the traffic lights at Washington Street and Fayette, and the one at Virginia Street. Every one was red. Finally we turned onto Virginia and went up its wide old arching bridge with our tires chipping on and off the gleaming unused trolley tracks. We were past the center and going down when York sighed and threw back his head.

"Quit it, Bruce," he said. "We lost. We lost two minutes ago."

Almost imperceptibly our pace slackened. Hammond eased, but very gently. "Are you sure?" he said.

"Yes. Just over two minutes."

We rolled, glided, coasted, stopped. Another red light. Virginia Street was busy, but not too busy; an ordinary afternoon.

"Now," said Hammond. "Where's the courthouse?"

"Just up there on the right. It's the stone building with the tower," Fooey told them. "It's too bad you lost," he added.

I scooted back and turned toward Fooey, full face. We looked at each other, and then he said, only to me, but loud and evenly, "Of course you could have won if you weren't so goddamn dumb."

Oh God, Fooey. He stared at me and I turned away and Hammond pulled over to the curb at Summers Street, stopping the car so that it rocked. He jerked down the bill of his ball cap and the two of them, Hammond and York, both turned around.

"Now, you just tell me, kid, where I was so dumb," Hammond said, low and angrily.

"Well," Fooey told him, like a lecturer, "first, you wasted a minute picking us up. You could have sandbagged the back of this car. And second, you could have driven at night and missed all the traffic. Your bet was for two hours—any two hours."

Hammond looked at York and I kept watching Fooey, but now he wouldn't look at me. And then Hammond sighed.

"I guess you're right. Damnation, you're right. But I don't like to be called dumb right after I lose a hundred dollars."

York laughed. It was the only time he had laughed since we got in the car. It was a high-pitched snorting. "That's the best time, Bruce," he said. "That's the right time."

I opened the car door and pulled my suitcase up on my knees. I was embarrassed, and, too, I was feeling the absence of sound. I seemed in a hollow. So I asked a question just before I got out, partly to fill in and partly to know.

"Tell me," I said, "who knows you lost? You only came in three or four minutes late."

"There's a guy in the assessor's office," York answered. "We were supposed to get up there and tell him. He has half the bet against us."

"I saw him," Hammond added. "He was on the steps. He saw us, too."

Well, we got out and they drove off. And Fooey and I were back in town at ten after three.

We stood on the sidewalk and I said, "Fooey, I hope you know why I cut you off like I did. I didn't want to go on Spring Street. I was afraid we'd get lost."

Fooey looked at me with great seriousness. It was an open overwhelming look. "It's all right," he said. "I knew you were afraid."

I've forgotten what I did the rest of the afternoon, although I expect I went over and bummed a ride home with Dad at five o'clock, when he got off work. But my memory stops with Fooey going up Summers Street beside the discolored bulk of the Kanawha Hotel and me standing and watching him out of sight.

Sometimes I still think, though, what might have happened if we had crossed at Spring Street. Probably we would have made it, and Merv York and Bruce Hammond would each have had a hundred dollars, which was a lot more then than it is now.

But I console myself by thinking of the infinite number of other ways we could have come. An infinite number, as the Kanawha County Courthouse, thought of in those terms, was at the very center of everything.

About The Authors

Stephen Vincent Benét (1898–1943) Yankee son of three generations of professional army men. He, brother, sister, wife, sister-in-law all writers. Benét lived in Georgia for a time. Wrote novels, short stories, poems, radio plays, operas, and, during World War II, anti-Fascist propaganda. Best known as glorifier of American past. His most famous work, *John Brown's Body*, written while in Paris, was awarded the Pulitzer Prize for Literature in 1923.

Elizabeth Bishop (1911–) Born in Massachusetts and educated at Vassar, but spent four adult years in Florida, from which experience and environment much of her best poetry originates. Bishop writes short stories, but is best known for poems and in 1956 she won the Pulitzer Prize for *Poems: North and South*.

Arna Bontemps (1902–1973) Poet, novelist, author of short stories and juvenile literature, critic, anthologist, playwright, librarian, and educator. Central figure in Black American literature and NAACP. Born in Alexandria, Louisiana, educated at Pacific Union College. Returned to live in South after publication of first novel. Later associated with Harlem Renaissance, and, during the sixties, with the University of Illinois, Chicago Circle.

Sterling A. Brown (1901–) Born and reared in Washington, D.C., educated at Williams College and Harvard. Professor of English at Howard University and Atlanta University for a time; writer, and editor. Called by contemporary critics, "The Dean of American Negro Poets."

About the Authors

Kate Chopin (1851–1904) Born in St. Louis, Missouri, of Creole mother and Irish father. Education emphasized Catholic teachings and French intellectuals. Married man of French and Creole parentage, and went to live in Louisiana, where she became intimately acquainted with Cane River Creoles, Cajuns, and Negroes, of whom she wrote. Widowed at 32, moved, with her six children, back to St. Louis. Began writing—short stories, essays and novels—all of which were strongly criticized on moral grounds. Personally ostracized by friends for liberal attitudes toward women's roles in society and the importance of sex as expressed in her work.

John William Corrington. From Shreveport, Louisiana, Ph.D. from the University of Sussex. Has written three novels, four volumes of poetry, and a collection of short stories. In collaboration with Joyce H. Corrington has written five filmed screenplays, including *The Omega Man* and *Planet of the Apes.*

James Dickey (1923–   ) Born and reared in Atlanta, Georgia, where lawyer father read aloud to him while he dreamed of football, which he played in high school and at Clemson College in South Carolina. Education interrupted by World War II, in which he flew one hundred combat missions with USAF in Pacific Theatre. Returned to school (Vanderbilt), taught and lectured at several colleges, and wrote advertising for five years, quitting highly successful commercial career to write poetry. Pulitzer Prize winner and currently Consultant on Poetry for Library of Congress. Primarily a poet, he is also the author of *Deliverance.*

William Faulkner (1897–1962) Born of distinguished pre-Civil War Mississippi family. High school drop-out, but prodigious reader. Served with Canadian Air Force in World War I. Afterwards took courses at Old Miss, but did badly. Supported self with odd jobs, becoming something of "town character." Tremendous literary output between World Wars, but not well received until after the Second, when, having returned to Oxford, Mississippi, after a stint in New Orleans and some time in Hollywood writing for movies, he became famous American author, pride of the literary South, and dearly beloved citizen of his home town. Winner of both Nobel and Pulitzer Prizes for Literature.

Mercedes García Tudurí De Coya. Cuban-born and educated poetess, essayist, and teacher. Received Ph.D. in Philosophy and Letters from University of Havana, where she began her distinguished career as writer, lecturer, and educator, a career which she has continued in the United States. Now lives in Miami, Florida, where she is a professor at Biscayne College.

238

Nikki Giovanni (1943–) Militant black poetess, anthologist, essayist born in Knoxville, Tennessee. Reared in Cincinnati, Ohio, educated at Fisk University and the University of Pennsylvania. Has lectured at several colleges, often reading her own poetry, which is highly oral as well as visually composed. Appeared in series called "Soul" for National Educational T.V.

Shirley Ann Grau (1929–) Born in New Orleans, reared there and in Alabama, educated at Tulane. Has written four novels and two collections of short stories. Married, mother of five. With her family divides her time between winters in New Orleans suburb and summers on Martha's Vinyard.

Langston Hughes (1901–1967) "The poet laureate of the Negro people," born in Joplin, Missouri. Son of lawyer, lived until age thirteen with grandmother, who was the widow of a martyr in John Brown's raid. After her death went to live with mother in Cleveland and began writing poetry. After graduation from high school went to Mexico, then Europe, earning way by doing odd jobs. Returned to America where he became associated with Harlem Renaissance, the Negro cause, and poetry, for which he won the Pulitzer Prize in 1925.

James Weldon Johnson (1871–1938) Born and reared in Jacksonville, Florida, educated at Atlanta University. First Negro to pass Florida bar exam, but never practiced law. Instead returned to home town as teacher and then principal in public schools. Went to New York City to study literature and drama at Columbia University and wrote songs, with musician brother Rosamond, for musical comedy. Became active in administration of various Negro reform groups in U.S.; served as American Consul in South America 1906–1913. Associated with Harlem Renaissance, wrote a novel and critical essays, but primarily distinguished as poet.

Wallace E. Knight (1926–) Born in West Virginia. Educated there and at Ohio University. Lives at present in Kentucky where he is public relations executive for Ashland Oil Company. In 1969 began writing poetry for fun, moved on to short stories, and now engaged in writing a novel.

Sidney Lanier (1842–1881) Son of lawyer, born and reared in Georgia. After graduation from college, enlisted in Confederate Army. Spent last few months of War in Yankee prison camp, where he contracted tuberculosis, which he fought unsuccessfully, along with poverty and frustration, for rest of short life. Accomplished musician (first flutist with Peabody Symphony Orchestra in Baltimore) and for a time lecturer on poetry and the English novel at Johns Hopkins. Had trouble getting poetry published during his lifetime, but now regarded as South's most important poet.

Carson McCullers (1917–1967) Novelist and short story writer born and reared in Columbus, Georgia, where she lived intermittently (there and in New York) for most of tortured adult life. Planned to become concert pianist and went to New York to further studies in music, but turned to writing for a living. Always in poor health, suffering, after age thirty, one crippling illness after another. Writer of many short stories and a number of novels including *The Heart Is a Lonely Hunter*, *The Ballad of the Sad Café*, *Reflections in a Golden Eye*, *Member of the Wedding* (two of which she rewrote as plays, and three of which have been made into movies).

Flannery O'Connor (1925–1964) Short story writer born in Georgia where her family had lived since before Civil War, and where she lived most of her life. Educated at the Women's College of Georgia and University of Iowa. Not much concerned with secular values, wrote from Christian bias of Roman Catholic background. Work consistently shows penchant for violence and grim Gothic humor of the grotesque.

Josephine Pinckney (1895–   ) Novelist born and educated in Charleston, S.C., with graduate studies at Columbia and Radcliffe. Writes mostly of her southern landscape and people, with much warmth but little sentimentality. First novel, *Hilton Head*, published 1941.

John Crowe Ransom (1888–1967) Born in Pulaski, Tennessee, educated at Vanderbilt and Oxford University in England (Rhodes scholar). Professor of English at Vanderbilt and at Kenyon College (Ohio) where he helped found *The Kenyon Review* and the New Criticism of the forties. A distinguished coauthor of *I'll Take My Stand*, an important statement on southern agrarian conservatism. Wrote only a few poems, and those mostly within a five-year period.

Beatrice Ravenal. Scant information available. Born and educated in Charleston, South Carolina. Some of her poetry can be found in a book no longer in print: *The Romatic South*, edited by Addison Hibbard.

Sonia Sanchez (1935–   ) Born in Birmingham, Alabama, and educated at NYC and Hunter College. Main themes are assertion of blackness, freedom from white culture and especially from drugs. Though familiar with white literary traditions, writes often in black dialect as in *We a BaddDDD People* (1972).

240

About the Authors

Mark Twain (Samuel Langhorne Clemens) (1835–1910) Born in Hannibal, Missouri, of poor but proud family which claimed to have descended from Virginia "bluebloods." Soldier, miner, reporter, Mississippi riverboatman, writer, legend in his own time, rising from poverty to great wealth and international fame. One of our most enigmatic literary figures: a great humorist, but a brooding pessimist; a coarse country fellow and a cosmopolite; a hack journalist and author of perhaps our greatest single American prose work, *The Adventures of Huckleberry Finn.*

Robert Penn Warren (1905–) Born in Guthrie, Kentucky. Graduated *summa cum laude* from Vanderbilt at age sixteen. Originally chemistry major, changed to literature. Further studies at University of California at Berkeley, Yale, and as Rhodes scholar at Oxford. Has taught at several important universities. Author of several volumes of prose and poetry, winning Pulitzer Prizes for both genres. Served as Chairman of Poetry for Library of Congress 1944–1945, elected to American Academy of Arts and Letters, 1959. Best-known novel, *All the King's Men;* latest is *A Place to Come To,* published in 1977.

Booker T. Washington (1856–1915) Born a slave in Franklin County, Virginia. After Emancipation moved, with mother, to Malden, West Virginia, where he worked in salt furnace and coal mine while getting elementary education. Graduated from Hampton Institute, 1875. Taught there, and later founded Tuskegee Institute (Alabama) for blacks. Educator, statesman, advisor to presidents, orator, and until his death the most influential Negro in U.S. His autobiography, *Up from Slavery* has become an American classic.

Eudora Welty (1909–) Born and reared in Jackson, Mississippi, in well-to-do family. Always a prodigious reader, began writing as a child, but for many years believed herself primarily a painter. After studies in Mississippi, University of Wisconsin, and Columbia, returned home to live with mother. Worked for a while as newspaperwoman, and then in public relations for W.P.A. Left work to devote self to writing. Has published several successful novels and many short stories.

Tennessee Williams (1911–) Born Thomas Lanier Williams, in Columbus, Mississippi; grew up there and in St. Louis, Missouri. Studied at Washington University, University of Missouri, and University of Iowa. Has written poetry and novels, but known primarily as giant of post-World War II theater. After becoming financially secure as Hollywood scriptwriter, won Pulitzer Prize for Drama for *A Streetcar Named Desire* (1948) and *Cat on a Hot Tin Roof* (1955). Spent some time in New Orleans, but now lives primarily in Key West, Florida.

241

About the Authors

Thomas Clayton Wolfe (1900–1938) Born and reared in Asheville, North Carolina. Educated at University of North Carolina and Harvard. Traveled for a time in Europe, then went to live in poor section in Brooklyn, teaching a little at Washington Square College. Author of a few short stories and four prodigious novels—*Look Homeward Angel, Of Time and the River, The Web and the Rock,* and *You Can't Go Home Again.* The last two were published posthumously, after he died of pneumonia.

Charles Wright (1935–   ) Born in Pickwick Dam, Tennessee. Educated at Davidson College and State University of Iowa. Fullbright scholar, and then Fullbright lecturer in Italy. Served in U.S. Army (Intelligence Corps) 1957–1961.

Richard Wright (1908–1960) Born on plantation near Natchez, Mississippi. Spent youth in Memphis, Tennessee, and then moved to Chicago. Frustrated with plight of American blacks, became communist for a while, but then split with that ideology. His *Uncle Tom's Children* published in 1948, the autobiographical *Black Boy* in 1945, with a number of short stories and a few poems in between. But his high place in American letters came with *Native Son* (1940), the first novel by a black to become a Book-of-the-Month Club selection, and now considered classic in American literature. With his family travelled extensively in Europe and Africa, living last fifteen years of his life in Paris.

Acknowledgments

(*continued from page iv*)

ARNA BONTEMPS, "A Summer Tragedy." Reprinted from *The Best Short Stories by Negro Writers*. Reprinted by permission of Harold Ober Associates Incorporated. Copyright 1933 by Arna Bontemps. Renewed.

ROBERT PENN WARREN, "The Patented Gate and the Mean Hamburger." Copyright, 1947, 1975, by Robert Penn Warren. Reprinted from his volume *The Circus in the Attic and Other Stories* by permission of Harcourt Brace Jovanovich, Inc.

ADRIENNE RICH, "Charleston in the 1860's" is reprinted from Poems, *Selected and New*, 1950–1974, by Adrienne Rich, with the permission of W. W. Norton & Company, Inc. Copyright © 1975, 1973, 1971, 1969, 1966 by W. W. Norton & Company, Inc. Copyright © 1967, 1963, 1962, 1961, 1960, 1959, 1958, 1957, 1956, 1955, 1954, 1953, 1952, 1951 by Adrienne Rich.

ARNA BONTEMPS, "Nocturne at Bethesda." Reprinted from *Personals* published by Paul Breman. Reprinted by permission of Harold Ober Associates Incorporated. Copyright © 1963 by Arna Bontemps.

THOMAS WOLFE, "The Child By Tiger" (pp. 132–156) from *The Web and The Rock* by Thomas Wolfe. Copyright 1937 by Maxwell Perkins as Executor, renewed 1965 by Paul Gitlin, C.T.A. Administrator of the Estate of Thomas Wolfe. Reprinted by permission of Harper & Row, Publishers, Inc.

WILLIAM FAULKNER, "A Rose For Emily." Copyright 1930 and renewed 1958 by William Faulkner. Reprinted from *The Faulkner Reader*, by William Faulkner, by permission of Random House, Inc.

TENNESSEE WILLIAMS, "The Long Stay Cut Short, or, The Unsatisfactory Supper" from Tennessee Williams, *American Blues* (Dramatists Play Service, Inc.). Copyright 1946 by Tennessee Williams. Reprinted by permission of New Directions.

RICHARD WRIGHT, "How 'Bigger' was Born." Reprinted from *This Is My Best* edited by Whit Burnett. Copyright 1942 by Dial Press. Reprinted by permission of Doubleday & Company, Inc.

JAMES WELDON JOHNSON, "The Creation." From *God's Trombones* by James Weldon Johnson. Copyright 1927 by The Viking Press Inc., © 1955 by Grace Nail Johnson. Reprinted by permission of The Viking Press.

STERLING A. BROWN. "Sister Lou." Reprinted by permission of the author.

FLANNERY O'CONNOR, "The River." Copyright, 1953, by Flannery O'Connor. Reprinted from her volume *A Good Man is Hard to Find and Other Stories* by permission of Harcourt Brace Jovanovich, Inc.

MERCEDES GARCÍA TUDURÍ DE COYA, "Maestro De Emaus" (Translated by Marian Smith). Reprinted by permission of the author.

LANGSTON HUGHES, "Daybreak in Alabama." Copyright 1948 by Alfred A. Knopf, Inc. Reprinted from *Selected Poems of Langston Hughes*, by Langston Hughes, by permission of Alfred A. Knopf, Inc.

EUDORA WELTY, "Lily Daw and the Three Ladies." Copyright, 1937, 1965, by Eudora Welty. Reprinted from her volume *A Curtain of Green and Other Stories* by permission of Harcourt Brace Jovanovich, Inc.

CARSON MCCULLERS, "A Tree. A Rock. A Cloud." From *Collected Short Stories and the Novel, The Ballad of The Sad Cafe*. Copyright 1955 by Carson McCullers. Reprinted by permission of Houghton Mifflin Company.

ELIZABETH BISHOP, "Little Exercise at Four A.M." From *Complete Poems* by Elizabeth Bishop. Copyright, © 1965 by Elizabeth Bishop. Reprinted with the permission of Farrar, Straus & Giroux, Inc.

Acknowledgments

SONIA SANCHEZ, "right on: white america." from *We A BaddDDD People* Copyright 1970 by Sonia Sanchez Knight; Broadside/Crummell Press, Detroit, Mich.

JOHN WILLIAM CORRINGTON, "Old Men Dream Dreams, Young Men See Visions" was first published in the *Sewanee Review* 80 (Winter 1972). Copyright 1972 by the University of the South. Reprinted by permission of the editor.

SHIRLEY ANN GRAU, "The Other Way." Copyright © 1962 by Ann Shirley Grau. Reprinted from *The Wind Shifting West*, by Ann Shirley Grau, by permission of Alfred A. Knopf, Inc.

JAMES DICKEY, "Cherrylog Road." Copyright © 1963 by James Dickey. Reprinted from *Poems 1957–1967* by permission of Wesleyan University Press. "Cherrylog Road" first appeared in *The New Yorker*.

CHARLES WRIGHT, "The Daughters of Blum." Copyright © 1967 by Charles Wright. Reprinted from *The Grave of the Right Hand*, by permission of Wesleyan University Press. "The Daughters of Blum" first appeared in *The New Yorker*.

NIKKI GIOVANNI, "Nikki-Rosa." From *Black Judgment*. Copyright 1968 by Nikki Giovanni; Broadside/Crummell Press, Detroit, Mich.

WALLACE E. KNIGHT, "The Way We Went." Copyright © 1972, by The Atlantic Monthly Company, Boston, Mass. Reprinted with permission of the publisher and the author.

PICTURE CREDITS

Page 3: Library of Congress.

Page 6: Al Stephenson, Woodfin Camp & Associates.

Page 12: Courtesy of Savannah Chamber of Commerce.

Page 20: *Caricature of Mark Twain*, by Max Beerbohm. Courtesy Wadsworth Atheneum, Hartford. Ella and Gallup Sumner and Mary Catlin Sumner Collection.

Page 40: Courtesy of Florida News Bureau, Department of Commerce.

Page 57: *Prisoners from the Front*, Winslow Homer. The Metropolitan Museum of Art, Gift of Mrs. Frank B. Porter, 1922.

Page 104: *Field Workers*, Thomas Hart Benton. Hirshhorn Museum and Sculpture Garden, Smithsonian Institution.

Page 122: Owen Franken, Stock, Boston.

Page 135: *Raftsmen Playing Cards*, George Caleb Bingham. The St. Louis Art Museum. Purchase: Ezra H. Linley Fund.

Page 148: United States Department of the Interior, National Park Service Photo.

Page 164: Owen Franken, Stock, Boston.

Page 181: Courtesy of Chamber of Commerce of the New Orleans Area, P.O. Box 30240, New Orleans, Louisiana 70130.

Page 190: Peter Menzel, Stock, Boston.

Page 196: Jacob Lawrence, "In the North, the Negro had better educational facilities" from *The Migration of the Negro*. (1940–41). Collection, The Museum of Modern Art, New York. Gift of Mrs. David M. Levy.

Page 221: Courtesy of Environmental Protection Agency.

Page 232: Courtesy of Environmental Protection Agency.

244

Index

Index